# WITCH HAIRS
## MIRTH, MIRACLES, MAYHEM, & MUSIC

# WITCH HAIRS
## MIRTH, MIRACLES, MAYHEM, & MUSIC

by
Dixie Gamble

Working
Title
Farm

*an imprint of River's Edge Media*

Witch Hairs
Mirth, Miracles, Mayhem, & Music
Copyright © 2019 by Dixie Gamble

Working Title Farm
6834 Cantrell Road, Suite 172
Little Rock, AR 72207


Edited by Shari Smith


Cover design: Lili Gamble/Michael Robertson
Cover photography: Dan Heller


Witch Hairs/Dixie Gamble — 1st ed.
ISBN 978-1-940595-70-2 (Softback)

# ACKNOWLEDGMENTS

At birth we're not issued a guidebook advising and advancing our journey like Douglas Adams foretold so well in *Hitchhikers Guide to the Galaxy*. Had I taken a peek at the plethora of extraordinary gifts the Universe would bestow upon me in the form of family, friends, frienemies, mentors, colleagues and truth stalkers neatly packaged in miracles and mayhem, I would have blazed into oblivion.

Just as the various manifestations of these pluckings rendered the woman I am, the following far from uncommon beings underwrote the materialization of this book.

In the mid '90s New York agent Lynn Franklin, of Franklin and Siegal, encouraged me to consider writing a book. A therapist at the time, I fell in then out of love with that notion by writing about my work. During this time frame, Caroline Myss published her first book, the informative and inspirational bestseller *Anatomy of the Spirit*, which paralleled my subject matter, yet far surpassed my knowledge and skill. My friend Lynn planted a seed that took twenty years to sprout. This book is imbued with your ubiquitous spirit, Lynn.

A few years back, long-time friend and confidant Rodney Crowell masterfully penned a life-defining autobiography called *Chinaberry Sidewalks*, whetting my appetite to pull out an armful of 55-plus volumes of journals, revisiting my own trials and tribulations. Three years later when I mentioned that a rough draft of my book was nearing completion, without taking a breath, he put me in touch with fellow North Carolinian, Shari Smith, a fierce writer/editor/publisher in the process of revitalizing Southern book culture through her publishing imprint, Working Title Farm.

That introduction led to a mess of a manuscript for Shari to wade through, followed by an offer to edit. In a single conversation, an inspirational leave-behind for my beautiful grand girls exploded into determination to reach out to other women, and men, who might use an emotional leg up, a belly laugh, or spiritual elixir. Shari Smith made that happen. As an habitual soother of ruffled souls and creative hand-holder, I've often longed to feel the comfort of having someone do that for me. Shari Smith made *that* happen.

A visionary publisher transforming the literary arts with creative passion and zeal said "yes," and here I am gratefully buoyed in the wake of her soul's mission. Namaste, Shari Smith, Namaste.

Invitations to the furrow of first draft reading went to trusted bibliophiles, Lili Gamble, Arunima Orr, Susan Loudermilk and Leann Barron. Bless your hearts and thank you, but bless your hearts.

Post edit readers Rodney Crowell, Lynn Franklin, Lauren Braddock Havey and Pam Tillis, you gave me permission to breathe again.

To the maven of punctuation, fixer of gaffes and purveyor of make-us-look-good, Dr. Nicole Sarrocco, Ph.D., you were the rock we leaned against. Michael Robertson, who labored to lay out a ghostly manuscript, thank you. Shannon Gamble, without whose creative skill in lighting a tiny mirror, photographer Dan Heller's capturing it, Ella Gamble missing class to PA the shoot and Lili Gamble's design, we wouldn't be holding this beautiful jacket. And without photographer Claudia Church's spot on facsimile of who I am, you wouldn't know where to place my voice.

Arms full of gratitude to my fellow Working Title Farmers for the heavy lifting, and to SIBA and Independent Bookstores for the invites.

To my beautiful coven of witchy women, your Light and Love spark hope for the planet.

To *The Five*, I know you know.

And for My Everything, first reader/believer in *Witch Hairs*, my heart beats with yours yet again. May it always.

*This book is dedicated*
*to budding witches,*
*Lili and Ella Gamble*

Mother shaved hers.

At least until she could no longer hold a razor after she stroked
out. They then sprouted into a light and dark pronouncement
of loss of control and inability to protect herself from shame.
She was dozing the first time I saw her after her stint in rehab,
a futile attempt to put her flailing life back together. There
was no rebooting Mama's brain. I stood at the door gazing at
her skeletal frame outlined by the setting sun, looking like an
illumined corpse. All I could see was her chin beard. I shivered
in shame, once for her, once for myself seeing my loving mother
so vulnerable that she couldn't fend off an encroaching lady
beard. I touched her face, careful to avoid the obvious. She
awoke and smiled a half smile, the stroke having robbed her of
the other half. I cradled her bony frame, hoping beyond hope
that my mama was still in there somewhere, then picked up the
razor and went to work on her crop.

That was 1996, over twenty years ago, and now I have a generous
crop of my own. No shaving for me, though. I pluck them one by
one by one every day, sometimes twice a day. Adding a dose of

insult to humiliation, most have, like my mother's, turned harsh and white with deeply imbedded roots that cling tight. Others are thin and dark and seem to slip out on first pluck. Be they black or white, I am self-nagged to loosen their grip freeing their wit and wisdom to plow my path forward. Like shame haunting the light, like memories escaping the dark, they grow as symbols of savvy. Self-reproach alchemized into self-awareness, renders a venerable wisdom that can only come to witchy women. Witches, the suffering sorcerers transforming humankind, one woman at a time, reign supreme as the symbols of feminine wisdom, one chin hair at a time.

I share these experiences from the light, some defying credibility, and from the dark, baring my shame quotient. The former come easily, bouncing from the pages of fifty-six journals preserved for forty years. The latter, more challenging to tweeze, a sore surrender. One incomplete without the other, just as the Universe is not the totality of Existence without the dark matter that binds it.

In revisiting my early journals, I hear the complexity of my own voice . The voice of my mother echoing a blue-collar progeny of pain and heartbreak, and that of my father, a brilliant healer, wrestling with a mighty shadow. The bumpy ride through clashing dualities may feel as though you are blasting through prismatic light straight into the density of dark matter ... and so it is with the Yin and Yang of Witch Hairs.

I committed to a daily meditation practice in 1984 after a personally challenging divorce from a music mogul. At the time I was a music mogul in training. My husband ran a record company for a major corporation, while I ran the publishing division. My songwriters were his artists, and vice versa. Entwined and prosperous for years, we shared the single-minded purpose of elevating the consciousness of country music.

After the gauntlet fell, our separation and divorce landed on the front page of the local paper, a level of personal exposure that was the tripwire to my journey inward.

As we split, so followed the two companies. The unraveling was difficult in the gossipy small town business of those days, the divorce had become so awkward that rather than speaking directly, colleagues slipped notes under my office door. "Dixie, are you ok?" Nobody quite knew what to say or do, but one of us was far more powerful than the other – career-wise, anyway.

Vacating a 5,000-sq.-ft. mansion to set up a three-bedroom condo further eroded my dwindling sense of self. I felt vulnerable and vague, as if I could never speak with authority again. So much so that my throat completely closed and I could no longer swallow, and I fought to squeak out words. When I could barely take breath in and out through my massively swollen tonsils, I drove myself to the ER and was admitted to the hospital for a 'lancing.' Throat Docs, in dubious allopathic protocol, announced a plan to cut into my tonsils without general anesthesia the next morning, releasing buckets of toxins back into my rapidly thinning, divorce-besieged body.

My ass.

Critical dalliances with conventional medicine, which I intuited as perilous, seemed to follow me through life, emerging just when I least expected. Fortunately, steep indoctrination from my old Daddy, one staunch advocate for natural healing, set me up never to give over complete control to a system that "practiced" medicine. As I lay alone sick, divorced, and without a job, with not even saliva passing through my jammed-together nodules, I recalled another zero hour when I had to pull myself out of a medical situation that I felt could have sent me flying to the other side.

At seventeen I briefly tangled with a telephone pole on a rain-slick interstate while double dating with a novice driver. After losing control of the steering, the car spun out several times, then smacked the pole full force at the back passenger door where I was sitting. My pelvis was fractured in three places, resulting in damaged kidneys and shock. A few days later, because of kidney dysfunction, I spiked a dangerously high fever. (If you have inherent concerns about your life being jeopardized by hospital stays now, try subtracting medical advancement and knowledge by fifty plus years.) Without warning my mother and I were told I would be taken to surgery the next morning for 'an exploratory look at what was going on.'

My ass!

Through a Demerol fog, I told my Mother—herself a nursing assistant—there was no way I would do that because I would die. So we prayed. Well, she prayed, and I visualized my kidneys to be normally functioning, happy kidneys. We worked together like this all night with her keeping cold washcloths on my burning head. Neither of us slept. With our feminine healing powers united, we defied gravity lifting the issue to another dimension, my mother with prayer, and me awakening the budding witch. When first light broke into the darkened hospital room, so did my raging fever. I felt hungry and, not counting three pelvic fractures, relatively normal.

So now, twenty years later, as the throat scalpel was about to come out, I again resorted to help from other dimensions. Not with any sort of the rituals I would learn much later, but from a raw sense of believing there is something out there so much bigger than this situation, and in that something my throat is normal and happy so, okay, I'm going there.

Early the next morning when the throat doctor barged in rolling the ominous steel cart with a plethora of shiny cutting tools in plain view, I swallowed and spoke for the first time in days.

"My throat is OK now; I'm ready to go home."

The years of the Big Split were the most expansive of my life and therefore some of the most painful. Since my psyche leans far more toward control than to addiction (we're all on the spectrum somewhere), I decided once and for all to understand why I was an addict-marrying magnet.

As if falling straight from the cosmos, words came along that turned my outward focus to an awaiting inner sanctuary. Sure, continued sanity required healing my childhood wounds and unsavory attractions, but before I ventured down the rabbit hole of the unknown, I needed a spiritual tether. It was through a seminal book that I let go and fell into the vastness of countless other waiting worlds. Savoring every unfathomable word and experience, I read on, saying out loud over and over, "I knew it, I knew it!"

So that's my intention with this little crop of Witch Hairs, to offer a lifeline to spiritual dimensions you may have experienced without recognizing the truth of their existence. Maybe you called it a dream, an illusion, or delusion. You may have a secret yearning for access to other dimensions or curiosity about what the hell is out there. In the simple act of acknowledgment, truth prevails and boom we're one with our intention. Each essential life narrative be it light witch hairs or dark witch hairs, creates synchronicity with our soul's mission to expand. It's the natural state of the Universe and it belongs to us all.

I hope at the end of this read, you too will let go and fall, proclaiming out loud "I knew it, I knew it!"

# WITCH HAIR #1.

Siring in the South breeds existential bounty, palates whetted for savory foods like slow-cooked pinto beans, fresh turnip greens and iron pan cornbread—forget about flour or sugar—and lean-living folk accustomed to giving without expectation, especially anything edible. Ours were noses aroused by the scent of cotton plucked straight from the boll and soppy summer days infused with honeysuckle and humidity, all cosmically concocted to distract from the ruthless chiggers, ticks, and mosquitos gnawing at your skin.

The cardinal rule of southern cultivation, besides tea so sweet you could stand a spoon in it and loving Jesus but fearing God (at least in our house) was that a simple yes or no never stood as complete sentence.

'Yes, what?' Daddy sternly demanded.

'Yes, Sir!' Dutifully chimed, seething with empty esteem, setting up my first act of rebellion.

Quietly waltzing with the regional rewards of being a daughter of the South was an inbred shame, and its dance partner, pride, fertile and thriving like kudzu in my former Confederate States of America. The social mantle seeking to make right of something as inherently wrong as the buying and selling of human beings forged a shellacked veneer of hubris that has been silently passed from generation to generation, forming a festering wound. Although politically lanced by the Civil Rights Act, a gash that continues to seep. A sanctimonious 'southern pride' has been birthed out of the human ego hard at work at making it all palatable. Like most sons and daughters of the South, I did not part that particular veil of illusion for many years.

Our southern 'plantation' was actually a two hundred acre cotton farm inherited from Julius Augustus Cauble, my grandfather, which Dr. Gaither Grear Cauble, my father and the youngest of the seven Cauble children attempted to work as somewhat of a 'gentleman' farmer. He hired most field labor to be tended by African American neighbors, whom he treated fairly and with what I perceived to be kindness and respect. Although he referred to our dark skin neighbors collectively with the softer term "Darkies," infinitely embarrassing to recall now, I never detected a hint of loftiness or judgment, and I don't believe they did, either. To Daddy they were Cauble Road folk. Like many who farmed the big field crops, wheat, feed corn, cotton or tobacco, Daddy had a barter system around sowing and reaping time and all seemed obliged to work the crops along side whoever was harvesting. The African American families seemed grateful to have the cash and he was thankful to have them there, as was I.

I loved summer's end when it was picking time and the white-capped fields were dotted with neighbors, both black and white, dragging heavy sacks behind them down the sweltering rows, while we played. As a preschooler, with a brother too young to keep up, cavorting with a field full of children was akin to what real school playground might be like. I don't recall having a preference about the skin color of my playmates, only that I was sad and shocked when I finally made it to the long-awaited classroom that none of my black friends came to my school. In fact, in twelve years of education in North Carolina, not one day did I attend with an African American.

Later in life and deep into personal processing, the biggest challenge in reshuffling my ego to the back seat was the mother lode of shame I found, partly from the Southern cross to bear, but painful topical wounds as well. Big hurts to buy, ,then pare into bite size pieces to digest without retching them into my relationships became my daily bread . First course was my father. My evolved, brilliant, healer father was old enough to be my grandfather. Fifty-two when I was born, and deeply in love with my twenty-six-year-old mother, he carried his stout frame well and his considerable charisma better. When I started first grade and all of the other children's fathers were young and handsome, my classmates wanted to know if my grandfather lived with us.

The fact that this man who looked every bit his age and more, a shiny bald head rimmed with silver hair and matching moustache, warranted being called my grandfather was a hard enough burden on a six year old, but his casual around-the-house attire was baggy boxer shorts and a white muscle shirt. Probably why I do it to this day.

The bookmobile and the school bus, pull in as aromatic triggers back to this same preschool period. Gratefully my developmental years, with a few bruising exceptions, were the most stable and joyful of this life. I was a precocious smidge of a poorhouse princess, who fell in love with books and radio, in that order. There was little else to stimulate a budding brain on the farm. Excitement for the bimonthly arrival of the bookmobile was second only to my eagerness for real school. A small, green van-like vehicle with double back doors that were thrown open to vivid worlds outside the farm held a particular bouquet that defined the smell of words. The entire back of the panel truck was lined floor to ceiling in shiny hand made oak shelves with a look-alike footstool so I could reach beyond the children's books on the first shelf. As a four and five year old, I don't recall being drawn to preschool books, skipping over Dick, Jane, Spot and Dr. Seuss, for anything and everything by Edgar Allan Poe.

A television didn't become a coveted piece of furniture in our sparse living until the early '50s, so I learned what I liked to watch by visiting neighbors. My brother Butch, two years younger, and I watched *The Lone Ranger* with our closest playmates, Scott and Chris Shoaf. The Sunday *Ed Sullivan Show*, which I loved, and wrestling, which I loathed, we watched on Saturday nights with friends of Mama and Daddy's a few miles up the road. Aside from the Lone Ranger picking off bad guys, I had no exposure to violence and certainly not the macabre. Then Edgar Allan Poe uprooted my innocence and forever changed my psyche with "The Pit and the Pendulum" and "The Tell Tale Heart." "I think it was his eye! Yes, it was this! He had the eye of a vulture …" I couldn't stop until I read them all. None of which was vaguely appropriate reading material for a developing personality. Looking back, I could have ended up a Lizzie Borden.

A pitiful pining and whining to venture where learning lived consumed my days, and the school bus was the means to get there. I waited every morning on the front porch to watch as the schoolbus turned around in our driveway then threw down a screaming tantrum when I couldn't get on. To appease her willful waif, Mama asked the driver to sneak me on and let me sit on the front row while he turned it around. When I finally earned my spot on the bus, it was another aromatic event, a blend of diesel fumes, sweaty little bodies, bologna sandwiches and spray starch all rolled in to a ubiquitous smell of knowledge.

Far too soon, the shadow side of the school bus carried an anxious dread of Daddy's alcohol-fueled tendency to park his green 1949 Ford at one of the stops and sneak us off when he and mother were partaking in one of their exercise-in-codependency separations. I was never afraid of my father, but I sat in dread of the embarrassment of having my grandfather-looking father exposed to the rest of the kids. When I spotted Daddy lurking in the car at one of the bus stops, I would freeze in dread. Torn between standing up and telling Daddy I was not going with him, creating a ruckus, and sneaking quickly off the bus before the other kids noticed, I always opted for the latter. This sort of craziness never happened when my proud father was on the straight and narrow, so the daddy that showed up was not only old, but unkempt, and reeked of a month-long alcohol binge.

Kindergarten didn't seem to be an option for me, even though I constantly begged to go to school, likely because it would mean a seven mile trip into town by Daddy or Mama and the consistency wasn't there for a commitment. I was jealous of my first cousin Larry, who did get to attend at five, and wondered if

I'd be less smart than Larry because of it. His sister Jean was a shining star to me because she had just started first grade. She was a real schoolgirl! Their mother, my Aunt Dorothy, was my mother's youngest sister and we were all close. Aunt Dorothy was like a second mother to Butch and me, opening her home and her heart to us when Mother and Daddy were on the alcohol outs.

I think it might have been the second day of the new school year when our phone rang with a jarring blare that I hear to this day. Just after she said 'hello,' I watched the color drain from my mother's face and tears spring to her eyes as she screamed, "oh, God, no!, I'll be right there."

"Jean has been hit getting off the school bus and Aunt Dorothy needs me with her. You and Butch stay here with Daddy," she yelled as she ran out the door.

Deeper into the evening, Mother came home with red-rimmed, swollen eyes and the unbearable news that Jean did not live because her brain was too badly hurt. Having yet to experience death, I felt confused as to what this meant. Mother's relentless crying over the next days told me more than I wanted to know. I followed her around the house hugging her legs, trying to comfort her heart. It would be another fifty-five years before I understood the depth of her grief.

Barely four years old, struggling to make sense of what was happening, I wondered if I would ever play with Jean again or if she would still pass down her outgrown dresses. In that pivotal moment, understanding death and what it actually meant somehow imprinted as a life goal. I felt sorry for my teary mama and an overarching dread of what might be coming next, but strangely not sad for Jean. I didn't feel her gone.

A few days later, Butch and I were decked in our Sunday best to go "visit Jean for one last time." My heart was turning somersaults as we stepped inside the quiet living room stuffed with sadness. The women crying softly whispered to each other and hugged Aunt Dorothy while the men huddled outside smoking. My eyes landed directly across the room on a small open box piled in layers of fluffy white silk a thin veil draped over the upper half. Mother held my hand so tight it pinched. I winced but stayed quiet as she guided us over to see my Jean. An urge to cry surged, my throat lumpy and tight, but no tears came. I didn't know what to expect when I stood on tiptoes peering in the silky container, but certainly not to see my sweet cousin lying very still with her eyes closed and a grown up hat on her head. I was all confused by the way she looked—not my shining Jean, but dull and gray with grown up makeup on and wearing an old ladies hat. What had this thing called death done to my Jean? Later, when no one was paying attention, I snuck back over to the casket, lifted the veil and pulled off the stupid looking hat.

Some grown up grabbed me from behind jerked me away, then gently refit the ugly hat and replaced the veil. I felt small and shameful that I had done something wrong in front of so many sad adult people, especially Mama. But I had the feeling that I wasn't the only one who didn't like the weird hat. It was in that minute I realized Jean was not in the white silky box.

"All you kids need to go on outside and play, then we'll have some cake," the shell of my Aunt Dorothy called from the kitchen.

Larry, Butch, and I, followed by a few other cousins, bounded for the back door and as soon as we hit the yard, Jean was there with us. I couldn't see her but I *knew* she was there and I *knew* she hated the hat.

The story of how Jean died getting off the school bus was defined over the years as, I suppose, Mother felt we could absorb it. It was Jean's second day of the first grade and Aunt Dorothy, as she had the day before, walked onto the front stoop to wait for Jean to scramble off the bus, maybe pondering if she should go walk her across the road. Their tiny frame cottage sat a small yard's length back off a busy four lane highway, connecting China Grove with Salisbury. As Aunt Dorothy carefully watched, Jean ran around the front of the school bus, with the STOP flag out. Just as she stepped into the inner lane, a speeding car veered around the flag, striking Jean full force. Her tiny body, was knocked high into the air and tossed far down the road. Aunt Dorothy had to buy a crazy old lady hat to hide Jean's shaved head and stitched skull after doctors labored hours trying to save her. Mama said no one could find a little girl bonnet for her.

That made me cry.

"If little Jean had lived, she wouldn't be right," Mother, attempting to rub some balm on the story, declared repeatedly.

But who was never 'right' was my Aunt Dorothy. After that day, she changed into the slightly crazy aunt, who did and said stuff that everyone thought was weird but me. I loved how she accepted Butch and me straight to her heart, plus she was one of the best cooks in our family. Unlike some of Mama's other siblings, I could trust her never to cook rabbit, squirrel or possum camouflaged in white gravy. Larry became a Mama's boy who slept with Aunt Dorothy in a double bed every night until he was twelve, while Uncle Walter slept in a twin bed on the other side of the room.

My happy yellow school bus quickly carried a mighty shadow after Daddy's antics and Jean's death. When it pulled into our drive way and opened its doors to me with my grownup school girl notebook, stiffly starched crinoline petticoat, and twirling baton, I never again hopped aboard with the same innocent joy. And the exciting mobile libraries bringing knowledge to those hungry to learn, gifting me with a preschool education far beyond what any kindergarten could have offered, are now mostly available to the Amish and isolated rural communities without libraries. Be it in the form of school buses, bookmobiles, or rampant racism this child of the South felt Poe's ponderous pendulum drawing her heart between the light and the dark, a never-ending sweep.

While school age children from any region of the country might carry a cache of chagrin, heartbreak or bruises from similar experiences, being Southern deepened my burden. My name is shared with a place of immense beauty and aberrant history. My maternal grandmother, Sallie Dixie, and my paternal grandmother Eliza Jane, tendered my family-brewed name, having nothing to do with the anthem of the Confederacy. In my first year of high school barely settled into puberty, in a jubilant morning ritual, following the Pledge of Allegiance, the entire school belted out, "I Wish I Was in Dixie." Clusters of budding bad boys turned to leer in suggestive snickers. On the outside, I remained resolute, singing along with everyone else, but inside, shame flamed. I am a daughter and microcosm of the South. Generational pride carried by hobbled souls like mine denudes to underlying disgrace; whether inflicted by personal humiliation or cultural dishonor, any child aches, any culture suffers.

# WITCH HAIR #2.

*"Your biography becomes your biology. This biography
includes the totality of your choices, the things you feed
your body—your thoughts, your actions, your food—
the thing you feed your life."*
Caroline Myss

The old Cauble farm place, carefully nestled in a grove of oak
trees, offered a haven for Sunday wanderers escaping summer
heat, hoping to snag a sugary watermelon from our patch.
Everyone spoke of the beauty and bounty of Daddy's childhood
home. The hundred year old trees formed a canopy around the
front porch dropping the temperature a good ten degrees while
dropping acorns for hog family. For the pigs, acorns tasted like
candy corn. Daddy bribed us to gather the tree seeds for a nickel
a quart, a daunting task for small hands trying to avoid a razor
sharp point on the head, not to mention the vicious yellow
hornets that took up residence in the trunks. Danger pushed my
curiosity right to the edge, so every so often I'd venture a little
closer squatting down to eavesdrop on evil sipping sap out of
the holes. I don't recall ever being more afraid, yet at the same

time fascinated, by anything on the farm as the cranky hornets. One sting could inject enough venom to kill a twenty-pound towheaded calamity in waiting.

The extended arms of the oaks offered enticing rope swing limbs, the perfect place to practice being a circus performer, which I insisted to Mama I used to be. I'd expertly shinny up to the highest low hanging limb by wrapping the rope around my leg pulling myself up, then show off by hanging upside down by my knees while swinging a good fifteen feet above the ground. My high-flying antics were calculated to scare the begeezus out of Daddy's histrionic, aristocratic sister, my Aunt Edna—as punishment for calling me Dixie Jane, but also because I could.

Once Mama took us to a traveling tent show on the edge of town, a rare happening around Salisbury, excited to show us real lions, bears and elephants. But what caught my full attention were the trapeze artists flying from swing to swing across the top of the tent. Mesmerized, I craned my neck to not miss a single move. Someone was going to fall! I held my breath, as my tot head followed back and forth. There was a big net under them but danger fell all over me.

"Mama, I did that when I was in the circus!" Trying in vain to get her attention, "I did, Mama, I promise and my friend… "

"Let's go get some cotton candy. Then we can see the tigers and bears outside in their cages," Mama prodded, no interest at all in my child's tale.

The magnificent beasts frantically pacing in wagons with bars not much larger than our chicken coup made me shiver then break out in a sobbing spree that would not be soothed. I could feel their souls, and they were dying. I begged to leave as Mama stuffed brightly dyed pink spun sugar in my mouth to stop the embarrassing racket.

Some thirty-five years later in Nashville, after enlightening dinner conversation with spiritually-centered friends, the three of us were in a joyful end of the evening embrace. The competitive but adoring husband and wife, the king and queen of the country music mecca at the time, were my touchstones during a fish bowl divorce.

Out of the blue, the male among us suddenly jumped back in shock, "Oh, my god, the three of us used to be in a circus together! I was the catcher on the trapeze, when you, pointing to his wife, swung over ... and ... oh, god, I missed you. You slipped from my hands and fell, I ... I think you may have died."

Pointing to me, "and you were there on the platform waiting to swing over next."

Well, there you go, Mama.

The farm, a fertile environment for sprouting and growing a couple of new human beings without environmental pollutants, toxic pesticides or chemical fertilizers, molded my penchant for food straight from the belly of Mother Nature. I was the only kid in my first grade class who looked forward to the vegetables on my tray and balked on hot dogs. Our mineral-laden well water, nutrient dense organic food, plump healthy chickens who scratched and pulled worms out of the earth, all added to a cornucopia of biblical daily bread that went under appreciated until many chapters later. Dotting the edges of the kitchen gardens were small orchards of apples, peaches, apricots and persimmon trees along with Scuppernong and Muscadine vines, all sustaining our culinary needs while honing my palate for clean, unaltered food.

The noble princess part of me found a way to attempt to understand, but never quite accept, friendly clucking hens being wrung by the neck, desperately squawking, wings flapping madly in a flurry of fight until finally falling silent, hanging limply in the air. I trained myself not to hear or see this murderous carnage carried out by my softhearted mother when requesting the 'pully bone' at Sunday dinner.

Fall was killing season on Cauble Road. Many farm essences displeased my snobby little nose, but not the sweet milk breath of baby calves or the delicate pink skin of newborn piglets.

While still in training panties (when I would leave them on), I'd wander to the pasture behind the barn to visit Bossie, our lonesome milk cow, and her newborn I called Honey for her golden color. Early one frost-nipped morning, as the green leaves switched to the color of my Honey, I was warned in no uncertain tones not to leave the porch.

"Do you hear me, Dixie Jane?" Daddy never used the dreaded two names unless things were deadly serious.

Leo-born prospective witches infused with impetuous spirits encounter a certain level of personal defeat in doing what we are told. Thankfully, neither Mama nor Daddy was a swatter, even though the 'fly swat' or an occasional 'dogwood switch' was trotted out as a threat. Safe to say, I did endure my share of 'good shakings', which Daddy doled out as a brain-rattling prelude to banishing me to 'go lay on the bed, until I tell you to get up' or both, depending on the gravity of my offense.

Off the back porch, down the well-worn path from the kitchen steps to the barnyard in two-year old defiance I trotted. Climbing through the gate, across the barnyard I scampered, clearing the edge of the barn and … BANG! a bullet pumped right into the heart-shaped white spot on Honey's head, sending my sweet-smelling new friend crashing to her knees in horrifying silence. The piercing sound of my wails as they echoed around the barnyard made Blackie and Blacksilk bark warnings, besieged Bossie bellow, and the pigs in the nearby pen squeal in mournful protest.

Needless to say, mine was an easy coast to vegetarianism, where as an adult I remained for nearly thirty years.

Barefooted splats in copious piles of animal excrement and the hellish smelling slop bucket, ever present by the kitchen sink, mocked my early born elitist sensibilities, but the reality that our century old house had no indoor toilet was a deal breaker, prompting many tirades to go home with Aunt Edna and Uncle Strick, two hours away in Warrenton. Uncle Strick a soft spoken gentle giant who was President of the Warrenton Railroad, a pulpwood hauling short line, loved nothing more than having me in the engine room with him. He assigned me the job of bell ringer. As the engine approached a crossing, he'd whistle through the gap in his front teeth, and the crewman would lift me up to pull the string to ring the bell. What a mighty job for a little twit! The smell of creosote, the seductive sound of a train whistle in the dark night, the clickity clack of the steel wheels against the smooth shiny rails sweeps me right back to those visits with my Uncle Strick. He even managed to find me tiny blue ticking stripped coveralls to match the crew's.

Uncle Strick had just built Aunt Edna a beautiful new brick home lovingly filled with family heirlooms, which suited my princess fancies far better than our dowdy farmhouse. I loved Aunt Edna in spite of her staunch schoolmarm personality but I adored Harriet, my version came out Carrot, their winsome black housekeeper who ironed their sheets and tea towels. All in all, I felt more at home in the pristine, comfortable waif's idea of a palace, than I ever felt in the venerable home my grandfather built for his family. For Aunt Edna, though, it was the home of her heart, where she was born and raised. She longed to be there with us as much as possible, mostly to Mama's dismay.

Dirty floors, dog paws, I insisted on cleaning Blackie's paws after I'd try to milk her, clothes, shoes, stalls, anything that smelled or felt gross was beyond my endurance. I could not wait to get my itchy behind out of cumbersome diapers, so by the time I could walk at eight months, I walked myself right out of the nasty things. At night I learned to use an enamel potty, a kid version of the white beast by the bed that they used at night. During the daytime Daddy dictated he wanted me trained to use the outdoor toilet, what he lovingly referred to as the 'johnny house.' I rebelled against the scary, foul outhouse with holes way too big for my tiny bottom, convinced I'd slide butt-first in to the stinky, dark hole teeming with black widows. There was always a story hanging around about some man who got a widow bite on his ass and died. Unless Mother went with me and held me up far above the spider pit, I defied entry.

As part of my self-applied potty training, I squatted outside for both number one and number two, which my oh-so-proper daddy didn't take kindly to stepping in or cleaning up.

"Young lady, did you do a 'bad job' in the yard again?" he'd quiz with one of his steely stares, frantically rubbing his shoe against the grass.

"Nu-huh." Dramatically shaking my head.

"What did you say?" Daddy's face reddening at improper vocabulary more than the lie.

"No ... "

"No, what, young lady?"

"No, Sir! Maybe Blackie?"

"Are you telling Daddy a fib right now, young lady?" Leaning in as the situation grew more serious.

" Yes ..."

"Yes, what, young lady?"

"Yes, Sir!"

BOOM! "Go get on that bed and don't get up until I say so!"

A better discipline by far that the dreaded 'good shaking' combo.

Swirl together all of my shit phobias in a haughty, redneck royal and voila, you've spawned a compulsive hand washing 'germy Annie' who wretches around most any brand of feces.

As did all living beings on the farm, the hogs ate well and bacon tasted good. Gratefully, it was many years before I associated bacon with the curlyque tail piglets that became my favored wards. I loved nothing more than loitering by the hog pen studying a dozen or so sucklings as they squeaked and squealed while nursing … mostly minding Mama to stay out of their pen.

One day, one of the babies, a scrawny white runt with pink eyes, lost the tit and scrambled off in the wrong direction. Straight through the wire fencing I bolted, bound for the north end of the sow, plucked up the squealing sibling, jerked a little round sister off her tit, attached my puny friend, then decided the whole family needed to learn better table manners. Greedy bullies were relocated to the south end while the smallest of the squirming litter was efficiently reassigned to a bigger spigot. I well understood the importance of a good flowing tit. Having her fill of the hungry brood being rearranged the massive mama slowly raised her head, glaring over her shoulder, let out a roaring snort in fair warning to stop with the nonsense. About the same time, Mama darted around the barn wiping her hands on her flour sack apron.

"Oh my Lordy, Dixie Jane Cauble! Don't move—that mama sow will eat you alive!"

Well, I couldn't move. Boney bird's feet attached to match stick legs were mired knee deep in hog wallow, a steaming brew of poop, pee, and mud rooted into slimy black sink holes where the pigs cooled down on hot days. The look of terror tinged with rage on Mama's face as she hiked up her dress to climb into the pen, me up to my thighs and sinking fast, left a hardy gash in my memory. The sty stench of the sticky mung oozing down my legs triggered gagging, which started me bawling, which then launched a full on hissy fit screaming to Mama, "get it off me, get it off me," clawing at my legs, then digging at my eyes, flailing against my poor rescuer doing her damnedest to hoist me out of harm's way.

Fixing shit covered me in shit, and The Fixer was born.

I'm guessing this bit of pandemonium ended in a 'good shaking' and an extended afternoon nap.

Sugar pea shelling on the screen porch with Mama and Aunt Alice, Daddy's ancient aunt, popping more in my mouth than ever landed in the bowl, instilled a lifetime of pea cravings. Aunt Alice and Mama parting their legs, poured the peas in their aprons, which I tried to imitate with my tee shirt. I don't remember much about Aunt Alice except that she was my Grandmother Cauble's sister, and that she dipped snuff and spit into a spittoon at her house, but at our house, she spit ever-so-discreetly into a Coke bottle kept under the hem of her dress. My grandmother died many years before I was born, so Aunt Alice was the closest thing to a grandmother I had. The Hartleys were the English nobility line that flared my pious princess DNA.

Daddy was aging and his health hampered, not only by alcoholic binges, but arthritic inflammatory issues, likely brought on by the binges. As if by some sort of osmosis, either Ray or Jim Ward would suddenly appear as upstairs tenants, tag-teaming each other without so much as a phone call. Daddy opened the spare room for them in exchange for help around the farm. For the most part the 'Ward boys' as Daddy called them were gentle and kind drunks, who doted on Butch and me like their favorite cherubs. I adored them both when they didn't reek of stale alcohol and chewing tobacco. Usually with the first whiff of alcohol breath, Mama ran them off, but sometimes they'd sneak behind the barn where their bottle of white lightning was stashed. Jim was the good-looking one and Ray the more pathetic, so it's likely that I felt sorry for Ray as I did most drunks, especially Daddy. One afternoon Mother asked Ray to put me down for a nap. He lay down beside me showing me pictures as he flipped through a *Look* magazine. Magazines gave me, my first window to a world outside the farm.

I was between two and three so, as usual, wearing nothing but little girl panties.

I remember so clearly a picture of a beautiful little baby posed with a large pink rose turned up on the page. As Ray was showing me the image, he said, "look at that sweet baby, just as sweet as you are."

Out of the blue, my trusted Ray touched me through my panties. I froze for a few seconds as victims do, then jumped up and ran out of the room to find Mama. I'm not sure what, if anything, I was able to verbalize about what had happened, but I forever avoided Ray and so did Mama. What buttons were pushed for Mama, I see in the rearview, and Ray was never alone with me again.

We both saw to that.

I suppose the farm was a utopia of sorts for city people, but for me, animal husbandry aside, the farm had a way of cultivating shame in our daily life style. During the summers I sometimes rode shotgun while Daddy slowly drove our green Ford up and down pristine downtown streets hawking whatever fresh-picked produce was lovingly displayed by Mama in tin dishpans in the backseat.

"Fresh-shelled butter beans, tomatoes, corn, okra, and black eyed peas," he'd call out to whomever happened to be rocking on their front porch in the sweltering late afternoons.

I found myself feeling a confusing glut of pity, piety and mortification around my proud daddy, especially when forced to peddle the fruits of his labor when his soul longed to be healing his devoted patients. My father was a healer, a unique human being charged with a task only his soul understood. He strained and struggled to hear guidance to help the rural, mostly undereducated neighbors and patients who found their way to him word of mouth. But the disconnecting static of addiction kept tossing him back down the rabbit hole, where he stayed one month out of every year. Only looking over my shoulder did I understand the path his soul created and the torture he endured to follow it.

Slipping away from moorings seemingly without provocation or announcement imprinted as a lifelong pattern, be it sinking into the night from family porch gatherings, stumbling from seemingly committed relationships, escaping deep into Mexico to avoid the earth's violent shudders or disappearing into the ethers to cavort with other Beings, the same independent spirit that walked me out of my dirty diapers shadowed my life.

# WITCH HAIR #3.

Thirty years after the home place had been sold to developers all that remained was a carved wooden sign vainly proclaiming "Cauble Acres." I began to grasp the profound significance of not only my father's health-centered consciousness, but of the power infused into my being by the environment itself. My capacity for Houdini-like disappearances was well established by the time I moved about on two feet. Mother had her hands full with a miniature escape artist, so the frightening malady that attacked my brother after only a few months on the planet must have driven her into a state of overwhelm, especially with Daddy's unstable presence. I chattered to anyone who looked down about my baby brother being "all broke up." Eventually he was diagnosed with infantile eczema, likely an allergic reaction but his entire little body was covered in oozing itchy red patches for the first six months of his life. It was during this trying time for Mother that one of my escapades could have been my last.

I visually recall some of the bee encounter from behind three-year-old eyes. On a whim, I decided to take a stroll up to our closest neighbors house, where Carrie and Sadie, a couple of white-haired sisters, lived with Sadie's husband Fred. Frequent escape to a world beyond our cozy front porch, whetted by an appetite for how other folks went about their lives differently or better, was daring and exciting. Our closest neighbors, the Josey trio, was a frontier to be conquered, even if it was a quarter-mile barefooted hike on gravel. The journey to the Josey's all-dirt yard, meticulously manicured with stick brooms, was adventure in it itself, but four white square boxes all in a row between the yard and field caught my attention. My curiosity called me toward what I reckoned to be some kind of animal houses. The last memory I have was standing in front of one of the boxes.

Mother filled in the rest of my misadventure. My screams could be heard for miles, bouncing around the treetops causing the dogs up and down the road to kick off a barking frenzy, and Mother's world to stop spinning. Scrambling as fast as two old ladies in hand-sewn ankle frocks and homemade sun hats could, Carrie and Sadie barely beat Mother to the hives, scooping me up, trailing swarms of crazy mad bees behind them. Mother wiped mounds of bees off my near naked body with her bare hands. The stingers, with bees still attached, were stuck in my eyelids, my ears, and even in my mouth, wide open from wailing.

Mother raced back down the road with my limp body splayed in her arms begging Jesus to let me live, wanting nothing more in the moment than to hear me scream. Holding my body up to her face she checked for a sign of breath as she scooped dead bees out of the back of my throat, praying as only a mother can pray for her baby to live long enough to get help. With my baby brother asleep in his crib and Daddy on a binge, she was left to a mother's intuition to save her child. She grabbed a towel and box of Arm & Hammer baking soda, filled a lard bucket full of ice water, moistened ravaged new skin with the chilling water, then patted my entire body down with baking soda until I was caked in ghostly white from hair to toes. Without a car, Mama's only choice was to get help to come to us, so she frantically dialed the operator, or *central* as Daddy called her, to get the family doctor on the line. After what seemed like hours to Mama, Dr. Coffey, some ten miles downtown, called back only to say nothing more could be done, and that if I lived for the next few hours, he was 'purty sure' I'd be OK. I didn't regain consciousness for a full twenty-four hours. When I came to, it was as if nothing had happened, with the exception of looking like I had fallen into a flour bin. No swelling, no redness, not even one itchy spot.

A miracle, or an inoculation for a life to be lived on an increasingly toxic and acidic planet where honey bees would not only never be recognized fully for their immunity-building, inflammation-reducing, powerful healing properties, but in my lifetime would be slowly poisoned by corporate greed. I suppose my soul created the bee mayhem as a vaccine against inflammation. So was it a child's curiosity goading me off the porch that day, or the voice of my soul putting me squarely on healthier life path?

Maybe it was the chaos of the colliding genes, but with the exception of the honeybee blackout, I can vividly see patches of most of my childhood, as far back to before Mama's tit segued into cow's tit from Pepsi bottle with a rubber nipple attached. Mama was likely trying to wean me because of my incubating brother who arrived twenty-three months after me. I wanted nothing of it. When I saw him snuggled up next to Mama sucking away in my spot, I mic-dropped the Pepsi bottle and latched on to the other tit.

Exactly why I was so determined to attach the tiny piglet back on his tit.

Once my mouth full of teeth had taken a toll on her nipples, I was banished to crib jail while Butch nursed. Since there was no central heat, everyone gathered in the room with the warmest heat source, either a fireplace or the propane stove. The fireplace room had a double bed, dresser, crib, bassinet and several rocking chairs. The heat-stove room was more or less a living room, which morphed into a bedroom in the winter. In this cozy family setting, my first taste of jealousy reared its ugly head. My big-sister heart hovered in pity for the first months of Butch's life, but when his skin began to clear, he was fair game for competition. Shoving the Pepsi bottle out between the slats, it crashed to the wood floor in perfect timing to interrupt my sucking sibling.

In that instant, peeking out between the bars at my young mother nursing baby Butch on the bed while Daddy rocked by the fireplace smoking his pipe, I had a harsh realization for a newly-bound soul. No one in the room was going to waltz me through this thing called life. I had to go it alone. Fifty years later, relaying this tot-sized thought storm to my mother, she came back with her own story.

Weather permitting, the family, along with any resident inebriated farm hand, rocked in tired silence after suppertime on a sleepy porch. As we lost light, we all fell silent to see who could hear the first whippoorwill call. The smoke from Daddy's pipe and Mama's cigarette curled around our heads while the soft clanking of the swing chains lulled us. This sweet time every summer evening became a ritual to flee a steaming hot, unlivable kitchen. Mother used to say we were waiting for the kitchen to cool down so she could wash the dishes, but usually that took place the next morning at the crack of dawn.

According to Mother one muggy evening, I once again stole off the porch into a soft moonlit night and it was quite a while before anyone noticed. Mother explained on her part it was because she was nursing Butch and Daddy was dozing, which he called "clearing his mind." Her telling triggered a memory of hearing both my names echoing through the dark over and over again: "Dixie Jane, where are you? Answer me right this minute!" Then a pungent smell of freshly deposited cow poop fired up the memory of plunging both tiny feet in a huge cow patty as I wandered through the pasture looking for my friend Bossie.

Daddy, spotting me with a flashlight, ran up on me sweating and panting in his underwear, jerked me up dripping cow shit everywhere while Mama hollered louder than Bossie mooed, "Dixie Jane Cauble, don't you know the BOOGIE MAN will get you out here?"

"He WILL NOT, Mama; the space people take care of me."

# WITCH HAIR #4.

*"All suffering is caused by ignorance. People inflict pain
on others in the selfish pursuit of their own happiness
or satisfaction ..."*
*The Dalai Lama*

My Lutheran-reared Mama finger pointed and raised her voice a few notches to scare the word "hate" out of our vocabulary.

"It ain't a nice word. Jesus wouldn't say it, and I don't wanna hear it".

I've remained abstinent under the most trying circumstances particularly when it comes to certain political figures, but ...

I *hate* pine trees.

If I or if any "we" combination checked out a house to buy and there was even a lone pine tree on the property, I refused to leave the car, for years claiming an allergy. As witch hairs sprouted and demanded plucking, my allergic reaction became an itch marinating in emotional content.

Until second grade, my childhood was fairly idyllic eleven months out of the year. Yes, my daddy was old and looked his age, and though I was a born princess-and-the-pea, the stark Federal style farmhouse my grandfather built for his wife and eight children was made livable by my young mother. Breathing love into every pea she shelled, every biscuit she baked, and every diaper she changed, the woman was love incarnate: unbuttoned and unconditional. As an adult coming home for a Mama fix, the first thing I'd do was plop on her lap until aging bones became too fragile to hold me. No doubt Mama was in love with my old daddy, and the way his blue eyes lit up and held on her face told me he adored her.

By the time I was eight, Daddy was only seeing his patients part time so he had moved his practice into our house. This was not so much about his sixty years, but the toll alcohol was taking on his body. For eleven months of the year, he was a strict, by-the-book, all-respecting husband and parent, proud of his lovely young bride and his only two children out of four other marriages. My gifted father was not only a full-on fifty years ahead of the holistic healing curve, but was a professor without a podium, lecturing me before I could walk about how many bones were in my foot … twenty-six, one quarter of the entire body. Not surprising at all that I have spent my entire adult life chasing natural healing and health.

Any image of Daddy around the time I came on board would not reflect a ladies man, but women flocked around and fawned over his stout, bald-headed self. According to family lore, substantiated by photos in his family album, he married two actresses, two nurses, then finally my mother. The truism that opposites attract played out almost comically in my parents, injecting my DNA with soul-stretching dichotomies that grew more pronounced and irritating with time.

The Caubles, a hard-working straight-laced German clan, settled in the Piedmont area of North Carolina in the late 1700s. My grandfather managed to afford six of his eight children advanced educations. Two were doctors, one an engineer, one a nurse, one a teacher, one died at four years of unknown cause, one died at twenty-two possibly of suicide … or a train hit him. My grandmother, reputed to be English nobility, storied in rare yellowed photos with her chair back posture, taste for fine linens, shiny silver, perennial flower gardens and based on her children, the English language properly enunciated. Both grandparents departed long before my arrival, but in a treasured photo of Eliza Jane Hartley Cauble posed elegantly on the edge of a chair in her flower garden surrounded by cascading blooms of every species, I see my mouth, eyes, nose, the long shape of my face, and a big chunk of my spirit reflected back to me.

The Morgans all wore blue collars, perpetually dirty fingernails, tobacco in their cheeks and as Mama used to say, "didn't have a pot to piss in."

Another well-used decree of Mama's was that her daddy was "the meanest man that ever walked God's green earth." I barely recall meeting my maternal grandfather only once, standing in our front yard by the tree swing waiting for Mama to come out of the house. Did she ever come out? I recollect a dark shadow of a man with few words and wild, unsettled eyes. Mama's roomy heart harbored deeply interred secrets, carefully guarded from Butch and me. When she finally escaped her slave-like existence and legally married a man twenty-six years her senior with Dr.

in front of his name, her denial fertilized the sod over the grave that safely preserved the family secrets.

Fifty-five years later, when Mama had been with Jesus about ten years, two of her skeletons rose from the grave. One would forever change the fabric of my life and the other was a spark that lit a burning brain.

During my teenage family history assignments, I'd quiz my Mama about what happened to her beloved mother.

"She dropped dead in the tomato patch, is all I know," The end of the story programmed into my mama from the time she was eight years old.

The skeleton that raised my life to new heights forged a path to the real story of what happened to my grandmother in the tomato patch. She didn't just drop dead of a heart attack at forty-two, as the biblical version was passed down. My namesake, Sallie Dixie Barnes Morgan, was brutally whacked on the head by her husband who, in the grip of one of his rages, grabbed a nearby singletree. She died instantly amongst the ripening tomatoes. Her death left six children under the age of thirteen with a severely mentally ill alcoholic father, capable of murder, to fend for themselves. By eighth grade my book-smart mama was yanked out of school to care for the rest of the brood.

Mother had no inkling when she married my much older, successful father that she had reunited with the shadow of her daddy standing in the mirror. Truth is, women have been marrying their daddies, the light, the dark, and the gray, since time immemorial, and they will tread that path until the male psyche evolves to understand and meet a little girl's need for a fully expressed unconditional love from her father.

My daddy's benders were brutal for us all, not just psychologically and emotionally, but financially. Daddy would up and disappear into town, I suppose when the tug of addiction grew stronger than his will, sometimes not showing back up for days or weeks. He came home dragging his guilt behind him, using it vilely to trash Mama. Even as a preschooler, I knew he was accusing her of doing exactly what he had been doing.

Alcohol converted my proud, holistic, articulate gentleman daddy into a raging dervish whose brain had been soaked to liver mush.

To Mama, it all had a familiar ring.

I learned the ancient art of codependent behavior from her ever-loyal, ever-hopeful ways and practiced it faithfully for nine years of my first marriage. That humble woman, openly loving and unfailingly compassionate, endured more than seven Mormon wives could ever fathom. But sufferance has its zero hour and Mama finally reached hers.

She had already rented the horrid-house when she told us we were moving out of our forever home. A dull green stucco square box surrounded by sad droopy pine trees, the dark and foreboding hovel had two closet-sized bedrooms and a postage stamp bath. Insulting the drab, depressing setting was a radio station next door with a huge tower emitting all manner of toxic shit into our young brains. Even the evergreen pines hung in a perpetual state of brown. Although I understood why we were leaving and more or less accepted our fate, my heart dropped to my toes when she opened the door on moving day. Up went my hackles.

"We're going to live here?" the haughty little princess mouthed off.

The look on Mama's face has forever haunted my heart.

"It's the best I could do," she whispered through wet eyes.

"Well, I like it!" chirped my five-year-old brother as he bounded to the backyard covered in rotting pine needles where grass ought to grow.

Bad things happened in that house.

Real. Bad. Stuff.

# WITCH HAIR #5.

*Those who see a vision that is withheld from those
lacking the necessary equipment for its apprehension
are regarded as 'fanciful' and unreliable. When many
see the vision, its possibility is admitted, but when
humanity itself has the awakened and opened eye, the
vision is no longer emphasized but a fact is stated and
a law enunciated. Such has been the history of the past
and such will be the process in the future.*
*An unknown channeling found in my journal.*

What triggers a soul's yearning for expansion? Is it the inner
longing for cosmic contact inherent in every human psyche? Is
it pain? Is it spiritual deprivation, engulfing fear, or perhaps a
slippery descent into such a vulnerable state that the ego simply
surrenders, stepping aside to make room? For me, it was time to
deal with my healthy dose of Southern shame varnished over by
fleeting affluence. Thirty plus years had ticked away; I could buy
most anything I wanted. Never had I visited that paradigm. I'm
not suggesting I spent extended time in poverty, but in various
stages of lacking. For the most part I managed through creative

means to make home and life look presentable. There was also a generous gift that afforded a bigger house when my Aunt Edna, bless her stock market shrewdness, passed in the early '70s, but by this time there were two little boys to feed, clothe, and educate. The inheritance temporarily took the heat off a couple of too-young-to-be parents trying to make ends meet with a guitar, a song, and in-laws who owned an Esso station. For two eighteen-year-old small-town kids who met in a drugstore parking lot, we dove into some pretty deep doodoo. Without a pot to put it in.

Jesse Bolt Gamble, an Elvis doppelganger, was a shiny big star in a small town. He had the same sexy, sleepy, brown eyes, full lips, and crooked smile and sounded seductive like Elvis, landing him the role of Birdie in his high school production of *Bye Bye Birdie.* Our early dates were in a bright red used funeral hearse with *Variations,* his cover band, emblazoned across the sides in white. My heart wants to be inspired to sing about my first marriage, the father of my beautiful boys, grandfather to my sweet girls. Suffice it to say, it was, as all is, a merging of the dark and the light, but with a deep undertow of addiction, control, and emotional, psychological, and random physical abuse as a deal breaker.

There was little breathing room between my split from the boy's father and my musical merging with the renowned record producer Jimmy Bowen, who prodigiously had produced Dean Martin, Frank Sinatra, Sammy Davis, Jr. and virtually every country artist you might name. We married in 1977.

We divorced in 1982.

My interior crash in 1983 was more dramatic than viewed from the exterior. A four-thousand-square-foot house on an old-money, tree-lined street (appropriately called Golf Club Lane) complete with guesthouse, tennis court, massive heated pool, fancy company cars, expense account and five-day-a-week domestic help came easy. Add in a career crowning title— President of Elektra Asylum Music—for a woman in the 1980s version of the country music business, my life trajectory was upward. Definitely these six years could be described as riding the crest of a phantom wave with no shore in sight. The shore reference reminds me of a comical photo that, for me, became the microcosm of this life chapter.

On a company-sponsored trip to Oahu, my new husband and I ended an evening picnicking on Sunset Beach. With my prized Nikon he bought me for the trip, a perfectly packed basket from the chic hotel, and new love that had not succumbed to the slightest tinge of tarnish, we settled down on the sand to take in a romantic sunset. Within minutes, a rogue wave several stories high exploded on the shore with the velocity of a small bomb, scattering romance into a heap of soggy sand with a camera lens and half a sandwich poking out of the rubble. Except for the camera, we savored the humor in the frame of the scene I managed to snap just before the waterlogged, sand-grinding Nikon succumbed. Forty years later, I found the image and only then realized the prophetic prognostication.

Yes, it was a butt-burning slide from the power of being the first woman given the corporate title of President in country music to the sky dive out of quasi-royal realms into a commoner once again. Nothing I could not withstand, had my ego not still been wedged between unresolved personal and cultural shame. As my ex frequently reminded me: I was an incomplete circle.

Day-to-day operation in a masculine-oriented corporate world in the late seventies to early eighties when women were barely sanctioned to sing in Nashville—not to head companies or produce records—body-slammed me into an underdeveloped, inexperienced masculine part of myself. I suppose my immaturity mirrored my daddy's on-again, off-again success as a before his time natural practitioner. I had no solid male example of how to master success, yet I had leadership status in an industry cinched in a kicking and screaming transformation from a good ol' boy network into what was to soon become a major moneymaking mecca. I carved my chops with the cowboy hat and shit-kicking boots at Tree Publishing Company, worn by the likes of Willie Nelson, Hank Cochran, Harlan Howard, Bobby Braddock and Roger Miller, all on paths to the legendary walls of the Country Music Hall of Fame. They were not incumbent country music messiahs in my mind, but friends to hang with, smoke weed, and witness the birth of their newborn poems set to music. The original 'guitar pulls' started when Roger blew into town. He'd invite any and all of the above-mentioned writers along with Larry Gatlin and Sonny Throckmorton, Kris Kristofferson, and other scribes of that era to his suite at the Spence Manor or his lair at the King of the Road Hotel. First call to business was the passing of a joint, and for some, disappearing to the bathroom where white powder piled in quart baggies, I knew even on innocent glance was enough to send us all downtown to jail. When the collective high found perfect harmony, out came a guitar and the introduction of the latest offspring from country music master scribes. One guitar was passed to the next and the next and the next until the wicked morning sun crested across the Nashville skyline.

What I learned from those auspicious Friday nights, a fence-hop across the alley from Tree, was that songwriters are the backbone of music. Without a song scribe there is no poetry, no chords, no notes, no record, no money, no fame. I hung on as a neophyte in the room with my fledgling-but-attuned ears pedigreed by WLS in Chicago and WSM in Nashville piped from a radio stuffed under my pillow. I had *ears*, as it is called when you know what you hear is what needs to be heard by everyone else.

Tree International, the world's largest country music publishing conglomerate, was my first gig outside of a few model shoots when Jesse, the boys, and I moved to Nashville for him to star in a show written for his good looks at the brand new Opryland Music Theme Park. I labored over a hot phone console as a sexy-voiced receptionist luring songwriters to incoming calls, then as an Assistant to the Writers, meaning I typed lyrics, held hands and, unbelievably, suggested fixes. The staff writers passed me the words to their new creation scrawled in long hand, and lo and behold, sometimes, I'd hear what my ears considered a 'better word' suggesting they try it. 99% of the time they'd love it, and a Pig Fixer, Mama Fixer, desperately trying to be a Daddy Fixer, Delusional Husband Fixer turned Audacious Song Fixer was born.

Roger Miller and I rendezvoused between his marriages to Marys when he was in town and sometimes at his shows around the South. When we first met at his Nashville hotel, The King of the Road, where he would oftentimes grab a guitar and hop on stage with Ronnie Milsap, the houseband at the time, I blurted out, "oh, my god, I used to watch you on TV when I was a kid!"

One of the funniest men I've ever met, he shot back, "well, come on over here and sit on grandpa's knee, little girl."

Most of our time together was spent with other writers and his posse. In that environment he was a clever, subtly charming, self-effacing Texas boy, but hiding beneath a masterful performer was an insecure brilliant poet who wrote first verses and choruses, then, deciding he would finish the song later, stuffed them in the hole of his guitar. One night he turned his guitar upside down and shook out one of the most compelling songs I'd ever heard, one that as far as I know was never rendered whole. Obviously, Roger created artfully- written but unusually short songs, "Husbands and Wives," for example: "It's my belief pride is the chief cause in the decline of husbands and wives" may be one of the most perceptively profound lines ever in country or any music.

I could name-drop ad nauseam about the Tree years and the close friendships forged in those hallowed but tacky halls, especially with close friend and writer—along with Curly Putman of "He Stopped Loving Her Today"—Country Music Hall of Fame member Bobby Braddock. His daughter Lauren was the daughter I almost had, and we have remained a close family throughout the years.

In 1974, Buddy Killen, the owner of Tree with Jack Stapp, called me in his office to tell me that he had arranged for Paul and Linda McCartney and their kids to stay at Curly Putman's farm in Lebanon for six weeks, and would I like to be their "Girl Friday"? Are you fucking kidding me? Hang with a Beatle?

A few weeks later I found myself impatiently waiting in the lobby of Soundshop Studio where Wings was recording with Floyd Cramer, Chet Atkins, Boots Randolph and other Nashville hierarchy to meet Paul and Linda to start my new job. Newly divorced from the boys' dad, making $146 a week take home pay, and I'm going to work for a Beatle. Yes, I am a rabid Paul groupie, but I ain't about to show it now. For over a nerve-racking hour, I waited in the lobby for Paul's personal manager Alan Crowder to escort me to meet music royalty. Finally Alan came out all apologetic that I couldn't come in. Linda did not allow women in the studio.

"Oh, my god, Alan, I'm a single mom and I NEED this job. If I don't get in there, Buddy may fire me," I pleaded.

"Well, I have an idea," he offered after a couple of snarky British musings about the whole charade of Linda's. "Wait until she comes out to go to the loo and ask her if she wants to go shopping."

I did, and she did, and we ended up sharing girlfriend stories about clothes, kids and photography as I showed her around Nashville's many unique boutiques in my little yellow Toyota. Alan and I stayed in touch for several years, and as a Christmas card I got a photo book from Linda called *Linda's Pics for '76*, a personal treasure from a once-in-a-lifetime experience. Signed, a Beatle fan.

During my most career-challenging chapter at Tree, I met Bowen. My goal was to segue from Assistant to the Writers to Song Plugger, bucking Buddy's 'only fuckable women can get into country producer offices' mind-set. When I asked for the position, he sweetly fawned that women would not be able to get a foot in the good ol' boy, hanging-out-drinking, cigar-puffing network. My words, not his. I have long discarded his pedantic explanation; alas, the bottom line was he didn't see women as cut out for song plugging, even though he had one woman,

Judy Thomas, on his staff as his 'pop developer' to fulfill his female quota conveniently. Belated kudos to Judy for signing the brilliant John Hiatt, but there was space for no more females on Buddy's good ol' boy staff.

I was smitten with song writers, and where they drew inspiration to write particular stories. Every chance I got to stay late I'd sneak in the 'tape vault' where three-inch reels of single demos lived, suss out a title that piqued my interest, thread it on the Wollansak (an ancient tape recording and playback device no longer in existence) and immerse for hours in a country music masterclass.

I randomly pulled a title by Willie Nelson, whom I had never heard of. When the song finished playing, I figured I'd just been baptized in the future of country music by the strains of that one song called "Nightlife." The next morning I bounded up to Buddy's office, tape in hand, hawking brilliance.

"Yeah, Willie's a good writer and vocal stylist, but he will never fit into Nashville." Buddy schooled the unschooled.

Every week a 'cut sheet' circulated around to all the staff pluggers, listing artists and producers on the prowl for songs that week. I noticed a new producer, Jimmy Bowen, needing songs for "Treat Her Right" singer Roy Head. I knew Bowen had produced hits on Sinatra and, more interesting to me, Dean Martin, my mother's favorite singer, so again I hid away in the tape library to reel off a few songs for Roy. A week or so later, a phone call.

"Hey, Woman, this is Bowen. I listened to the songs you sent and I want to put two of 'em on hold for Roy. You're the only goddamn motherfucker in Nashville with any goddamn ears; next time I'm in town, I'd like to hear more."

Knowing that wouldn't exactly be easy to do, I punted back. "Let me know when you're going to be here and I'll take you to lunch." Figuring I'd corral him somewhere away from Tree.

"I'm coming in next week—I'll do you one better, I'll take you to dinner," Bowen wasn't about to let a woman be on top. Not yet, anyway.

He did, and halfway through the meal, our eyes caught in midair over a plate of bad pasta. We fled back to his place barely making it to the bedroom … not quite a wall fuck, but close. Within six months we had moved in together and were married a year later.

Bowen's sex appeal extended far beyond his pants. I crushed on the respect bordering on reverence he held for songwriters, their creations and the artists who recorded them. To my yearling ears, his production was nothing short of inspired genius: Sinatra's "That's Life" and Dean's "Everybody Loves Somebody" being perfect examples. But the way the man loved me was the persuasion to finally flee the co-dependent clutches of my first marriage. Outwardly Bowen was not only not in the least threatened by feminine power, but relished spotlighting it. That's what he did for me. He positioned me center stage in an industry that did not turn the beacon light on women, especially as label executives, producers or managers. Background singers were the embraced comfort zone in the '70s.

After Bowen and I coupled, he took a stab at convincing Buddy that I should be a staff song plugger. A final headshake and I departed Tree.

I acted as Bowen's song stalker for a few years stocking his coffers. He was quickly ordained the new ruler of the studio realm with technical skills, arranging talent and a pop hit factory far surpassing the average Nashville producer. My deep connection to the cabal of brilliance in the songsmith world that I had come not only to venerate but digest from the soul out, compelled me to accept an offer to create Elektra Asylum Music as a grooming den for songwriters with artist potential. Because of their uniqueness, artist/poets like Willie tended to fall through the cracks in Music City. Many of the writers I signed, like Pam Tillis and Josh Leo, went on to realize their artist potential. Elektra Asylum Music was the first corporate company of its kind to step out of the old business model, where writing your own songs was not at all a requisite for being a recording artist, to open the door for writer-artists of today like Taylor Swift.

We made a cohesive professional team, Bowen and I. My boys adored his unconditional presence in their lives after an on-again, off-again father, and I relaxed into a non- threatening household. At night after dinner, usually left prepared in the refrigerator by Annie Mae, our all-around keep-the-house-in-functional-order person, we'd take a few hits off a joint and I'd play him my latest demos or new songs from my writers, and he'd play me his latest Mel Tillis or Conway Twitty production. The problem rose for me after Bowen started running record labels; he'd have to sign what he called 'tonnage acts' who had established enough name value to pay for the 'baby acts', who were the developmental artists next in line to be a tonnage act. Some of the latter were K.T. Oslin, Bobby Braddock, Pam Tillis, and later for other labels, Steve Earle, Lyle Lovett, Dwight Yoakam and Lewis Storey. Though Bowen picked stellar songs, the more commercial country singers were not who stirred my soul. Eventually I grew bored with Bowen's show-and-tell part of our night, and I surmise that he, therefore, became less attentive to my demos.

Was there a point where our romance sustained a stress fracture and my love and respect for Bowen as a producer, record label runner, stepfather, and husband tarnished overnight? It's possible. Suffice it to say, there was a heartbreaking incident where I unknowingly stumbled into questioning his ethics. A choice he made to go to the dark side made me question if I ever knew the real Bowen. Some in the business had a disdaining opinion of Bowen, but for the most part those people never worked for him. His employees, like me, tended to bow in deference to his genius. Actually few music row peeps escaped working for Bowen, since at one point or another he took over almost every label in town, in his words "upgrading the output." As a record executive who found the songs, arranged, produced and engineered his own recordings, he had total control of the outcome, and yes, it absolutely did evolve the Nashville sound.

Because of his label-hopping, Bowen fired a lot of people, leaving him vulnerable to verbal assault. My perception may or may not have been correct that Bowen did indeed cross an ethical line in the sand, but in my heart he breached core standards of what is good and right and that was close enough. When my respect dimmed, so did our marriage; when our marriage split open, for Bowen, who had never been without a woman in his life, it was time for number five.

The perks of merging with a mogul, from a stately two-story mansion to not having to gas up my own car or stand in line at grocery stores or get up after a late night in the studio to take my boys to school were, in hindsight, a source of confusion and chagrin. Not having to consider money when moving forward or when making a choice were lifestyle-altering habits turned addictive. Adapting to wealth was a smooth transition, but reconciling my noisy ego to a downgraded lifestyle was a rocky slide.

It took five years of playing on a silent field, out beyond right and wrong, weak and strong, or black and white, to pull myself out of a free fall that may or may not have been survivable—not inferring physical suicide, but soul annihilation.

The years at Tree were the developing cocoon where I earned an undergrad on how to treat creative beings. The naturals, the authentic, the real good ones are insecure vessels of light, hungry for an open-hearted receptacle for their new story, ever-ripening, ever-adapting children all held captive by the muse. The years as President of Elektra Asylum were a proving ground for my masculine, who may not have been thick skinned or devious enough to compete in the cold raw world of corporate chess. Certainly observing the ease Bowen reflected in manipulating and strategizing the pieces around the game board without involving his heart was not in my wheelhouse. Nor was bullshitting.

Somersaulting out of a rarified world, careening out of my marriage and vanquished from the safety of a corporate umbrella to plain ol' solitary Dixie Gamble with no Bowen attached, no title to follow, was a slow motion plunge inside a glass cage, taunting me to let go and plummet into a vast unknown or to continue to suffer the boot of my ego pressing on my soul.

Plunging in a free fall like I had never imagined possible, I could barely breathe. To survive the maiming, I dove deep into the simplicity of silence. I began meditating.

In those years there wasn't a lot of how to, and I craved guidance, not only in how to meditate but how to discern relevance from gibberish floating around in the cosmos. In the start-up stages, stray disembodied, sometimes ominous faces stared back at me when I focused through my third eye: that's the invisible inner lens between the outer. In 1983, with no Internet, tracking down meditation instructors or viable gurus was out of reach. I felt envious of friends trekking off to India seeking or to meet with their guru. I briefly dallied with the idea of dropping out to India for an ashram stay, but with errant rock and roll teenagers vying for my sanity button and health concerns in an unknown environment, I decided exotic travel might not be a good fit for this sensitive mine canary.

The willful little hussy—determined to waylay the biting fear circling life like a buzzard on a carcass—stayed put. Since early childhood, I touched the hem of answers but never reeled in the questions to pull them down. In a field where every soul is free to assemble their life puzzle piece by piece, question by question, intention by intention, my questions were: *who am I, where did I come from, and what am I doing here?* I ached to frolic in that field as a soul, not a personality with an ego attached.

Every morning, instead of prying myself out of bed, I let go to an urge to stay horizontal and breathe. A structure evolved naturally as I practiced my breath. I began to count three as I inhaled, filling my abdomen. Then another count: one, two, three, as I pulled the breath up into my chest. Still not satisfied

I was connecting outside of my ego, I upped the breath through the top of my head and voila! it worked. I noticed something completely different as the breath flowed out through my crown—a vast, free, light-infused sphere where someone or something bigger reached out to touch me. Bliss. Nirvana. God. I had ever experienced this kind of ecstasy. Different than an orgasm, not intense and physically induced, but an everything-all-at-once sensation, like breathing in tandem with the entire Universe.

Until that inhalation, I had been sequestered on the first three floors of an infinite structure then suddenly swooshed to the fourth floor, dropping into a space bathed in energy that felt like quiet bliss.

I wanted more.

Some gurus teach meditation breathing only to the chest/neck area, which will not access the fourth floor, or to use a term that blends science and spirituality, *higher frequencies*, entrenching the guru as the spiritual voice. So, in retrospect, I understand why no gurus for me, although I love the meaning of the word "guru" as the dispeller of darkness.

Deciding an inner ashram was my safe place, I committed my mornings to exploring what was out there in the inner sanctum. A discerning voice, a patient, distant, detached voice, who over a period of years I accepted as some part of myself, reached me across space and time. My capacity to hear that voice grew more adept with practice. The energy carried by the voice felt similar to mine except unattached to a body. Who exactly might it be, and what floor did the owner of the voice hang out on? A year or so into my practice, I concluded the voice as that of my *unconscious Self*, the part that immerses into and is a part and particle of all Universal energies. Was the owner of the voice a sliver of my spirit left behind on an upper floor shining a light on my path as I navigated to loftier levels?

With the help of the work of Dr. Carl Jung, I designated that aspect as *The Self*, signifying the reuniting of the conscious and unconscious mind, and my body clad ego as the *self*, responsible for spontaneous emotion, necessary defense and self esteem at the personality level. Where is the top floor and how do I get there? With no particular perception of what perks might be coming or what a long-term commitment to being silent and breathing every morning might yield, I surrendered to the escalating climb.

I am reasonably certain that in human form there's no express elevator to the top floor except death. Lifting the veil on death at my cousin Jean's wake sparked a yearning for my soul's real home and a desire to know if a longing to visit those realms could be fulfilled outside of death. The five-year-old child knew that the body with the ugly hat was not Jean, that Jean was waiting to go play in the yard. It was time to prove her right.

My goal was to get there without taking the express elevator. My soul knew how to do it, but I had to get quiet to hear. Up until now, nothing about my life had been remotely subdued; it was time to hit the mute button.

According to my journal, my first ascent outside the dream realm to a higher floor was initiated during deep meditation on August 30, 1984. The content of the experience was daunting to describe even then, but you deserve to know what I know as best I can explain it, both through science and personal experience.

My first escape from three-floor awareness hastened by simply breathing was not only mind-subduing, but ego- releasing. The breath, a silent, smooth runway for shifting out of the *I/Me* personal realm to a connection with *otherness* waiting on higher floors took flight. The separation happens when the brain is soothed out of the normal active beta state into a slower alpha state, the brainwaves in motion seconds before falling asleep. As I breathed deeper, leaning into the alpha state, I began to feel a sense of lifting out of my body, as if going from a prone position to a sitting position without my body's involvement. The environment felt instantly electrically charged, silently crackling in infinitesimal spurts, as I broke free of the confines of my body. Suddenly I found myself flying unmoored, like a genie whooshed out of a bottle. I was still me as I knew myself to be, but complete and free. My entire psyche condensed into a new form, all of me was contained in a subatomic particle, which felt miniscule, like a spark of light. Transported as if on a stream of thought that did not originate within me, but from someone or somewhere in the ethers where I was floating, I flew unbridled.

Someone somewhere beckoned me to them in my new state.

Since time was nonexistent in this state, I had no idea how long it took to find myself aboard an esthetically comforting vessel that looked like one might imagine a space ship to look.

Don't let this spook you into eye rolling; there's science here.

Backed by Dr. Stephen Hawking's theories, there are eons of parallel Universes and eleven known levels of consciousness in Quantum Physics. Since early childhood I have been comforted by the sense of being protected by familiar unseen Beings, be it from the boogeyman lurking in a darkened cow pasture or from hoards of agitated bees.

As I scanned the portion of the craft visible to me, it appeared to be constructed of a metallurgic fabric, refined to be almost translucent; solid as if made from some unknown metallic substance yet luminous and incandescent. Smooth and round, it was silent, except for the crackling energy causing a friction-like sparking, not so much a sound but a hyper-sensory disturbance. I suppose if my experience could be measured on a physical level it was my brain awakening to deeper wavelengths, or conscious mind letting go to the unconscious.

The mode of transport into the vessel was pretty much like some movies later portrayed. A beam of light streamed from the bottom of the craft bathing me in blue energy that was permeating every cell in my body. Instantly I was inside the vessel with 'them.' I have no idea who or what to call 'them,' so I'll call them *The Other*. Not us. Not human. Not angels; no wings or other appendages, just vague akimbo limbs with a few digits at the end, maybe three. The vessel, operated by several of the The Other was laid out in a circular pattern of what looked like massive curved *computer* screens with oscillating patterns. Remember this is 1984, so that word comes not from my journals but my present description. And yeah, I'm aware of how Star-Trekkie this all appears, but in deference to Gene Roddenberry's imagination and my personal experience, there was little similarity. My physical body was not disassembled then reassembled, but was left behind while my soul wandered.

In a flash, quicker than an inhalation but longer than a random thought, the vessel whisked to an unrecognizable planet. Nothing I had seen in photos of our solar system was familiar. I was posited somewhere that I understood to be an unknown star in another galaxy called the Pleiades. Earth could be seen as a star from where we were, as could Saturn as its rings. The expanse surrounding me looked, smelled and felt like another atmosphere. I sensed a strong presence of chlorophyll, yet there were no trees or grass. Perhaps chlorophyll equated to our oxygen. There was no density that I could see or feel, but I had no doubt that I was indeed on a planet or a star, an environment and an atmosphere that supported life, but a far less dense form of life than a human body.

My communication with The Other contained no emotional content, nor was I aware of any personality. They were *beings*, but not human beings. I understood through non-verbal communication that I, along with many others now incarnate on earth, was part of a plan or project having to do with saving planet earth. The Other were clear that the planet itself was in peril and may not be able to sustain habitation. Though I was not given any specifics about the project, my soul seemed to know and understand the plan and my role in it.

*What your soul knows and creates is what matters* was the message.

Arguably this phenomenon could be interpreted as archetypal in content, and a psychoanalyst like Dr. Jung might quantify the experience as a visual archetypal journey. Fair enough, but if true, it wasn't my last.

The Other were evolved beyond human intelligence and not brain- but pure energy-driven. If I could offer an equivalency, we would be Mesozoic reptilian to their present day Homosapiens.

Until these experiences I had never explored 'Alien' beings beyond an inner knowing of their existence since early childhood. Cavorting with The Other awakened me to the dimness of my everyday existence and to the truth of my longing to connect with family in another place in time. I felt home and an urgency to remain in the vast everything-ness with The Other. In that instant, I had a thought about my frequently rudderless teenage boys and wondered how they would continue without me if I stayed. When that single thought formed, I was jolted back into my body. "What the hell just happened and when can I do it again?"

I had no way of knowing how long I was out of my body, but every limb felt numbed out and fast asleep. For several minutes, I couldn't move anything but my eyes, the only frightening aspect of the experience. Like most everyone, I had experienced many lucid dreams where I was aware of dreaming and could operate independently or creatively within the dream. The extraordinary happening that had just occurred was clearly not related to the dream world, but to realms of consciousness beyond the conscious, subconscious, or Super-conscious mind, suggesting that this floor exists at a level beyond our space-time continuum, or way the fuck up there past the eleventh floor. Accessing Super-conscious mind, the aspiration of deep meditators, is considered to be the Omnipresent or One Mind expressing through all—in religious vernacular God, in a spiritual context, LOVE. All made possible by breathing.

If you have a curiosity about other realms or experiencing existence as a spark of light, focus is the key, in or out of body; it is the power of intention and consistency of focus that creates manifestation. Whether like me you want to know your soul and how it communicates, to understand death and what it really means, or to become pure consciousness and fly free form, the less dense you make your body, the easier it is. Eating a plant-based diet, living in a clean, chemical-free environment surrounded by nature is a great start, supported by detoxing emotionally from people, places, and things that weigh like heavy metal on the soul.

Suppose an aspiration is for simple manifestations such as a new car, new gig, new relationship—whatever you want, it is about clearly focusing and visualizing your intention, then applying passion, which adds action to the visualization. But then this is commercial awareness, and I have probably ventured way too far into self-helpdom, but it's how I left my body to visit The Other.

Speaking of my teenage boys, a few weeks after this cosmic ride, my youngest was stricken at school with an unbearable 'pain in his gut,' and according to the school nurse was vomiting, sweating and groaning. The nurse suspected a kidney stone and made arrangements for the ER and an ultrasound. While Garin and I were waiting in the cubicle, his pain became unbearable for me, since he had far surpassed his own threshold and was screaming. I put my hands on his abdomen and followed what a distant familiar voice said to do: breathe to open the energy center (chakra in Hindi) at the top of my head allowing the higher energies to flow down through my body into my hands, lifting his energy vibration to a level where his body was in perfect harmony. Desperate, I did what I was guided to do and focused with all my might.

Fifteen minutes or so into holding my hands on his abdomen, I felt a sudden sharp pain in my lower left side and back.

A few minutes later when the blue-uniformed person with a gurney came to take him to the ultrasound room, my son suddenly sat up and said, "It's gone; I'm going home." And we did.

I felt unwell for several days afterward, having trouble staying awake more than a few hours at a time. It took me several erroneous stabs at energy shifting before I realized if I was going to pull such spontaneous stunts, I had to get better at allowing the energy to move through me, not into me.

I'm sharing this snippet tweezed from my life because anyone and everyone can do this. It's about focusing energy. If you happen to be religious, it's bringing God or consecrated Love through you. Most religions postulate God as "out there." Experience that energy as residing within, and become One with the Source, whatever you choose to call it. I believe us all to be healers in the sense of an ability to shift energy at will, simply by changing the current conversation. Lifting an existing energy pattern to a less dense form is exactly how hands-on healing such as Reiki works. The higher or finer energy will prevail over the denser pattern where disease resides.

The Other prevail over our humanness for exactly the same reason: they are less dense.

I'm parting with these witch hairs not because I'm special or have any cosmically endowed gifts, but in hopes of igniting a recall. Sometimes it takes but a blip on the screen of conscious mind to open a quantum leap in the unconscious mind. Possibly to higher and higher floors, until we can commune with The Other, without an express elevator.

# WITCH HAIR #6.

*"If you want to find the secrets of the Universe, think in terms of energy, frequency and vibration."*
*Nikola Tesla*

*The goal of a spiritual quest is to put our selves back together, reintegrating the self that acts and the Self that observes. To be split is to be in pain. We feel our inner separation as a wound and we try to dull our pain with frantic or self-destructive methods. We seek wholeness and we'll achieve it only by surrendering to the sense of a reality that lies beyond ourselves.*
*Channeling found in a 1984 journaling*

A friend aware of my before-arising, two-hour meditation routine, suggested I might be vulnerable to becoming addicted to meditation. I thought about it for three seconds and took another drink. Addiction, rampant in my family fold, was never a personal concern since I imbibe more in the control end of the spectrum, but it occurred to me he might be on to something about the flying out of my body aspect.

Admittedly, *this* was more alluring than anything else life had to offer during the arduous ego-herding operation and getting the wheels back on my personal and professional life. Two unsteady teenage boys who looked to me as their anchor, having just lost access to a present step-father, kept me from flying off the planet and simultaneously made me want to snap the cord anchoring me. Both were called to the hormonal altar of alcohol, weed, girls, and partying in our house when I was away, filling my liquor bottles with colored water, along with any and every other imaginable challenge that comes to single mothers with teenage boys.

My gut stayed in a wrench personally and professionally, and the only solace came from silence and shenanigans on the upper floors. I'd been celibate since leaving my marriage – no libido knocking – and my energy had pooled in my upper body from compulsive meditation. My primary earthly responsibility was my boys. Shannon was a hot sixteen-year-old, nearly six feet tall, blue-eyed blond girl-magnet dallying with acting and singing in one of Garin's bands. Garin was a fourteen-year-old prodigious rock and roll drummer who had older girls hanging out in front of our condo in hopes of luring him to their car. How does a Mom protect good-looking boys from the perils of opposite sex adoration? A mere year previously in a heartfelt conversation, which usually came naturally with my boys, Garin vowed never to be seduced to Shannon's path of drinking, weed and smoking.

"I would never do that to you, Mom; I see what Shannon is doing to you and I'm never going there," promised my sweet, smart, charmingly seductive boy.

The three of us had moved into a condo in a lovely area of town to be near their high school after Bowen and I split. It quickly morphed into a sanctuary for soul stretching, as a psychic sledgehammer cracked open a leakproof urn holding my pain and heartbreak from two failed marriages to addicts.

I suppose my witchy soul knew there was no way I'd survive the toxic dump of my emotional release without a tether to the upper floors.

In February of 1984, I had scrawled 'third eye opening' into a scrappy entry to my journal. Each morning as soon as I was awake enough to know I was awake, I closed my eyes and breathed the meditation breath. Most of the time, initially, my mind preferred wandering around aimlessly in and out of random subjects before settling quietly in a corner. Not true for this particular morning. As soon as I made it to the fourth floor, I began to hear-feel a deep primordial stirring that started softly then grew alarmingly loud, a mixture of sound and vibration filling either my head or the room, as if the primordial OM had sprung to life. As in the first trip to the upper floors, the vibration itself was the escalator, but this time, I didn't fly off to anywhere. As the deep OM pulsation grew more intense, *Five Beings* (I'll call them *The Five*) surrounded my bed. Each of the Beings carried a distinct individual energy, as if they had names and personal identities, dramatically differing from The Other on the vessels. My first sense was that they were not on a floor from somewhere above the eleventh as were The Other, but were from a lower floor where incarnation into a body was no longer essential to their growth and they reigned as either a hierarchy or part of a hierarchy on their floor.

After I bypassed the initial jolt and was able to focus my vision, I saw an outline of their forms. Intimidated by an overwhelming sense of power, then awed by their personal focus, I finally simply felt comforted by their presence. Unlike The Other from sky piercing floors, *The Five* took more human body forms although transparent and ethereal. It occurred to me then that the Christian concept of Angels must have derived from others having similar visits through the eons of time. I ponder now if these types of 'visits' are what Native American and other indigenous people refer to as the Elders who guide them. Elders might well apply to the sense I had of them. Yet what did they want with me?

As *The Five* materialized around me, they energetically transmitted that they were on a preordained mission with a purpose, with my permission, yet certainly news to me in that moment.

In the showdown between ego and soul, my soul knew what I needed and what to create in heed of that pressing need. Curious to actually see them, I focused, refocused and squinted my sightline on the Being at the end of the bed but still could only distinguish the same shimmering light form, as if observing through frosted glass. Like The Other on the ships, The Five were genderless and radiated a beneficent magnificence in total attendance, humbling me with their presence.

As they maneuvered around the bed, I had no sense of what their plan might be or how it involved me.

One landed at my feet, one over my head, another to my right and two to my left. While still a bit disconcerted at the suddenness of their appearance, I felt myself lifting toward them, merging with their higher vibration, dissolving all my concerns. After that I trusted their mission whatever it might be.

I sensed that we all had known each other for infinity and counting, surrendering to whatever was before me, yet oh how I wished they had given me a heads up at what was in store.

The subsequent unfolding of the 'ritual' rattled my bones—literally! An intensely loud, vibrating noise swallowed the room. It shook the entire bed like a plane shudders encountering turbulent weather. The right side of the bed shifted under the weight when one sat on the bed. The energy felt somewhat sexual but not in the usual sense of sexual arousal but a whole being *activation*, as if every cell in my body had been plugged into an electrical source with the current arcing to a higher voltage. The rumbling vibration progressively increased to a near violent quake spreading to individual energy centers in my upper body. Beginning with my heart, it was as if a ginormous vibrating machine was being held over my heart yet I could tell it was only the hand of one of *The Five*. How was a hand, not a machine, creating such a tumultuous pulsing? I tried to question what was happening, but their energy over powered my concern. One of *The Five* positioned to my left then shifted his hand to my throat area. When I asked again what they were doing, they relayed they were 'working' and my role was to let go. *The One* at the head of my bed approached my forehead, and at this point the shaking was so loud and turbulent that I considered the disturbance that might be happening on the physical plane. Were the boys asleep upstairs hearing an altercation and wondering what was happening? The lengthy initiation became so intense that I found myself wondering if my physical body could withstand the process.

Just as I was about to express my concern, a resplendent shade of purple, like a fresh color on the spectrum appeared in the area of my forehead between my brows, instantly followed by a violet triangle-shaped orifice. At that moment, the birth-like intensity gave way to a radiant, comforting luminance, igniting a whole-being feeling of hyper-aliveness, more alive and more awake than I could ever imagine. Every cell in my body had been ignited and infused with light.

All I could see at this point was the triangular shaped opening in my forehead, as if the camera had moved in for a close up on all there is.

Tucked down in the right corner of the pull in, beaming across eternity, a solitary *Light Being* with a magnificent cobalt-blue aura extending three to four inches around the upper body, waited patiently. The view of this Being was not veiled; it was clear, distinct and mind blowing, yet on 'meeting' the *Light Being*, I remained unemotionally transfixed. The Being embodied pure, androgynous energy, was somewhat human in shape, and was condensed light.

As time is very indistinct and difficult to fathom in this state, I can't be sure how long I was able to observe, but it was long enough to pose a question. I sensed that the Being had overseen the entire procedure I had just undergone, and the purpose was not only to encounter the Being but be shown empirically of its existence and presence.

Since I had no notion of the identity of the *Light Being*, I asked for permission to draw a likeness. It was granted.

Ceaseless comfort, constant protection, unbridled peace, filled every pore, as if this Being had always been and would always be with me as Guardian over my soul's journey. There was no emotion present then, but as I describe my arduous but life changing experience, I can't stop tears from flowing. I guess it's why I want everyone to know of the existence of a personal overseeing aspect that I know is there for us all. Whether we have a direct encounter or not, is inconsequential.

When the arduous procedure completed, it took some time to acclimate to my body. I was still lying on my bed, but nothing about me, Dixie Gamble, felt the same, or ever did again for that matter. As I stirred into my day I felt an unrepressed confidence in my ability to express myself as a complete person, a realization that imprinted into every cell, as if an important part of me had been missing in action until then, and I'd been given the piece to complete the puzzle that was my whole identity.

As time and determination deepened my meditation, I developed a theory on the Light Being. I came to understand the concept of a continuous and personal higher guidance. This soul alliance, incarnating into a body served to imprint the concept of God. I frantically drew the image of the Light Being as soon as I came back to my normal brain pattern. Indeed, the image looked similar to The Other on the ships but younger in evolution. So, just in case my ego wanted to step in and wail on the cosmic roaming as anything personal to me, I was but a tadpole on the evolutionary scale of upper floors.

My understanding of my experience that auspicious morning eventually resolved into a private thesis: *the entirety of our Spirit serves as the over seeing soul lingering behind on higher floors waiting for and perhaps supervising the soul which comes into incarnation in a body to complete the tasks and lessons of each life. This Being, I will call The Higher Self, resides in a Pure*

*Consciousness state serving as observer, guide and protector to*
*and for the soul's progress and well being while completing the*
*lessons laid out for each incarnation.*

My theory, based on personal experiential understanding, is not
an attempt to project onto or erase any belief system already in
place. It's an addendum. As I mentioned, the myriad strata of
parallel Universes in our endless building with infinite floors,
some powered by light and others by darkness, mirror the
frequencies here on earth.

As long as we inhabit a dense body, I suspect we will all
meditate on and presuppose if and how we are cosmically
connected to Higher Guidance. We may not be afforded
personal affirmation while still in human form, but if awake, we
will attract enough miracles along the way to sustain a belief
in something bigger than we are. Many evolved members of
humanity comprehend an awareness of a Higher Self (in some
form) as their touchstone to hope, without assigning a name,
concept, or religious connotation.

I share my personal perceptions in the hope that it facilitates
a conscious quickening or personal curiosity to become a
stalker of higher Truth. The planet perilously awaits an
awakened humanity.

During my formidable encounter with the *The Five*, my life
and my understanding of how to live a healthy life forever was
transformed. I was offered a glimmer of insight into upper
floors, yes, but for me the most important encounter was the
introduction to my Higher Self. In my interpretation, I had seen
Jesus, the Buddha, Allah, and the Dalai Lama all stirred into one,
saturated in the purest Love most call God, and it was a part and

particle of me. Convincing me empirically that God or whatever the name applied to a higher Deity is not out there somewhere, but in there, patiently waiting.

We each can manifest our own unique versions of my spiritual adventures. We undergo an initiatory phase that opens our eyes (all three of them) and our hearts to a deeper level of spiritual understanding as we tread the path. This transformation or advancing of consciousness takes place on our current level of understanding or willingness to evolve. From an early age, I had a passion fueled yearning to understand more about life forms existing in other dimensions and I asked a question: "Who am I, really? I mean WHO AM I?" Once I had the question my soul created the bridge to an answer. We simply have to ask and then go real quiet.

A month or so later, *The Five* came again in my morning meditation, surrounding the bed in much the same way. By now, I was acclimating to these visitations and felt less uptight when they appeared. I still was initially a bit startled by their presence, but this time I completely trusted whatever was in store.

One of *The Five* at the end of the bed began to blow warm air into my body though my feet. I felt myself unhinging from, then lifting forward and out of my body. I had the sense I was being led by The Five to an upper floor not previously available to my level of consciousness. Interesting because I am not now, nor have I ever considered myself to be a Christian, so to my surprise I saw the Master Christ standing in a glorious light-filled round-shaped space. His presence was so ethereal and beautiful that I was startled. He resembled not so much what we know from art renderings as an angel with wings, but an

Enlightened Being, similar in form to The Five, whose energy felt ageless, genderless and with no genetic identity. As with The Five, it was easy to sense the benevolence and highly evolved spirit that was before me. He transferred his identity without fanfare or hoopla. We exchanged Love. The highest form of love I could ever imagine. This special Being called Christ embodied Agape, or Spiritual love, the glue holding the Universe together and surely why so many proclaim, God is Love.

Many of *The Other* were milling about in the space. Proportionately centered was an open portal that looked like a clear convex dish on a podium, perhaps five feet in diameter. The physical vortex was easy to access, so I floated over to take a look in what was at the same time enticing and daunting.

Peering into the device, I could see in sepia tones what I observed to be my soul's journey in other dimensions, perhaps happening in real time simultaneously on an upper floor? I was viewing short vignettes, each holding the inherent lessons of a particular lifetime or parallel dimension. The device seemed like a time eradicator of some sort, yet as I mentioned, it also occurred to me that I could have been viewing parts and particles of my entirety beamed simultaneously in a hyper-alive instant on many parallel Universes. Was I actually observing the entire building at once? As I write, I sense a smiling Stephen Hawking over my shoulder. Not unlike watching various atoms emanating from the same source, the viewing seemed to present a continuance of life experiences, all existing in one tall building on different floors at the same time. The apparatus was in full view for The Other to use at will. I wish I could recall exactly what I saw in the portal, but I did have the sense that when I looked at the actions of many varied incarnations or stacked parallel lives, my soul somehow retained what was relevant its present mission. I reckon had I been able to remember and interpret what I was shown, I'd be shortchanging my own soul.

All the action happened in one fell swoop, as if all the information was contained in a blink of an eye.

For several days after the deep meditation, I was more aware of myself as a soul than as Dixie the personality. It was a confusing time in many ways, trying to rein in my fragmenting boys, keep them in high school when their focus was either in their pants or rock 'n' roll music. I felt torn between my mothering duties, my focus on my budding new music publishing and management enterprise, and going to a cave in India and sitting it all out in silence. So the shadow, the inevitable shadow that balanced all of my tripping the Light fantastic, was the untethered, ungrounded sensation that stalked every minute. I felt completely unhinged and disconnected from my body, especially from my emotions and from any sexuality at all.

I'd have nausea ghosting at the thoughts of food; even my favorite veggies felt extraneous. I began to lose weight, not in a good way, at 110 pounds. I thought of the lives of Tibetan monks, envious of the simplicity of waking up connected with Spirit day in and day out without the intrusion of the shadowy content of everyday life. I read about Breatharians, who believe they can live solely on deep breathing and energy from the sun, and because my relationship with nutritional sustenance had shifted, I marveled at how it might work, and, since I ate all organic, calculated the money I'd save. Gratefully, I wasn't tripped into trying anything that drastic, but it all swirled about while I was doing my damnedest to raise teenage boys who looked down on me, physically and psychologically, as their 'little mom.'

A nagging thirst for the upper floors and hunger to be with The Other began to feel like a delicate dance toward death. Was my friend right about addiction? I had never felt more awake, alive or authentic as a human being, no more ego driving me around, but also I had never felt more disconnected from emotional content. It's an airy-fairy, Pollyanna world up there in the upper floors when the lower are dormant. But The Five did not venture to the south end during their work with me, so aligning with daily life was up to me. Everyday tasks seemed like backstroking in blackstrap molasses but on the north end of my polarized life, I'd never felt more joyful or certain of my full identity. With no Google to rely on in those days, I had to buy books to learn visualizations for grounding. For example, seeing myself as a tree sending long roots digging deep into the earth, then pulling energy from the earth through my feet by walking barefooted, helped, as did exercise like swimming and power walking.

I decided to share these encounters, safely bound between journal covers for forty years, after a recent re-visitation from The Five. No meditation for this visit, they prearranged their appearance for the purpose of encouraging this book, not only giving permission, but urging me to the right words.

Souls need to expand. We do. The loss of my second marriage, my professional position, my social status, if that even matters, left me unmoored and feeling small, but all of this detritus paled in comparison to what was happening with Garin. More than drugs, booze or groupie girls, more than rock and roll, more than teenage doldrums, my youngest treasure began to exhibit a personality change that became progressively alarming. Rage without provocation, holes in walls, and a dimming of his personal light was before me, yet how could I begin to fathom what was to come.

Because souls need to expand, we do.

# WITCH HAIR #7.

*"Go placidly amid the noise and haste, and remember what peace there may be in silence."*
*Max Ehrmann, 1927*

Between 1982 and '87, it was time to pull my sweater over my head inside out and let my soul shine. As soon as my eyes parted on another morning, I'd slip in to my meditation breath, adjust my focus through the invisible indigo eye now opened between my two green ones and free my soul to fly. My boys and I were a threesome again, all searching for solid ground in our own way: I tethered to my spiritual empire, they to the strains of Led Zeppelin.

Dancing with the mystical, as inexplicable as it may have been, created surefootedness and balance as I debated a new job trajectory, once again adapting to shopping for groceries and pumping gas while downgrading my monthly budget to fit unemployment. Teenage boys groaning for more cars and independence while lacking emotional maturity to keep their lives between the lines added to mounting stress. Several cars having quickly lost their lives in the crosshairs of hormones and booze weighted the scales of my meticulous financial planning. I shadowboxed with chaos inwardly while Shannon and Garin blasted theirs outward.

Whether my ethereal wanderings and other world connections were objective or subjective, I did not and do not know. I suppose I assumed at the time that everyone had similar exploits with upper floor dwellers, especially avid meditators, and indeed it may be true that seekers remain reluctant to share highly personal experiences until time grants permission.

It took me forty years.

Since the curtains were flung open on my private life during the divorce from Bowen, I had lived a near exclusive interior life. Libido, the stranger, rang only occasionally with all of my life force corralled at the north end. When The Five pried my upper centers – heart, throat and third eye – ajar, they discussed opening my lower centers, which would have not only freed but amped emotional and sexual energies. The power center at the solar plexus was not considered one way or another as far as I can remember. I later understood when emotional, sexual bruises and wounds are released for healing, power flows naturally uninhibited. The Five voted thumbs down on cracking open anything below the waist. Mountains had to move before excavating sexual wounds and emotional co-dependencies, and I was yet to cross paths with mining maven Sharon Wegscheider Cruse. Her groundbreaking work coached us walking wounded that violations of sexual boundaries corroded into either acting out or acting in the physical, emotional and psychological intrusion. I had done both. My boy-crazy teenage years I acted out, but tucked safely inside a commitment, I acted in.

Bottom line: spiritualizing emotional trauma can be hazardous to your health, and I was still in the rabbit hole. The all- knowing Five were conscious of my wounds awaiting cauterization and left the rest up to me.

I was not particularly accepting of my celibacy and scarcity of social stimulation, so every now and then I'd latch on to it as a self-esteem issue. One afternoon Garin and I were on one of waning car talks, when I found myself seeking advice from my wise youngest.

"Garin, you're an opposite sex magnet. Why do you think it is that men don't seem to be in the least interested in me?"

"Well, Mom, you look like you have it too all-together; we like to be the leader."

No retort for truth. In the cave I remained.

As my energy density waned, my sensitivity trigger waxed. My awakened senses could detect a speck of thistle down floating in darkness. The celestial roaming and years of silent exploration had heightened my five waking senses. I grew more alert to life's dots and dashes; I could peek around corners and had zero tolerance for negativity or toxins in my space. Not only could I taste pesticides in foods, but I could feel the burn on my hands, especially raw strawberries and apples. My daddy was right about DDT being an extreme hazard to all living beings fifty years ago, yet now thanks to Monsanto's glyphosate, we continue to be lab rats for chemical conglomerates as cancer runs rampant.

While I was hold up in my monastic cocoon, my tribe played musical chairs. Friends that hung out with the President of

Elektra Asylum Music now stood in line for Bowen's attention as a new tribe answered the call of my heart.

Some members of my witch coven were lesbian, smack in a comfort zone where my first prepubescent crush shifted my gender awareness. Virginia Team, Music Row's maverick designer dropped into my orb, joining Dale Franklin, ex-rock road manager turned consciousness of Music Row—not gay, but also celibate while valiantly managing a cancer diagnosis. Pam Rose and MaryAnn Kennedy, writer-artists whose art and souls drew me in first professionally, then personally were inducted by Virginia, and, thanks to Dale, I had John D and Susan Loudermilk close to my heart. John D and Rodney Crowell easily embraced their feminine sides as honorary witches. My friend and later business partner Katy Bee, a former music journalist and radio personality, never wavered her loyalty, nor did my first pop signing and beloved friend, Pam Tillis. A new tribe of creative like-minded seekers joined Rodney Crowell and Rosanne Cash, sturdy anchors during the most vulnerable, valuable years of my life. I was swaddled in love and acceptance for who I was, not what I did. For the first time, I felt wreathed in forever friendships.

Some months into my third year of sweater wrenching, my finely tuned radar detected a blip of earthly love on the horizon. Not that any potential suitors clamored for lingering candlelit dinners or long moonlit walks, nor were well meaning friends casting any bait for hook ups, but something aroused my heart. I persisted as a hermit on a tiny island with the curtains drawn, but after reams of self-help and spiritual immersing, explosive emotional, sexual paradigm shattering followed.

I had transitioned into a shiny bright landmark in a vast sea of nothingness ready for love to find me.

My consciousness-raising romps consumed my mornings. After meditation, I'd dive into yoga, then our condo pool for physical exercise, all seemingly a life of leisure, but my bank account clued me I needed to shine some light on a career path. An offer to start a Nashville branch of a West Coast management company whose roster boasted the crème of what we now call Americana artists initially tweaked my interest, leading me down an investigative path for six months or so. A half dozen Los Angeles meetings with the reigning king of that particular world later culminated in enlightening new friendships with artists I had tapped for a possible Nashville roster, but no contract. Again I bumped up against ethical standards which, in my perspective, were not reflecting the level of integrity I'd been working my ass off to bring to the business of music. I wasn't programmed to bullshit artists, which looked to be the criteria for corporate success.

Katy Bee and I huddled, deciding we'd form a managing, publishing co-op to see if we could lift it off the ground. Between us we'd had twenty years experience, and it sounded fun, so eventually we stopped talking about it and taxied down the runway.

Then I picked up on a presence lingering on the rim of my day, nothing I could distinguish or define, but I knew it was there. Once in a while, the elusive energy hovered close and as if someone was physically in the room with me, watching, smiling ... waiting. Determined not to crank up any desperation, I'd chalk it off to a too sensitive too wishful antennae and let go, but I wasn't about to discourage something that felt like it could be love.

I remember as a child being wistfully fascinated by couples in love, falling in love with their love. I never envisioned myself living a solitary life with an all-consuming career, bounding around the streets of a bustling city toting a large expensive bag of daily life. Nor can I cop to early visions of a white picket fence, aprons and ringing laughter, certainly not shrill screams, of little voices. I straddled somewhere in between. I loved being married, had tried it twice with no regrets, now I was clearing the slate for greater love, a healthy love stripped of condition, out there somewhere, waiting.

March 17, 1984, I noted in my journal:

*Lucky day today because I awoke thinking about you, you've been around me all day. I don't try to make you go away anymore, I accept your presence as my gift for the day. Sometimes it brings tears of the purest love I've ever felt, joyful in essence, because you are the essence of joy. I will not tuck you away or deny your presence anymore. I relish your light and bask in the warmth you create inside me. I can feel your soul so clearly and there are no words, only feelings ... beautiful, colorful, soft feelings. I wonder if you can feel my presence the way I feel yours? Sometimes I know you must or you couldn't be so present with me. How truly blessed we are to be able to experience the essence of unconditional love. I hear your music speaking, yet I don't know the song. Will I ever know you on the earth? Will I ever know who you are?*

Some months after I wrote this passage, I was in my morning meditation when again I was ousted out of my body, then settled on the floor beside the bed. In a flash, an all-encompassing presence lowered down on me, as if merging with me. The presence was distinctly masculine with a beguiling innocence and open benevolence.

Startled, "Who are you?!" I snapped.

A distinctive chuckle, then audibly, "well, I'm John."

The implication in the tone of what he said was, *I'm John, I've been waiting and waiting for you and I can't believe you don't know who I am.*

My immediate response was: *"It doesn't matter who you are; this is EVERYTHING."*

As quickly as he came, the energy swooshed away and when I came out of the meditation, I was lying on the floor beside my bed, aghast and slightly embarrassed at how I got there.

After that magical masculine drenching, every man who ventured near my orbit was named JOHN. There was an attorney, a comedian, a couple of songwriters and even a one-percenter—I stretched my parameters on that one—but not my John. If anyone even vaguely mentioned someone named John, I walked over coals to meet each one, to the point of once flying to San Diego to meet a friend of a friend. With only a glance, handshake or hug, one by one I eliminated Johns.

I had mingled with forever. I would find my everything.

For the better part of two years, I tracked Johns. No matter how discouraged I grew in my quest to find him or for him to find me again, I trusted our cosmic convene more than I've ever trusted anything in my life.

# WITCH HAIR #8.

My rock and roll boys raised the ante on surviving my rootless life. Wooing my heart with unconditional love then jilting it with hijinx had me flirting with a jaunt to a cave levitating with the gurus. My illusions about guiding their life paths from the siren call of Medusa to something resembling a college education were wrecked by reality, and simply getting them through high school became a lofty goal.

Their father, a twenty-one-year-old in his early teens when they were born, disappeared first into his own rage, then alcohol, and finally religion when they were in middle school, then my boys lost Bowen as a father figure just when he was most needed.

Beautiful boys, every mother says this, but those two turned heads and melted hearts. Blue-eyed, tow-haired, Spock-smart Shannon arrived first with little provocation about ten months after Jesse and I eloped. Two years later Garin found the arms of relatively aware, welcoming parents. With flashing brown eyes tuned to his hair, he was a shining bright star from the time he struck three, and a simpatico little Leo spirit for me.

Shannon came in with my wandering wonder for what else might be in the world, or at least the neighborhood. Reluctant to leave the womb, he was nearly a month old when he was finally booted out. From the time we brought him home from the hospital, he slept all night without demanding a bottle, but as soon as the sun split the horizon he was up and at it making sure we were too. When he could barely stand, he figured out how to scoot his crib across the floor to our bedroom door for a six o'clock wake up call. By nine months, he maneuvered a way to escape his cage, toddle to my side of the bed, lift my eyelid, and speak into my eyeball like a microphone.

"I'ont some ceral." Little dude could talk at six months. First word: not Mama, but bird.

Jesse and I hatched a plan to teach our little ingenious monkey how to grab his bowl from a lower cabinet, cram it full of Cheerios, no GMOs then, and heave a milk carton off the bottom rung of the refrigerator, in an effort to halt the early morning eye-speak .

Quickly we surmised that turning on the television to Sesame Street had to be added to his schooling in self-sufficiency, salvaging an extra hour snooze for young rock and roll parents.

Shannon easily mastered the break of dawn routine, then grew bored with Big Bird and worked out how to unlatch the front door. With his blankie dragging behind him and nothing on but training pants, he'd solo venture in the hood. We'd wake up to the TV blaring but no Shannon anywhere, panicking the entire block. On one of his morning walk-abouts, we got a call from a neighbor two busy streets away.

"Is this J.B. Gamble's residence?" A concerned voice on the other end of the line was both relieving and embarrassing.

"Yes, we're Shannon's parents; is he there with you?" I was inches from calling the police to help us find him. "How did you know to call us?"

"Oh, we asked him who his Daddy was and he said, J.B. Gamble, but he wasn't sure of the name of his street, so we looked you up in the phone book." Helped that Jesse (I insisted that he be called by his birth name Jesse Bolt) was a 'rockstar' in small town Salisbury.

Clearly today Jesse and I both could have been jailed for child endangerment and Social Services would have absconded our boy. Our style of rock-and-roll parenting would not be an option in the 21st Century!

Truly, Shannon's DNA was saturated with my Houdini genes and lust for independence. Gratefully there were no beekeepers in our neighborhood.

Jesse and I experimented with just how far a total lack of parenting skills could get us toward not mucking up our bright little boy, muddling through to the choice to procreate another human being. Audacious, I know.

I got pregnant with Garin while holding down a job at the hospital across the street as a Respiratory Therapist to supplement Jesse's meager income from his roving-hearse cover band *The Variations* and his day job at the Esso station. Problems arose when I was appointed Chief of the CPR team, which meant responding to Code Blue calls to resuscitate patients in death's grip. Morbid as it sounds, I loved the powerful feeling that came with actually pulling someone back from the brink of the afterlife. Not only had I always been fascinated with the truth of our journey home, but with each soul I coaxed back to the body, I learned more and more about the journey.

One patient whose heart had stopped unexpectedly flat-lined for several minutes before I finally got a blip on the monitor, always an emotional, soul-shuddering relief, came back with a story.

"You worked hard on me, young lady, and I 'preciate it so much!"

"I'm glad, you're back with us and with your family, but how did you know I was working on you? You had no heartbeat for nearly two minutes!"

"Oh, I's watchin' you from up there in the corner of the room and I knowed how bad you wanted me to come back."

So this is how it works! I thought of my cousin Jean waiting to go outside to play with us at her wake.

Then, early in my pregnancy with Garin, when even a whiff of cheap coffee could send me reeling to the toilet, I was called on a Code Blue for a baby, a beautiful new being with anguished, young parents, who did not come back to his body.

That was it for me. I left the profession never to look back.

If nature combined with nurture hatched a sagacious, pragmatic Mr. Spock in Shannon, we spawned Jon Bonham in Garin, a soul who knew exactly who he was and where he was going. He taught us how drums were played when he'd pick out the right size pots and pans, turn them upside down using spoons to sort out perfectly timed beats, if torturing tones. For his third birthday he begged for a real snare drum; for his ninth, he got a professional drum kit. Garin was firmly on his path.

During my disembodied outings, when I felt compelled to hang in the ethers or tempted to exile to India, my tall, badass teenagers fixed a spotlight on everyday life. Kind beings with generous hearts and more than adequate rock and roll edge, the boys and I huddled easily as a threesome until puberty scattered hormones laden with addiction genes all over our lives.

I decline to whine about the challenges of being a single mother with teenagers aspiring to follow rock's body-littered path. I'll leave it with anytime the phone rang after one a.m., I knew shit had hit some fan somewhere. Once I got a three a.m. call from the Franklin police department who'd detained Garin for having an open beer in his car, telling me I had to come get him because they had impounded his vehicle.

"Nope. You keep him." I turned over and went back to sleep.

Attempting to tame the budding beasts, I turned one of the garages in our condo into a soundproofed rehearsal studio where Garin, who had already been playing drums for several years, quickly gathered a talented band around him, with Shannon tapped as the lead singer. Shannon, a model-faced boy with sculpted cheekbones oozed enough sex appeal to get by without a Freddie Mercury voice. Garin, on the other hand, flew in a prodigiously gifted musician, along the way grooming looks and personality to match. I had no doubt that he would follow the golden glitter path to arena rock tours.

The garage band respite lasted less than two years when weed, alcohol and quite possibly other shit I never want to know about invaded my esoteric sanctum like Big Foot squashing grapes. I took a chair in every *-anon* group I could track down tackling addiction in my family of origin, the boys' father, my in-laws, and my Big-Split-pot-dependent-ex. Determined to learn why I attracted addiction-disordered people, I persevered through torrential emotional storms. Too soon, the boys' behavior added several more *-anons*, groups where parents go to preserve any modicum of remaining sanity when living with a child/boy using anything that messes with what little reason a teenage brain can muster gathered to moan. One of the weekly meetings was a Tough Love group, which bit me on the ass in the end. Treating suffering with muscle was sadly misinformed.

I navigated learning how to hang on to shaky boundaries, how to quit saying "no" then allowing it to happen anyway because it was easier, and, most importantly, about rehab. Blessed rehab, where for twenty-one way-too-short days, I knew where they were, and that they were not using anything stronger than 12 steps to sanity.

Shannon eventually pulled out of his teenage death spiral after spending forty-eight hours in the downtown jail on a dining-and-dashing ruse with friends. Like any true Kerouac/Burroughs fan, after breaking into tears processing his abject fear of the daunting environment, he wrote a brilliant piece about his experience, matriculating up to another life level. Shannon ended up following his passion and skill as a gaffer, designing lighting plans for film productions, to great success.

Garin never did.

A monster denuded his life with a much bigger footprint than any fear I could ever muster, and he was lost in the fray.

# WITCH HAIR #9.

*The Center is birthed from Chaos.*
*(found in my journal)*

A deep spiritual massage comes with a healthy dose of inner
security, a soothing sense of all possibilities lying in wait a
few steps toward the edge of everything. Rimmed in the soft
light of readiness, freed from tangled emotions, I took a walk
to the edge.

Jungian therapy introduced me to my preeminent shadow, I
devoured the enlightening tome of Yogananda's life, and hung
the iconic poster with it's ever-present dot of dark imbedded in
light balanced by a spot of light glowing in a field of darkness.
The Yin and Yang of life. No doubt my shadow and I were well
acquainted, but I downgraded the part I knew the least as a
condition to be feared or conquered rather than understood and
accepted as co-resident in a free will zone. A patient, impartial,
unbiased Universe doesn't probe or prod or goad or bend for a
kiss of approval on a job well done; that particular sacrament
was still mine to receive.

Cowering from the wicked witch part of me—obvious to others, oblivious to me—fabricated a personal conundrum. When the shadow whispered, 'there's a spinout on the road ahead,' was it fear talking or a heads-up, and how did I decipher the difference? In the end I suppose it mattered little, since either way my lessons would have their way with me.

Because Lewis Storey and I see our journey together as possibly having saved our respective lives, let the shadow dancing begin.

On the rim of the Big Split in 1983, while still with Elektra, a manila envelope with Dixie Gamble written across it appeared in my inbox. Out of self-preservation, I was not in the habit of listening to drop-offs, after once having been handed a demo cassette while I was dazed on pre-op drugs waiting for a surgical procedure, but this one called me. I tore it open and a handwritten note on lined notebook paper spoke to my soul in a voice humbled in authentic simplicity.

*'I'm a third generation Arizona farmer and English teacher, but music is my soul's voice and nothing would honor me more than someone in Nashville hearing my music.'*

The letter spoke of spending two years in the Peace Corps in South America with his wife and of their two young children. This brush with humility commanded my attention in a bubble where many rookies presented themselves as the next Kris Kristofferson, or snuck a cassette tape on your gurney when you were waiting for surgery.

I whirled around dropping the cassette in the deck. A verse and chorus into the first song, my career shifted into high gear. I was hearing not only one of the cleanest most powerful voices I'd ever heard but the words coming through that voice soulfully spoke a simple dirt farmer poetry, Wendell Berry set to music. A superstar had just docked on my desk and the trajectory of my life pitched skyward.

Elektra Asylum Music was a Warner stepchild, so when the gauntlet fell in my marriage my contract loopholes were already under scrutiny. As the last song sustained on the four-song demo tape, I knew, since one foot was out the door this music would tag along wherever I went. Sandbagging was not beneath me. I'd just heard Neil Young's stories, Bruce Springsteen's passion, and Wendell Berry's poetry woven into O'Keeffe landscapes, delivered in pitch-perfect soul-stirring contemplations of everyday human life.

The elusive once-in-a-lifetime package, the reason every music biz gambler plays the game, rolled the probability of high numbers my way.

Bowen's deep authoritative voice, damp with disapproval admonishing to 'learn to play the game,' shadowed me. A competitive sliver wanted to show my mighty mentor how a woman whose circle had sealed could beat him at the game. Never allowing for a thick layer of scar tissue that had formed around my healed wounds, I sat down at a high stakes table.

The process of forging a megawatt country star out of a copper-soil, bilingual, advanced-degree, modest, gifted, good looking enough teacher from a third-generation farming family did not strike me as particularly daunting. I was upper floor, upper energy center megawatt-empowered, primed with enough light to manifest any and all rewards circling my line of sight.

After hit upon smash hit of musical mediocrity, the country music business in the mid '80s was teetering on a precipice of artistic integrity, with writer/artists like Steve Earle and Lyle Lovett popping up on the radar. Lewis's heartland music furrowed from deep within his desert roots revived a sound everyone wanted to plug in to their system, and I had him under contract to my new publishing company.

I produced an industry-wide showcase, inviting all the major players and positioned A-Team session musicians behind him. The reigning king and queen of country, Rodney Crowell and Rosanne Cash, rocker John Hiatt, John McFee of the Doobie Bros, Nigel Olsson and Dee Murray from Elton John's Band and songbird Pam Tillis, all contributed to the demo of Lewis's masterpiece *Heartland*, and many turned out to sing it with him on the showcase. Musical ears from up and down the row, A&R or CEOs from the major labels packed the club, thirsty for authenticity. Even though Lewis's largest audience to date had been beer guzzlers and line dancers in dive bars in a tiny Arizona town, my nascent star readily rose to the occasion.

Lewis delivered a set of masterfully penned visual narratives wrapped in classically influenced, roots-inspired melodies to an enraptured crowd of cynical, seen-it-all professionals that commanded a rousing spontaneous standing ovation.

The CEO of my chosen record label leapt up beaming dollar signs and bear hugs.

"Which label under the umbrella do you want him on, and do you want a ride home in the limo?"

Lewis and I were on our way, with a few minor details to sort out, like who would be producing his music and who would be his agent, his publicist, and peep posse.

Fun stuff.

After the album was cut, which in my heart I knew lacked the earthy heart and soul of the demos he produced with his local band, the CEO called me in to pick a single. We agreed on the best song of the compilation and he started writing checks to live up to his part of the bargain to promote the project, hiring a well-known New York photographer to shoot the cover, and veteran publicist to hype the record and the top promoters to get it on the radio.

The first single release, a mid-tempo dance-ready charmer, squeaked into the top twenty, considered respectable but not optimal for a new artist. Now positioned among the 'rising elite,' Lewis not only garnered the respect of his peers, but picked up some die-hard fans.

In 1986, the Academy of Country Music nominated Lewis as a best new artist, coveted recognition for any artist with singles struggling up the charts.

Lewis and I were in Los Angeles for a taping of new artists clips for the ACM live show when Lewis's characteristically genial persona began to contort.

We were in makeup with Lewis and Dwight Yoakam, two of the five nominees, getting bronzed for the camera, when Lewis who had been amiably chatting with Dwight, not a particularly outgoing type, suddenly leaped up and knocked off Dwight's white cowboy hat, sending it bouncing to the floor. I'd heard rumors of Dwight being a chrome dome, but being a 'bald is sexy' type, I wasn't particularly curious about his cranium.

Lewis was.

Dwight was not amused and I stood there in dazed disbelief as Dwight picked up his hat, dusted it off then struck Lewis across mouth with deafening tight-jawed silence.

Lewis lost the coveted cowboy hat trophy for best new artist to Dwight Yoakam.

Far more subtle behavior changes in my talented progeny began rising up as I maneuvered him into the country music spotlight. His natural downhome charm and genial confidence devolved into an edgy egocentric posture, bordering on arrogance. A little wired, a little tight in the belt, and a big fondness for Molson's I chalked up to a small town boy squinting in big city glare. During our requisite country radio tour, a defining experience that made me realize I was so not cut out for managing, I found myself concerned about what Lewis might blurt out to conservative country music programmers, who worked to find a reason not to play a record.

We made it through the two-week tour with me forcing tight-lipped grins through being called 'darlin'' by beer-burping DJs who disdained music but coveted power.

Immediately after the first single peaked in the high teens, likely because of the ACM nomination, nobody was nervous but me. I was having trouble drawing a deep breath. Radar acutely attuned to addictive personalities was beeping like an urgent heart monitor in a cardiac unit. Father, brother, uncles, husbands, children—god, if I had any attraction pheromones left, they were hanging on sticky flypaper waiting for addicts.

My emotional excavation entailed shit-shoveling my way to why I was an addict magnet, and to the hope that this gut-wrenching dig would demagnetize my heart. For several years, I toiled with a codependency therapist, sat cross-legged for endless hours in a group for women intent on marrying addicts, and traveled to South Dakota for several ten-day workshops with Sharon Wegscheider-Cruse, author of *Understanding Codependency*. In my spare breaths, I drove to Birmingham twice a month to work with Nancy Qualls Corbett, one of the country's foremost Jungian Psychoanalyst and author of the seminal *The Sacred Prostitute*. I had all the psychological, emotional and spiritual bases covered and the Great Wall of China erected, defying any addictive personalities to dare transgress.

As I scheduled interviews for Lewis, I paced in mind circles, nervous if he'd make the interview on time or blurt out some hat-knocking insult derailing our career. An inner fiasco rumbled as I continued to pour personal money into Lewis's publishing and management. To the dismay of those who could spot the obvious smoke and mirrors, I shunned the wise advise of money management types warning me to get backing for my fledging company. I truly felt Lewis's first time to bat would yield a home run, or at least an easy walk to third.

Lest this all seem business as usual for the music industry with me as one more believer denied the hallowed halls, remember I was on a transcendent spiritual journey: meditating hours a day, celibate, pious, roaming around out of my body, and feeling as if the Light had beamed me up and posited me permanently on the upper floors.

I spiritualized my reality to the point of self-deception.

It's an established fact that my ego had to take a quantum step back or at least break open a crack for self-accessing. The Center, the elusive almighty Center that I spent hours a day inviting into my life, evidently had not awakened to my compliance. The church was not ready to accept my membership. The second single pulled from the album sitting on a shelf waiting for a reason to be released did not ignite the charts, dropping out a little below the first. I had been around the barn long enough to know the writing was on the wall for the project. At first I wanted to fight, meaning I had to knock on the doors of the other initially interested labels to dine on some crow.

But then something happened. Destiny perhaps, but I was jolted into a reality check. Lewis was in town to powwow about our next move and wanted to go to an arena concert, which I declined to attend. Against intuition, I let him take my car. The long-time married father of two never returned that night, but Lewis was a die-hard family man, so infidelity never loomed. Then I was slammed up side my head with "COCAINE!" How in the hell did it take me this long to realize his behavior was cocaine-fueled, the personality changes, the acerbic edge, the lack of soul in his demeanor that was so vibrant in his original note.

In that smack in the face realization, I stumbled not backward this time, but forward, grasping it was all a final exam to see just how well my dependency and codependency money had been spent. When I gently informed Lewis that I was pretty damn certain he had an addiction problem, he retorted that he was more than certain I had a Mother Theresa Complex. Oh my Good OM, was he ever right about that one. Lewis and I agreed to part ways in all the love and trust we could muster while standing in a puddle of awkward, awful truth.

Gone was a good chunk of my money, my pride, and my confidence as a businesswoman, what little there might have been. Gone was my superstar that would set me up for the rest of my life and send my boys to college, if colleges accepted students hogtied to a chair and dropped from a helicopter. Gone was a friend and business partner whom I trusted, not only for his integrity and curious intellect, but his talent. Hopes, wishes, dreams and goals drifted away in the disintegrating chemtrail of my ego.

For the first time in my life, I was truly free.

*Footnote:*

After some years of struggle, Lewis braved his addictive illness, deep diving in a program to free his bound soul. Twenty years later, a welcomed phone call offering beautiful amends for wrongs and hurts, was fully accepted in gratitude for my own growth in our journey. At the end of the conversation, I couldn't stop myself, out of love of his work, from asking to hear some of his latest music, since by then I was no longer in the music business, but making documentary films, and the request held no responsibility for an outcome.

Over thirty years after dropping in that first cassette, I slid a disk into my computer and once again was charmed and bedazzled. His trial by fire had not incinerated, but reignited his poet's voice. His singing voice was weakened on some of the tracks, but his spirit was vibrant and the authenticity of his stories, was enhanced by hindsight. In that choice validating moment, I realized I would do it all over again based on nothing but the man's talent.

In 2013, Lewis became quite ill with a chronic malady that threatened his ability to sing. I wanted him to have a definitive collection of his standout songs for history to evaluate, and arranged for two master guitar players, both fans, to produce a CD of some of our favorite Storey narratives. Lewis called the collection *Storey Road*. The recording experience, joyful for all involved, closed the circle on our souls' resolute dance for unconditional love.

I love Lewis Storey.

# WITCH HAIR #10.

*"I simply believe that some part of the human Self or*
*Soul is not subject to the laws of space and time."*
*Dr. Carl Jung*

Remarkably, considering my scampering genes, I had not yet
traveled out of the country, though not for lack of yearning. My
Big-Split-Ex had an aversion to Europe, to flying across oceans,
to foreign cultures; which Texas-bred letoff was real, I could
never drag out of him. He didn't want to be on a cruise ship
"trapped in a tin can with regular people," so though we could
afford travel, it was more often than not limited to work trips to
Los Angeles.

Longing for other lands came in waves of recognition or
familiarity with various touchstones. Australia topped my list.
I remember as an insatiable preschooler carefully flipping the
pages of a National Geographic, captivated by a luminous ochre
photo of Ayers Rock, a giant monolith in Central Australia.

"Mama, c'mere n' look at this! I wanna go here," thrown at an
unsuspecting mother with an eighth grade education.

"Why on God's green earth would you want to go so far away, young lady? You don't know what you might run into way down there."

"Cause it's sacred. I wanna go back." She later filled in my retort, sacred being a word Mama used for the Bible; a sacred book, she called it.

Forty years down the lane, I walked the entire 9.4 km circumference of Uluru, and yes, it was indeed sacred.

What inner narratives and soul-stirrings spark the unconscious to certain sojourns we can only suppose. Is it genetic memory searching for roots, or what we refer to as 'past life' recall, or is it all happening at once on upper floors? Whatever the impetus when strange lands call, the soul needs to wander.

Like many upper east coast settlers who drifted south after vanquishing the native dwellers, my genes scrambled into Northern European servings: Scots/Irish and Dutch from Mama's tribe and Brits and Germans from Daddy's.

On July 25, 1984, I traveled to my ancestral land of Ireland. Faster than a plane or a speeding bullet, I flew with the support of a beloved friend.

I met M. L. Benoit, talented percussionist for Jimmy Buffett, backstage after a concert. Buffet had exploded from a Nashville managed singer/songwriter, country artist wannabe, whining about lack of recognition, to amassing a fanatical following christened "Parrot Heads" after "Margaritaville" blew the charts wide open. Guitar wizard Josh Leo and I were flying in a too-tiny-for-my-comfort private plane from Nashville to somewhere in Ohio, taking Josh to play the show and introduce me to Buffet's drummer, Matt Betton. During my tenure as a publishing executive, I produced studio demos on songs written by my diverse staff of songsmiths, so was always on the look out for new talent, especially drummers, Garin's prodigiousness having finely tuned my ears.

Incidentally, this is the exact trip where my abject fear of flying upped the ante and never relented. A menacing cluster of cumulus clouds stacked like skyscrapers formed a death-defying wall that our pilot couldn't detour around, disappearing us into the belly of one of the ominous giants. The twin prop convulsed violently for longer than I want to recall, then sputtered. Our skilled pilot revved the motors attempting to steady the plane. Pretty sure we were downward bound, I grabbed for Josh, who had just survived testicular cancer.

"We're not gonna die, Dix; if I was gonna die, I would've done it last year when they cut off one of my balls and pumped my body full of poisons. We're not gonna die."

M. L. Benoit left a bigger imprint than the drummer, although he became my mainstay for several years, until my big time producer husband stole him for the big leagues. From the moment M. L., a slender, waif-like cherub with a mane of wild brown curls that scattered like birds when she played and doe eyes that dripped with infinite wisdom, cast her toothy smile my way, I knew we'd always be soul-bound witches.

Sadly, there was no always for me and my M. L. Four years later she exited her cancer-riddled body. One of only two friends I shared my cosmic exploits with whose eyes didn't glaze over, M. L. was a natural earth mama. Her soul ran deep and her spirit played in wide-open fields. When M. L. departed, her seven five-inch-long, well-used healing crystals and a pair of custom made cowboy boots (which I could never begin to fill) were her parting gifts. It became my habit to place one of the crystals on each energy center before meditation, being that science says quartz crystal is an electrical energy enhancer and conductor. Science is right.

Those crystals jump-started me to the home of my mama's Morgan clan. Close to three years into what esoteric lit referred to as 'astral travel,' I studied physics and researched voraciously to understand the neuroscience of how my brain was functioning to facilitate my cosmic explorations.

Because of the amplification from the crystals, I quickly dropped to a deep state, which I will quantify as somewhere between sleep and awake or theta waves. By now I understand the longer I stayed in each meditation session, the more pronounced the brain wave states defined themselves allowing me to identify the varying states. As I kept my breath consistent, I noted myself falling into the delta wave state. From there I felt my body let go and fall back.

I'll give a little instruction here, because when this otherworldly sensation begins to happen, the natural reflex is fear, but as soon as emotional energy is felt, you will pop back into your body. So the physical body must be in a state of retreat or decline as if giving over to sleep, but instead of falling asleep, you fall more awake than you've ever been.

Through trial and error I learned how to seduce my brain to an alpha wave by priming with consciousness-raising material before going into the meditation breath. Not possessing the

Biblical patience of Job or the serenity of the Dalai Lama, I accelerated the process by reading the ageless witchy wisdom of Alice Bailey: *A Treatise on White Magic* written in 1934, *Esoteric Psychology* from 1942, and the all-important *Ponder on This*, a brilliant compilation of her groundbreaking esoteric works. Thankfully Rodney was reading Bailey, too, and we'd meet for lunch to ponder a path to understanding her discourses. One accomplished witch, that Alice Ann Bailey.

A flight veteran, as long as I stayed out of planes, exiting this time was easier and smoother, a perfect takeoff. It was as if my physical body actually released my soul by lying back and letting it drift out. I am calling this part of myself my soul. Can't begin to prove what part of us leaves our body in a near death situation or at death, or during deep-ass meditations, but I do know it's the same aspect in each one of us. When the soul leaves on its final journey from its currently inhabited body to rejoin Pure Consciousness or God, or Source, reunion happens on the level of consciousness corresponding with our belief system. Christians may see Jesus, Buddhists the Buddha, and non-believers cherished loved ones. As developmental biologist Bruce Lipton, author of *Biology of Belief* asserts, backed by science from a petri dish, we truly are what we believe.

I'd say the soul is the personalized aspect of the entire spirit, soul plus Higher Self, that projects itself into a life-sustaining embryo for the purpose of its own lessons, returning to join the waiting Higher Self expanded by lessons learned. The circle of life has been pondered by far greater minds than mine, and if there is a definitive answer to be had, it awaits us all in Pure Consciousness.

Just as I lifted from my body I was asked by the same familiar distant voice, my Higher Self, where I wanted to go and surprisingly heard myself respond, "Ireland." Poof! I was floating down a pristine, narrow road near a curve arching a sparkling blue lake rimmed by an ancient stacked-stone fence. Growing alongside the hedge stone were vibrant blue-violet flowers radiating a hue and watery deliciousness so pure and essential that it blended with my soul. As a breeze stirred, a fragrance sashayed in a fairy dance of the senses, baptizing me in their essence.

Ahead I noticed a low-slung piled-stone village, crude but sturdy. I wondered what the village was called and the voice answered "Boheraroan." No villagers milled about, so when I asked where all the people were, abruptly I was inside a cottage made of primitive hand-molded logs topped with a thatched roof. A radiant, middle-aged woman scurried around the open room preparing food for guests. She stood slightly taller than I with short silvery/blond hair, brown eyes framed in wire-rimmed glasses, bathed in sun-kissed complexion as if she farmed. The engaging Irish lady overflowed with a lovely, positive countenance, her entire being bound in a soft smile. Hugging her, I felt warm and comfortable in her presence again and told her I loved her.

Without answering or acknowledging she said, "We'll be eating now."

On the sideboard a type of pudding, very thick and lumpy, was the main course, not dessert. Alongside the pudding an earthenware jug containing an unfamiliar liquid, dark, bubbly and bitter, uprooted my taste buds. Centerpieced in the room was a long rough-hewn table caressed smooth by time. Lying on the floor near the table were two handmade wooden paddles. The woman asked me to pick them up because the dog liked to chew them. Wherever I was, who ever this woman might be, I felt comfortably at home and settled, as if I had inserted myself in real time in another time and place while daily life was in progress.

The question of how long I had been gone from my body surfaced in the sweetness of the environment. At first I questioned if I wanted to go back, then thought of Garin and Shannon without me and knew I had to return to my children. But my soul's urge was to linger in the warm, simple home with the loving woman and strange food. That notion made me scared that I had been gone too long to return to my body, or if I had snapped the thread leading back, immediately releasing a rush of fear catapulting me in my body, on my bed in meditation repose. I opened my eyes all stove up, borrowing a Southernism from my blue-collar cousins: stiff with immobile, achy limbs. According to the clock, I had traveled around for only a few minutes, yet my body behaved as if it had been abandoned for days, and it took that long before I could move about without wincing.

As soon as my brain settled back down to waking awareness, I recognized the woman as my childhood neighbor, Mrs. Shoaf, a second mother to Butch and me, whose beautiful daughter Smith was one of the three women who showed me how to be a bossy pants girl, a confident young woman, then a badass woman—not that I learned it all, but it was there in front of me for the taking. I either plunged my meandering soul in a past life with Mrs. Shoaf or we had a simultaneous visit on an upper floor: this I know, I know.

Some Neuroscientists and depth psychologists tend to attribute the experiences I am describing to either brain anomalies or trained response, meaning if you practice enough, you get good at it; also some say the veils are too thin. I am fixing my chronicles as an outcome of many years practicing deep meditation with the intention of reaching parallel realms of consciousness, my soul bypassing my brain. Who the hell really knows, and I only exert authority over my own experiences.

Yet some forty years later, like a religious zealot spreading the gospel, I find myself sowing seeds for everyone to have access to keys that usher humanity toward a peaceful, harmonious existence. Not to say one has to meditate to be a peaceful person, but a peaceable planet naturally evolves when everyone has tapped a personal source of peace—whatever that may be.

To quote Dr. Bruce Lipton, PhD, "The planet's hope and salvation lies in the adoption of revolutionary new knowledge being revealed at the frontiers of science." Condensing the frontier to a petri dish, Dr. Lipton demonstrated the cells' inherent wisdom, when their fate, thrive or survive, was controlled by the environment in which he placed them. When goldfish are confined to swimming circles in a small bowl they don't grow in size, but put them in a large fish tank and they'll grow exponentially to the size of their container. Like the fish our cells are predestined for expansion as long as we don't inhibit them with limiting belief. In Lipton's words, "It is actually our perceptions that control life and by changing our perceptions we can get control over our lives."

Ten years later I nervously journeyed to Ireland in my body, inside the body of a plane. I visited the area and the township of

Boheraroan in southwestern County Clare. Though it was more populated than during my astral visit, the Gaelic villages had changed little. As a heady welcome back, the bluebells exhaled their sweet sachet bussing the misty magical air.

# WITCH HAIR #11.

*"The most common way women give up their power is by thinking they don't have any."*
*Alice Walker*

Three fiercely independent young women owning no compunction about putting their minds on display along with striking faces, bodies and personalities, deftly defined power for me. Each slipped into a life chapter when only their sway could shift the arc of my narrative.

Smith was the bossy big sister in the family living across a cotton field then another quarter mile down Down Yonder Lane from our farm. The Shoaf homestead, with its expansive acreage, nestled close enough for a long trek on short legs, a risky ride on Junior, our stubborn bedamned burrow, then later for a hellish bike ride down the treacherously rutted dirt road. No matter the mode it took to get me there, after harassing Mama to the point of a nervous breakdown for a visit, I skedaddled one way or the other. Smith, or Valerie Smith Shoaf, was half-sister to Scott and Chris, the same age as Butch and me. Ten years older and in my young eyes the most beautiful girl I had even seen, Smith, a statuesque well-developed sixteen-year-old beauty queen with softly bronzed skin, shiny brown hair with exact matching eyes, loved horses, music, and marching, in that order. She was an accomplished majorette, with impossibly shapely legs, who took the time to teach a five-year-old tow-headed squirt butt with comically skinny legs how to twirl a baton, do a backflip, and once even performed an acrobatic routine with me in a school talent show.

From the time I mastered my first cartwheel, I chose acrobatics as transportation from point A to point B, challenging myself to cartwheel up through the weedy path to our nearest neighbors the Jacob family, who had three girls, one my age. Back bends and backflips, thanks to Smith, came next, then standing on my head until blood collected, leaving me stumbling, light-headed and woozy. Mama birthed me flexible, which may or may not have anything to do with fancying myself a yogi without a guru, or a circus performer without a circus.

Once during one of our Sunday afternoon porch sits, I crossed my legs into a full lotus walking on my knees across the porch.

"What on earth are you doing, young lady?" Daddy asked peering out from his paper.

"Yoga."

So, we had no television, only a radio, which as far as I know transmitted no Eastern spirituality. Swami Vivekananda introduced yoga to American in 1893, but by 1950 Hindu spirituality had yet to land in rural North Carolina. Certainly none of the redneck Morgans or the straight-laced Caubles were yoga practitioners or meditators, making a pretty solid argument for past life recall or awareness oozing through cracks in upper floors.

Until I hung around Smith, I never related to my body as separate or mine. The body-confident teenager mirrored not only how to be in my body, but how to respect it. I miss Smith to this day when I smell baby oil, reliving how I'd slather myself into a dripping oil slick trying to copy the polished look it gave her tawny skin. Watching her buff instead of polish her natural fingernails and spread Pond's cold cream her face opened doors that my poor mama never stepped near.

More than anything I wanted to be Smith.

By the time Butch was old enough to walk hand-in-hand with me to Down Yonder, he was all about playing with Scott and Chris. Sometimes that was fun for me too, until it got too dirt-oriented for a tomboy princess and I'd sneak in the house to find Smith. If she was playing the piano, I'd sit on my haunches in the hallway quietly taking it all in. We had a piano in our living room, but unlike Smith, lessons were never discussed for me. No music in our house, just news, Gabriel Heater on the radio. I loved the sound of the instrument so much I taught myself to play several songs by ear until Mama, financially forced to sell my beloved piano without asking, punched a hole in the bucket of my creativity, foreshadowing a compulsive need to marry multiple music men.

Smith turned me on to recorded music too. We'd listen to *Hank Williams Sings* over and over again, singing along ... 'Hey, Good Lookin', what cha got cookin'' ... at the top of our lungs. Looking back, we didn't think of Hank as country, or Jimmy Reed as blues or Dave Brubeck as jazz; it was all just great music to Smith and me. Because of Smith's eclectic taste in music, my first album purchase was Brubeck's *Time Out*, then *I'm Jimmy Reed*. Living in my adult ears, I hear how the broad sweep of my musical baptism may have played forward to my uncanny discernment— infinitely arguable, of course.

I could be a girly-girl and had a favorite rubber baby doll named Judy, but as soon as Butch could stand upright, I'd dress him in one of my dresses, pretending I was Smith and he was me. He caught on quickly and I had to change the play scenario to gender-appropriate Scott and Smith. When we were Scott and Smith, I bossed him unmercifully, but with a soft kind voice, just like Smith. In those few years, she breathed life into an expression of my female persona that would play Scott and Smith with men, seeing many of them as boys in need of gentle training or, better still, fixing.

By the time I was twelve, threading in puberty, Mary Frances Walker, or Sister as family called her, took Smith's spot as female life coach, a role that my mother simply couldn't occupy, her life containing far too many potholes, some deep and dangerous. Smith left Down Yonder for college or marriage or both, and, without skipping a chapter, Sister entered my story. Another captivating woman in her early twenties, Sister was a blue-eyed, svelte blond so carelessly pretty she could have been a model: beguiling, yet not intimidating. A sweet human with a ready laugh and sparkling personality, she was everybody's sister, who treated me like a younger sister, not a sixth grader who followed her around constantly yammering at her back. Though more than ten years my senior, Sister communicated as a contemporary, allowing my sense of self to take form, mirrored through the eyes of a goddess-like creature that I idolized. I felt capable and mature beyond my dozen years in her orbit.

Sister's mother, my father's first cousin, worked at the VA with Mama. Mama looked up to Grace Walker because, unlike Mama, she was a strong, decisive woman who without a stammer spoke her mind and ruled her own roost. I found Aunt Grace a little intimidating, but again observed how far conviction, even with a little bully stirred in, carried her.

From the first time Aunt Grace brought Sister out for a Sunday porch and cold watermelon afternoon, she left an indelible imprint on me, a work in progress girl. Unlike Aunt Grace who wore her power outwardly, Sister's flowed naturally from a deep inner spring. My enchantress was strong enough to bend.

When I was considered to be among the first women to produce records in a man town in the early '80s, it never occurred to me to think of myself as a female producer or to expound on being not male in the studio. My goal was to get the best possible reflection of what I considered to be worthy songs. Nor did I get up in the 'women's lib' movement. Inner power to me is soft, yielding, and wields not a jackhammer but a strong heart, exactly what I mimicked in both Smith and Sister. Not to say I internalized their attributes to the point of accomplishment, just that I wanted to!

Just as Smith showed me how to be a bossy boots clothed in love and respect, Sister added the sugar, the natural sweetness that cushions power. When Sister married Ippy Ipolito (I love saying that name) quickly producing a first-born, she trusted me to change diapers and feed him a bottle, boosting Mama's naturally blueprinted nurturing skills. Maybe all Southern women are born nurturers.

Mama may not have cast the ideal female prototype that I hungered for, but her effortless unconditional love and nourishing heart penetrated soul-deep. Sister fertilized my hopes and dreams, though I had no idea what they were, and went out of her way to tell me I was pretty and special.

Under Sister's wing, *special*, which had up until then been an albatross, turned an asset. I heard that word frequently as a child, that I was a 'special' child. Problem was, I picked it up to mean I was special because of the hardships and trauma dramas in my family and special meant the same as 'bless yo heart' … you poor pitiful child, I'll pray for you. Sister translated all that into, "You're pretty. You're smart. Find your dreams."

When teenage insecurities set in, in hopes of validating what Sister infused, I asked Mama if she thought I was pretty.

"Pretty is as pretty does," she shot back, not even looking up.

That shouldn't have confounded me as much as it did. At first deciding she just didn't want to tell me that I was flat chested, skinny, carried way too much teased hair for one small head and, yes, my teeth were a little wonky. All I needed from Mama was a hint that the boy-crazy insanity that had taken over my body was going to either cease or pay off at some point.

I never got a clue from Mama, but then Mama never got a clue from anyone. Throughout my teens, I continued to be a walking contradiction, a certain amount of certainty on the outside, cascading doubts on the inside.

When Sister and the expanding Ipolito brood moved to Italy with Ippy's Marine regiment, another female star dropped from the galaxy. Wilson was there to take her place. Mother, Butch and I moved next door to Florine Wilson into another dark but nonthreatening apartment near Salisbury High School, after leaving my beloved bestie Billie and China Grove in our wake.

Wilson was a raven beauty, tall with cropped black hair, knowing cobalt eyes and a wide perfect-teeth smile. Her darling little girls Cathy and Anne crawled right up in my heart the minute I met them. Wilson upgraded my female consortium just when my boy-crazed festering wound could have hijacked me down a risky path. Newly divorced, Wilson was sole support of her girls and made the impossible look easy. Like both Smith and Sister, Wilson was what we southern girls declared 'sharp.' I homogenized their approach to fashion as casual, adornment free, and comfortable, supporting personal preference and mood, rather than mimicking *Vogue* layouts. I admired most everything Wilson wore, and even though she was much taller and thicker than my skinny-ass self, I bugged her to borrow her clothes. Being a professional seamstress and likely feeling sorry for me, she sprang into making me cute flared skirts and tank tops out of any scraps she had lying around. She'd whip up something stylish in an hour, hand it to me and say, "Here, wear this tonight."

Being an eager, age-appropriate baby sitter for Wilson, I had fun with the little girls and even more fun with the big boys that I'd sneak in after the girls were asleep. My boy insanity was second only to stealing Mama's old robin's egg blue Chevy for midnight drive-abouts, both a common form of rebellion, having everything to do with a too-old, emotionally unavailable father who offered little or no masculine mirror.

During this precarious edge-of-teens chapter, my latest walloping crush was Bill Humphrey, a hunky blond quarterback in the making. In 1959, even in my wildest imaginative romances, venturing beyond kissing never occurred to me. I mean, really, I was in the 8th grade. But boy, did I love kissing, especially Bill Humphrey. One baby-sitting night, he came over to Wilson's and we got bored with kissing and started giving each other hickeys. First on our necks, then faces, then arms, I mean, we turned into a couple of young blood sucking vampires before we realized that those gross purple splotches splayed everywhere were not going away anytime soon. Not a hint of sexual play other than sucking, no private parts below the neck included. All hell broke loose the next day in school, when sooner than later even people outside our circle of friends, put two and two hickey wearers together and voila, I had a budding bad reputation.

Bill Humphrey's hickeys were cool, while mine proof positive that I was loose at the least, and a slut that went 'all the way' at worst. This was my first brush with a shame-tainted reputation, and the infuriating unfairness meted out when it comes to gender. We sucked face and I got stuck in the shadow.

Wilson, not my mother, coached me through the angst of gender discrimination and shaming, knowing a lot about it as did most Southern women. Sexual shaming was a righteous past time, not only among peers but the self-anointed bless-your-heart Southern socialites, who turned an R into an A, prying beguilingly …

"Now tell me, dear, what does yo-ua daddy do?" I spent a lot of good money banging a bataka (think: padded baseball bat whacking a pillow) while those pandering female voices spewed their toxic shame.

By the summer between my freshman and sophomore year, the gusting gales of puberty threatened to capsize my life. Mother worked second shift to earn more money and Butch and I were haphazardly minded either by equally unsteady relatives or not at all. Danger crouched behind my still-looking-for-Daddy attraction to older college-aged men; good shaggers (shagging is a regional style of dancing) that they might have been, I was a fourteen-year old girl without a boundary or a clue.

Attempting to balance all of my external chaos, my inner voice spoke loud and clear that Butch and I were not playing in a safe zone and were teetering on a precipice that could dramatically change the course of our lives.

A miracle beamed straight from the ships of the Pleiades or the upper reaches of the tower aired an ad in *Life Magazine* for a boarding school called Pineland College and Edwards Military Institute near Fayetteville, NC. The private school boarded students from the fifth grade through the second year of college.

Butch and I both could be taken care of.

I dialed the long distance number and probed for all the information, including tuitions and boarding fees then had applications sent to Mama without asking. When the applications arrived, I filled them out for me and for Butch then laid them in front of Mama.

"Butch and I need to go to this school this year, please help me get the money so we can, it's very important, Mama."

She heard me. I wrote to Daddy in Virginia, knee-begging for help, Mama got a loan from her Credit Union and off we packed to Pineland and Edwards. Although saying goodbye to Mama was teary and heart-squeezing, what joy and relief I felt to be held in a safe, comfortable yet expanding milieu at such a vulnerable age and stage in my development. I could finally stop having to parent myself. Still too young to establish my own boundaries, the tenets of campus living did it for me. Butch and I loved everything about the phenomenal school. Butch learned military skills and disciplines at an early age, which pointed him toward a mechanical engineering path, and I basked in the closest replica I'd ever have to college dorm living. Edwards Military boys were still good shaggers and kissers, but I wasn't listing on the edge of a shadow that threatened to consume my youth. We stretched, we grew and excelled in a cocooned academic setting that offered life skills, proper social norms and a quality cultural education.

Because of the small classes, no more than forty girls in my class, I mined gold with cheering, majorette, homecoming court, and top of my class to the point of being allowed to teach some subjects as my assignments. My ability to esteem myself escalated at a time when it was poised to tumble into an abyss.

Pineland was not only my most memorable adult-in-training immersion, but that happenstance advertisement, if I believed in happenstance, saved my life, if not my teeth. The only shadow side of the tiny town of Salemburg being there was only one aging dentist who happened to be alcoholic. Instead of attempting to fill even a small cavity with far too shaky hands, he'd pull the tooth rather than risk impaling unsuspecting students on his drill. When I returned to Salisbury to a sober dentist, he was aghast that I was missing molars at my age. I traded two perfectly healthy teeth for an intact sense of self and a fostering ability to steer life's careering curves. A fair enough trade, in the rear view.

The boogieman was poised to pounce, but the ship people took real good care of me, when nobody else could.

Sadly, the unusual school closed their elementary and high school programs and the next year offered only a two-year college degree. My junior year, Wilson moved to Yadkinville, a one-stoplight town up near the Smokies that I'd never heard of. She'd copped a new position as manager of a company that made tee shirts and needed me to be at home with the girls when she was working. The plan sorted out perfectly because the girls and I were in school while Wilson was at the plant. She cooked supper for us in the evening, after which I tied up her phone line for hours chattering about nothing to either blond, blue-eyed quarterback Ronnie or brown-eyed halfback Phillip. No shagging, but good kissing. Still suffering from a smoldering case of boy-crazy, but with a good fitting lid, I observed Wilson closely. She played silky, enticing her suitors with a red lipstick smile and high meringue lemon pies, neither of which I had the lips or cooking skills to pull off. However, I scrutinized and respected the confident, self-sufficient businesswoman, who managed a warehouse full of sewing machine operators by day, then morphed into a yielding house goddess who loved to bake on weekends. Wasn't long until she had her forever man and I had a little slice of Wilson to call my own, though I never learned to bake.

Gratefully, Wilson stayed in my life until her girls were old enough to babysit my boys. I wonder if she had any idea what a force of nature she was in my life before she left the planet? Well, I'm telling you now, Wilson: you were a masterful sculptor of the feminine form!

Smith, Sister and Wilson. My three paragons of sisterhood sanctity never met each other, yet they lodged together in my heart to rendezvous some forty years later, sent by the woman who always understood exactly how much I needed them.

# WITCH HAIR #12.

*"When you do not seek or need approval,*
*you are at your most powerful."*
Caroline Myss

The first time I saw Billie—1958, standing in the middle of the China Grove skating rink, holding court like a well-seasoned jester—I was hopelessly hooked. Bright lights reflected off a skillfully oiled, impeccably coifed Elvis pomp. Head thrown back in a laugh being drowned out by strains of "Johnny, he's a joker, he's a bird, a very funny joker, he's a dog … he's a bird dog," the Everly Brothers' anthem to Billie, or it seemed that way in the moment.

Cowering behind the rail as a first time skater, I finally double dared myself to fumble over to him at the risk of squirrel splaying at his feet. Pondering what to say to the gutsy, good-looking boy who had the gall to come to the skating rink in a dress, I took a deep breath. Before I could muster up the courage to escape from behind the rail, he glided over to me asking if I wanted to skate. Too tongue-tied to answer, I held out my hand and our life dance began.

A few days later, Billie and I were wrestling in our front yard, when Mother came tearing out of the house, flailing a dishrag in the air.

"Dixie Jane Cauble, it is not nice for little girls to be wrastlin' with little boys!" The three-name thing meant serious shit.

"Mama, he ain't a boy, he's a girl!" I yelled from somewhere beneath Billie.

I never saw Billie in a dress again. It was a "Mama made me do it or I couldn't go" punishment that Billie braved with her head up. Always clad in carefully creased blue jeans, Izod shirts of many soft colors and spit shined Weejun loafers, she was the sharpest boy, next to Elvis, I'd ever laid eyes on, and she gave Elvis a serious run for my throb-prone heart.

Billie and I were inseparable. I walked right past her house ... and damn, if it wasn't another dark house ... to get to my sixth grade school. Billie joined me in the morning and I'd wait for her after last bell. My wobbly world felt safer with Billie in it. Mother, Butch and I had moved every year after Mama's emotional separation from Daddy finally chilled enough to take. I grew more and more anxious because the longer we were gone, the more unstable Mama became, as if being disconnected from love opened up a scar on her heart, leaving her defenseless against marauders. Drop-in men who all seemed to have one aim in mind, to get her drunk and do their bidding, were not rare. Mother was a lousy consumer of alcohol, losing all sense of her self with the first drink. I never dreaded anything more than watching my straight-laced Mama fail at being a social drinker.

I had zero doubts that we were all better positioned to make it around the bend without Daddy's month-long binges, but

Mother's dip into the dark side left me clinging to a loose root on deep drop bluff.

My diaper-clad crib bombshell, dropped by a crashing coke bottle with a nipple on it putting me on notice that in this go 'round I was flying solo, exploded into reality and bit down hard on my life of fourteen years. No one, not Mama not Daddy, was going to be more reliable for a decent outcome for it all than little twelve pound me. I was on my own, and I had a younger brother who needed a mother and father even more than I did.

Billie-hanging days bubbled with endless rowdy giggling and snarky snickers. Nobody was cooler or funnier or smarter than Billie, and it wasn't just me who felt that way. Hell, the whole goddamn town loved Billie. Her only so-called vice, which I found fetching, was her constant cussing. Once I met her mama and daddy, I got where it came from and never thought anything about it. Mother, not so much, especially when I budded into dropping goddamns like a well-honed adjective.

"Would you please pass the goddamn peas?" got me a finger poke and threat that I would never be allowed to play with Billie again if I didn't clean up my potty mouth.

"Mama, Billie's goddamn cool, like Elvis. I love it when she's here," my ten-year-old brother butted in, which I was pretty goddamn sure would seal the deal on Billie and me.

Our favorite hang spot was the Dixie DoNut Diner a couple of blocks from our dark, dinky house … still not as dark or dinky as the one in the goddamn pine grove. The whole tired diner sprang to life when Billie and I sashayed in: me, invisible; Billie, blazing like a rock star.

"Hey, Bill, I heared you up and mowed the church yard. I just wan'chew to know the Lord 'preciates you," one of the locals in blue bib overalls and a dingy white tobacco-stained tee shirt shouted past a mouthful of bright orange hot dog.

Billie, flashing one of her crooked grins waved "much-obliged" with the hand not holding mine, guided me to her stool at the counter, then ordered us hot dogs all with the swagger of a twelve-year-old superstar.

Nobody knew if Billie was a boy or a girl; nobody rightly cared, and as far as I know nobody bothered to ask. Men claimed her for their side and the women, well, they just claimed her as one of their own, even though her bountiful use of The Lord's Name in Vain must have driven those God-fearin', in-heat Southern Baptist ladies to their knees, clutching a Bible to their crotch.

In a red neck mill town in rural North Carolina, a female who dresses and looks like a male beguiles 1,200 prayin', gun-totin', tobacco-spittin' mill workers, who today would be vocal Evangelical Conservatives disdaining any LGBTQ rights as blasphemous. That's how goddamn bright Billie Ann's light shined.

Our love, our mutual adoration stretched over twenty years and, of course, the stories piled high. On a hot summer day in our early years, Billie and I were wilting around our house and I had to go poop. Not missing a beat, she was in the bathroom with me lounging with her back against the door, still talking about some goddamn thing that she didn't want to put on pause while I pooped.

I was straining hard when she popped out with, "if you could be anybody in the whole world, who would you want to be?"

"Yo-ou." I grunted.

Even during our teenage years, when Billie had girlfriends lined up and I was pulling in my fair share of hot footballers, she called pencil dicks, Billie and I still found time to shag almost every weekend, even if it in was my living room. For the uninitiated, shagging is dancing in North Carolina, not fornicating. Billie and I loved without condition and were never sexual.

When Jesse, Shannon, Garin and I moved to Nashville in the early 70s, we lost track of each other. I'd never missed anyone so much. Twenty-some years later during one of my infrequent trips back to Salisbury I got wind that Billie was working at the Dixie DoNut Diner and decided I'd drop in to see if it was true. There she stood rocking a cleanly shaved head, still wearing an Izod shirt with those ironed jeans under a nasty bib apron, slinging burgers and as always, holding court with the locals perched at the counter. Chills ran around my body as I took in all of my Billie, tears rolling down my face.

Barely breathing, I choked out, "Could I have a cheeseburger with chili, slaw and mayonnaise, please?"

"Oh, goddamn!" wheeling around lobbing hot grease, "oh, goddamn, it's YOU!"

For the next three hours we huddled in the frayed vinyl booth, Billie regaling me with her misadventures, as always blissfully oblivious to any world but ours.

Billie told me all about joining the Army after graduation and eventually being stationed at Fort Ord in California.

"I was good at that military shit, DJ," her affectionate name for me, which only ever came from her mouth. "Then out of the goddamn blue, I's called into my Commander's office ..."

"Corporal Mecimore, it has been called to my attention that you have been having sexual relations with female members of this government organization," mimicking him with hilarious conviction.

"Naw, Sir, I wouldn't know anything about that, Sir." Saluting smartly as she acted out the scene.

"DJ, the sum bitch turned around and stuck a goddamn cassette tape in and ... oh, goddamn, let's just say I was doin' her good enough, just not e-nough and the jealous bitch recorded us! Never been so goddamn embarrassed in my life. Lost my stripe, nearly lost my fuckin' job!"

The colors in my life paled compared to Billie's vivid display of jaw-dropping entertainment, so I peppered her with questions.

"What did you do after the Army?"

"Oh, I was a madam. Had my own house, real charmer, white leather couches, Tiffany lamps, best house in Charlotte, made us all a shitload of money. Me and the Dawns started the business together."

"The Dawns?" I probed.

"Big Dawn and Little Dawn, the most beautiful blonds you ever saw. I loved 'em both but was only doin' Little Dawn. Big Dawn was the money-makin' star of the house. One night Little Dawn had an out call and me and Big Dawn imbibed way past our better minds. We's goin'at it purty good when Little Dawn busted in, jumping on me like a Banty Rooster in heat, chomped down on my right cheek … see the scar? And wouldn't let go. I'm tryin' to sling her off and the next thing I know, she's sittin' on top o' me with a bloody chunk of my face hangin' out of her sexy little mouth."

I'm losing it so loud the entire diner deserted their frozen fries and flipped around to listen.

"I'm beggin' her, blood spurtin'out of the gaping hole … come on, Baby, now you gotta give me back my cheek so we can go get it sewed back on, ok?"

When I could catch a breath, I asked Billie what happened to the Dawns.

"Oh, goddamn, DJ, it was fuckin' awful!" A rare tear pooled in her eye. "Little Dawn was a downer girl, and I reckon she had one too many, washed down with one too many, then wrapped her little Miata convertible smack-ass around a tree. I had to go down to the morgue to identify her perfect little body. Puke started clogging up my throat before he pulled her out of cold storage. The first thing I saw was the red satin heels I'd just bought her and told that goddamn Dracula lookalike 'No more! That's her, that's Dawn Sheppard, I just bought her those yesterday,' then I hurled all over his wing tips before he could grab a goddamn bucket."

Billie proudly though haltingly shared that she had given birth to a son, raised by her mom and dad, who'd always wanted a boy, glowing as she explained how he'd decided to be a fireman so he could spend his life saving lives.

Noticing my shocked expression, (never in my wildest imagination picturing Billie beneath any male form), she chuckled uncomfortably.

"Aww, DJ, it was a drunken thang, neither here nor there, but I got a good kid out of the deal."

What I saw on her face was not so much a deal but an ordeal. Billie was always straight up with me, so for her to step in to the bullshit box said the pain was too much to resurrect. Though I was a practicing therapist and could easily have pried it open, I left the lid sealed, hoping one day she'd slit it and let the shadow fly. My mirthful, irrepressible Billie victimized, imprisoned by denial, scarred the moment but it was not mine to open; it was Billie's. I ached for her to have cracked it before she flew home but the steep decline of her health and early departure said she left toting the heavy shadow that conceived her cherished boy.

After hugging long enough to make up for our lost twenty years, I left the Dixie DoNut Diner drenched in Billie spirit, knowing what she had just spilled into my life had be a movie. I finished the script just in time for her to read it and laugh her ass off before she died at sixty-two from diabetic-related congestive heart failure.

*Talk About China Grove* has been optioned twice but not yet produced. Projecting Billie Ann Mecimore to the big screen where she belongs nags at me just enough to one day wring it down into manifestation.

Billie never exalted herself as a crusader or illumined visionary for the brewing LGBTQ movement, she simply danced through life unwilling to trade authenticity for approval.

I love you, Billie.

# WITCH HAIR #13.

*When you live in complete acceptance of what is,*
*that is the end of all drama in your life.*
Eckhart Tolle

Riding the rhythm-and-rhyme flummox of my five-year interior searching, self-awareness expanding, soulsummoning, sex-absconding, ego-shrinking, hurt-healing furlough, I bewitched no forecast of its aftereffect. In hindsight, the formula appeared simple: amp up my resolve to rip off the jumbo addict magnet clinging to my sore heart by burrowing back to my birth, then painfully prod forward through the emotional bog. I was imposing one of those simple-in-theory, excruciating excavations few people voluntarily undergo unless they have tripped over some sort of crucible in their life.

After my divorce from Bowen, then Elektra, then Lewis, then my sanity, (compliments of teen boys in chaos), I bum-bumped some bruising bottom. But peeling off scabbed hurts, some collected at birth, meant I needed a clear line to viable spiritual stock. Be it Mother Nature, the Buddha, the Bodhi Tree, or baking in a sweat lodge, I was seeking to find. My path would lead me to meditation, but before capitulating to vulnerability, control freak that I am, I had to know empirically that some omnipotent grand design was out there, and whether I could buy a ticket to ride.

God was not a resonant word for me, and Jesus had been tarnished in a Primitive Baptist holy-roller church when I was haggled into a Sunday service by my step-aunt's evangelical daughter-in-law. Somewhere along path of his pacing rant storm, the preacher ripped off his jacket, picked up a pitcher of water, dumped it on his head then fell to his knees bellowing 'Jeeee-suuuuus.' It scared the be-Jesus right out of a six-year-old Lutheran kid. I bolted from the sanctuary. How on earth could it be called a *sanctuary*? I anchored myself to the front steps refusing to budge until Vera delivered me back to the sanctuary of my mama.

From that fiasco, I figured I'd take my chances with the space people in the cow pasture, no boogie man could be any scarier than that preacher.

Mother, Butch, and I left the farm in 1953 for the shadowy pine grove house then returned home in 1954, for several years when Daddy, yet again, swore allegiance to his family not the bottle. May the good goddess bless him, Daddy tried. Pioneering what we now call the 'Healing Arts' in the early 1920s, Daddy nurtured and healed others, but sadly, denied the excruciating dis-ease nursing at his own soul. After two years of white-knuckling abstinence, he fell off again and Mama took off again.

Finally, by the time I hit my third year of high school, Mama was granted the house my daddy grew up in, that his daddy built. There is no justice in addictive illness and Daddy retreated to a sad solitary life in a Veteran's Domiciliary, still existing in those days for aged or infirm veterans.

Today their domicile is the street.

Following backward though my emotional, psychological heritage I unearthed both Mama and Daddy's deep hurts and broken hearts with no outstretched hand for help or healing. I remember Mama saying to me when I was deep diving in my past lancing all manner of wounds.

"Well, you have the help you need. I never did, and now it's too late."

I cried when she said it, and I weep now for my sweet mama's silent, solitary suffering.

In the last quarter of his life, Daddy, opted for self protection from most all stimuli including alcohol, sequestered in a small domiciliary room in Norfolk, Virginia five hundred miles from Butch and me, and from any remaining friends. I can only hope his inherent awareness of the centering adjustments of meditation cushioned his loneliness.

Both Mama and Daddy generously shared their hypersensitivity genes, donating thin veils as a component of my DNA. I passed copies of those genes to my youngest son, a hypersensitive living with *no* veils. We, and others like us, are the energy sensitive, complex calibrators for not enough or too much, rarely striking a middling or normal.

Oh, how I long for normal.

So the conundrum becomes: did arriving on the planet as a recipient of a hyper-aware, energy sensitive genetic code part the veils for The Other to hear my plea for sanctuary and grant me a ticket to ride?

I supposed along the way in those bright-light years, the multiple getaways from my physical body were, if not common, not particularly rare. The high gear shift in consciousness fit my previous mode of manifestation. When I applied passionate activity to a tightly focused goal, I managed to ground some version of my vision. My goal was to expand my awareness, and soon after beginning meditation I knew empirically I was only borrowing a body for my soul's use, accelerating a leap in consciousness.

For the first time, I was privy to experiencing a complete form of myself compacted into a spark of light. I frame it this way because on one of the other quickie flights, I projected in the kitchen of my condo peering up at the bottom of a lower cabinet from a four inch space between the tile floor and the base of the cabinet with ample space above me, allowing me to deduct my reduced size minus my body. Later through the years, I'd notice when I sensed the presence of an individual energy around me, I'd first catch a spark of bright light out of the corner of my eye just before being aware of the presence of someone I knew. My sense is many experience this same exchange with complete acceptance.

*Must truth be that Pure Consciousness is but a spark of light?*

Alice Bailey lectured in 1928 that evolution was "the unfolding of a continually increasing power to respond." Are we evolving to be able to respond to The Other without a horror movie fiasco?

Owning my feelings of abject vulnerability and exposure, I hold the gift of knowledge gained during my reconnaissance flights as truth. Not to share my conviction as to whether or not we are alone in the Universe, but to impart my personal experience that may or may not be supported by science or coexist in a context of collective truth. Whether you or I regard my discoveries as factual is inconsequential to us or to The Other. They are existence as we are existence, residing on different floors. Their relevance to now, to the stand between good and evil, conscious and unconscious, truth and illusion, offers a broad suggestion that consciousness is ever-evolving, ever-expanding upward toward their floor and when we are in close enough proximity to their rate of vibration their presence will be apparent. I was offered a glimpse; I am sharing a glimpse of the other side of the veil. In the meanwhile, our lives move forward one day at a time: we get up, sip our coffee, put on our armor and parlay with our day, with or without knowledge of them.

Visitations with The Other schooled me to be not on the earth, but with the earth, one with the organism. In that spirit, I will share one more adventure, bowing to all the risk involved.

Perusing my early journals, this voyage sadly seems to have been my last with The Other. By this time, I surmised the contacts would continue on and off through out the rest of my life. I had no idea I would never be in their fold again.

I again found myself as a spark of light hovering over a red top clover field buttressing our old home place on Cauble Road. As a child, I found the field comforting and somewhat magical as the clover blooms beckoned the honeybees to wine and dine and me to frolic barefooted as soon as spring allowed. The essence of the sweet clover blooms infused mine, like the fragrance of the bluebells in Ireland, I didn't just smell the aroma but became the perfume.

As if it had me in its sight, an electrifying vibration pulled my attention up to a round, almost translucent module or hovercraft of some sort. The craft looked small, more like a two seat shuttle. A beam of bluish light streamed out from underneath and the next thing I know, I'm seated on the passenger side of the Being at the controls. A complex panel with a plethora of lights and toggles of varying colors a mind-boggling bank of what I would now call computers lit up screens in front of me. Although silent, everything seemed charged by an oscillating current, including me. I felt no apprehension or excitement, only calm and matter of fact, as if leaning in to normal.

The communication, as usual, was telepathic and in simple direct thought forms. As soon as I formed the thought 'where are we going?' a familiar Other, who resembled the previous Other yet who seemed decidedly like someone I knew and who knew me, relayed back, "Arrival imminent."

There is no way to frame time in this state, so I'm guessing imminent could be relative to somewhere between seconds and millennia. The smaller craft entered a massive vessel ping ponging my next thought to, 'How could anything be as huge as this and not be seen by half the state of North Carolina?' The airy space was similar to the other vessels, circular and occupied by maybe thirty Other dispatched around various wave forms with pulsating lights and panels lined up alongside what appeared to be an advanced bank of computer screens. According to my journal, this rendezvous was in 1984, at least ten years before my limited acquaintance with commercially available personal computers.

"What are all of you doing?" I communicated. As with the pick-up pilot, all in the immediate vicinity felt like family, albeit deeper, more rooted in tribal connection than my family of origin.

Maintaining his/her no-apparent-gender face directly on the screens, one of The Other volleyed back.

"Trying to help planet earth."

Like The Other in previous encounters these beings were slightly translucent, androgynous, decidedly not human yet non-threatening and approachable. Visually clear to me in this encounter, their forms included head, torso, arm and leg assemblages, but no mouths and slightly slanted eyes. All exuded an aura of essential peace and an inclusive oneness with all existence, as if they were, like me, a microcosm within the macrocosm and simply unremarkable.

Peering into one of the computer like screens so carefully monitored by The Other, I was transfixed by quick flashing movie clips of thick dark smoke billowing from stacks upon stacks in what seemed to be a cloud enshrouding China. Large fish, whales, and dolphin choked in sullied oceans, inhaling plastic discards while their pale eyes rolled up, as they lumbered in near death toxicity. On the deck of a massive nuclear-laden ship, a trash can fire glowed out of sight on an abandoned deck. Buildings poked out of brown water like dead Cyprus stumps in a murky swampland. Masses of tribal men, women and children toiled, parched and skeletal as they desperately dug for water in barren red sand, cow carcasses baking in the heat. The sun, dulled by a thick haze hung powerless in an anemic sky while water inundated what looked to be large islands.

In a single glance, a snapshot taken without the confines of time reflected a dying world: death by strangulation, death by ignorance, death by greed. This beyond-the-pale communication took place twenty-two years before Vice President turned environmental defender, Al Gore, informed us of our collective inconvenient truth. Some ten years later Bill McKibben, environmentalist, journalist, and scholar, advanced to the forefront of the clean earth consciousness with visual symptoms of global heat up. Fortified with scientific equations, McKibben offered fair warning that once we pass 350 parts per million, the safe concentration of carbon dioxide in the atmosphere, non-adaptable human beings are slowly toasting.

Is this why The Other were focusing their energy directly on the earth? Do they care more than we care?

The viewing aboard the vessel rendered me raw and bleeding, yet determined to find a way to contribute a sliver of hope, not only for myself but for my grand girls and theirs to follow.

A few days later, I was describing my vessel visit to Rodney and what I'd witnessed on the screens. As is his way, he breathed action into my sad sack of a soul, the only antidote for grief.

"Well, so happens Rosanne and I are organizing a movement to bring recycling to Nashville. Come on board!" As usual, Rodney was a match-striker.

Our collective efforts succeeded in starting the ball rolling to get recycling trucks rolling around the streets of Nashville, collecting renewable trash. Later, plastics were numbered according to sustainability for reuse, paper products remade into strong corrugated cardboard and recycled glass ventured into vogue as art.

One small step forward for humankind, yet the earth suffers more than ever. Catastrophic effects of a climate crisis no longer threaten or hover, but have descended. I will continue to breathe seemingly healthy air, but will my grand girls? At the time I was shown a glimpse of forecasted disaster, we had not yet collided with the reality of our seas helplessly strangled on massive islands of toxic plastic waste, swallowed for food by food we eat.

I'm on deck here as a temporary traveler, and while on board, I hold personal responsibility for keeping my portion of the ship clean. The Other did not rescue me from myself, but did and I'm guessing still do continue to infuse Light from way up there on the topmost floors, casting downward on the congestive masses huddled on the lower decks. I had to jiggle the latch to luminosity, a choice I was destined to make, either from an ass crash on a hard floor, from thin veils and a softer approach, or from acceptance that all life is, indeed, but a spark of light emanating from an infinite Source.

Fragility and vulnerability – cracks where light filtered in illumined my personal path, and I bounced upward after striking bottom. I can only hope this trajectory applies on a planetary level. Hitchhikers on a now dangerously-imperiled earth are nearing the end point, the 350 of my parable. When this beautiful ball bounces off the underside, the reverberation will send souls seeking another place to drop anchor for thousands of years. There may be other options. I stopped by a few of them.

But nothing I experienced equaled the unparalleled majesty of this beautiful old ship.

I weep now for her wellbeing.

Even my rabbit knew never to shit where he lived and fed.
May all who think planet earth is a pretty decent place to sleep choose to stop soiling their own bed.

And so it is.

# WITCH HAIR #14.

*"The moment one definitely commits oneself,*
*then Providence moves too. Whatever you think*
*you can do, or believe you can do, begin it.*
*Action has magic, power, and grace."*
*Goethe*

The Big Marrowbone Valley, nestled in a 'valley within a valley,' meanders along the pristine Big Marrowbone Creek. On first glance, I saw, not a holler but an enchanting English countryside paradise perfect for a recovering monk. By late 1987, stretched from four years of meditation, I no longer romanticized cloistering but craved light, open vistas, and sex, in that order. Feeling tangled and claustrophobic in my urban condo, my dream body cavorted with Mother Nature, frolicked naked under the Milky Way, and planted Bradley tomatoes with my new friend, Virginia Team.

Virginia wore her scintillating soul inside out, gathering admirers like ants to honey: smile, fall in, and, when not diluted with alcohol, behold her shining light. Maybe loving an androgynous, trans, bi, or gay being exalts love to a higher form, making them banner bearers for unconditional acceptance. Virginia washed me in that kind of love, as did Billie, soul without gender surging love to a higher floor.

I met Virginia's house at the tail end of my monastic years in 1986, when I was there for a psychic reading from Hillary Ellers, our prime time psychic who drove up from Atlanta every few months to lay hands on our blistered souls.

"I want to know whoever it is that lives here," I remarked to Hillary. "Why don't I know the person who lives here?"

"It's Virginia Team, the art director at CBS. Can't believe you don't know her; everybody else does."

What I had heard about Virginia didn't match the vibration of her eclectic, arty, homey, no-frills space, making me even more curious. I left a note on her kitchen counter that said something like: 'I don't know you, but I would certainly love to know the being who created the beautiful vibe in this house. If you are so inclined, call me sometime.' I signed it with my phone number, having no idea she was gay. That term was not bantered about in the country music field in those days. Still isn't. I never really expected to hear from her.

The next afternoon I played back a call on my answering machine, dripping with a thick South Carolina accent: "Hey this is Va-gin-ia Te-am. I got youra sweet note and would love to meet you, but right now I've got to go to Jor-ja for treatment. I will call you when I get back in a few months."

I loved her already.

I think it must have been only a matter of days after she got clean when she called to ask if I wanted to ride out to see some new land she had purchased on the Little Marrowbone Road.

"Ah made a little pimento chea-se, so we can sit on the front dam and enjoy the peace," she drawled.

Virginia never sat, not to eat and only occasionally to pee, and to this day I'm not sure she has penetrated peace, but she sure opened my heart to what a shining example of unconditional love looked like in the same way Billie had when I was eleven. Chain saws and weed whackers were her knife and fork, and that beautiful slice of property splitting two bluffs sheltered her sanity after weaning from cocaine and alcohol.

A lover of birthdays who generously celebrated all of our birth milestones, VT, as we called her, insisted on throwing me a party on her new land in the Leo heat. I was forty, single and well lit-up. We invited not only our circle of mutual friends, but also Shannon and Garin. Shannon showed up early with his sheltered, boarding school debutante, who unfortunately had stumbled into a witch's lair. I was escorting them from the front dam of the property to a lean-to in the back decked out with hammocks, tables, and fluffy down comforters dressing up makeshift cots. A charming well-organized primitive glampcamp adorned with bright zinnias from VT's garden, the outdoor compound hitched Davy Crockett right up to Martha Stewart.

The three of us were halfway down the gravel lane when we heard a rustling up on the ridge and paused to see if we could spot a deer. After a yowling 'fuuuuuck' bounced around the holler, Virginia first rolled, then tumbled, then butt slid down the side of the steep bluff completely naked except for combat boots, (the snakes) and goggles, (the stones), pelted with shards of grass clinging to all of her sweat-soaked body parts. Pendulous breasts flopping like grapefruits in gym socks, a giant weed whacker loudly protesting as she tried to use it to stop her bare ass slide, she hurled down toward us, barely catching her footing before splaying right in front of Shannon's debutante.

Ashley sent a blood-curdling scream echoing around the ridge for what seemed like several minutes. Shannon grinned, grabbed her hand and said, "Oh, don't worry, Ash; it's just Virginia," and kept right on walking.

Before loving Virginia, I never knew how to actually look forward to being a year older. She managed to make it an event almost every year. Mother, father, sister, brother, soulmate, friend – like me and Billie, Virginia and I we were everything we could be to each other except lovers, and that I'm certain we'd already covered in another place in time.

Though VT was the primary reason I wanted to live in the area, my hypersensitivity made it mandatory. Cursed with acuteness genes from both parents, I already responded to toxins like a canary in the mine, then years of meditation heightened my sensitivity to the point that standing in crowded grocery store lines became challenging.

Not only was I coaxed by Virginia's natural gardening skills, but the fertility of the Marrowbone Valley dared me not to garden.

After years of slathering soothing balm on my daddy deficits, I found myself diving into unfinished business with country living and organic farming. No better metaphor for healing my shadowy relationship with farm life than digging in my own dirt to see what I could make bloom. Three open green acres rolling into a clear flowing creek in an ancient first settler valley was the perfect container for gestating my new found center.

From the outside my house, hand-built by a carpenter, appeared a dramatic downgrade from Golf Club Lane or from my condo. A simple redwood square box topped by a tin roof, it had a well-constructed south facing deck perfect for sunbathing, journaling and sunset dinners, but was not princess digs. The inside opened to a blank palette that whetted my appetite for decorating. A large expanse held the kitchen, dining and lounging area warmed by a hand-built creek rock fireplace climbing to the ceiling. I had the floors and walls painted a shiny, soft white, plantation-shuttered the windows, then cozied the space with a cornucopia of comfy pieces. A cushy red velvet couch, antique wicker pieces, and a huge heart-shaped braided rug I found at a flea market hatched a *hygge* life (the Danish ritual of enjoying life's simple pleasures) that cradled my newly birthed soul. The day I moved in, I vowed I would grow old there with CT, my Gucci loafer-chewing sole companion of the last four years, after adding a soon-to-be-found yellow dog.

The owner of the Gucci loafers once went so far as to threaten, "it's me or the goddamn rabbit, woman!" after we had replaced our thick juicy vacuum cleaner cord for the fourth time. With a lumbering eye roll, I calmly informed him that he was treading on dangerous ground, the rabbit stayed.

For the first time in my life, I was an empty nester, responsible only for my own wellbeing and that of any four-legged companion. Or at least that's what I thought was sprouting in my new life.

Both boys were somewhat capable of surviving on their own at this point. Surviving, not thriving. Nonetheless, it was time for me to escape the role of lion tamer for rock musicians who were more or less still entangled in a scuffle with maturity.

Another more unconscious prod for moving thirty minutes into the remote Cheatham County countryside was the impulse to make myself hard to find. After years of on-demand chit-chatty business clusters, I felt a righteous right to embrace my introverted self. If anyone was willing to drive that far out to see me, it was likely someone I wanted to see. More urgently, I carried tomato- growing genes, worshiped at the altar of anything organic and freshly picked, especially Silver Queen corn and okra, so now dense nutrition was going to leap from my garden straight to my fork.

Daddy's rants and raves about DDT poisoning all the bluebirds, which of course it did, and how pesticides would deplete the good microbes in the soil were pounded into my tiny brain forty years before Monsanto created the current cancer boom. Then again in those years, farmers dining directly from their kitchen gardens used coffee grounds to acidify the soil, lime to alkalize it, and chicken manure to fertilize it, leaving no use for the term *organic*. Adamant that Butch and I be raised on nutrients, not convenience, Daddy could be a control freak when it came to nurturing his children, demanding that Mama cook tomato soup for us from her home canned tomatoes. Acidic tomatoes leached harmful metals from the Campbell's cans. Yes, he knew that seventy years ago. Of course, Butch and I much preferred soup with the BPA and sugar, considering it a treat when Mama could sneak it past his ever-ready eye.

My bountiful first crop gave Findhorn (Scottish commune infamous for gigantic vegetables) a run for the green. Looking back I have no idea how I planted, alone and by hand, multiple rows of corn, okra, green beans, squash, tomatoes, potatoes, radishes cucumbers, carrots and watermelons. Gratefully, a mature asparagus bed, backbreaking to dig and set, was there on arrival. Demeter whispered in one ear and Daddy in the other, guiding the planting and protection, with fair warning to encase the entire garden with eight feet tall giant sunflowers as fodder for the birds and deer in hopes they might allow me some leftovers. After the initial plowing, so as not to upset the worm population, I didn't use any tilling machines. I weeded and hoed by hand, in suffocating humidity, in a swatting-at-mosquitos, tick-skirting naked nymph dance. Now healthy enough to allow memories and lessons from my garden angel daddy back into my consciousness, I toiled empowered with his spirit backing me.

A working-while-naked ethic rose to my new environment; weather permitting, I farmed wearing underwear or nothing at all. Daddy had spent most of the days of my youth in boxer shorts and a muscle tee, so the nurture factor was there, but I defiantly disdained clothes from the get go, with or without Daddy's influence. The house was far enough from the sparsely-traveled lane not to put my body on exhibition. I figured, as it had been for Daddy, it was about comfort and freedom. I got caught a few times. A UPS delivery surprised me while I was harvesting okra, gingerly snipping spiny, itchy pods in nothing but a thong. I dropped into a crouching position pretending to pull carrots when delivery dude jumped off the truck placing my package at the front door. All was going well until he saw CT hopping about in the asparagus bed and ambled over to talk to him—fair warning: pet rabbits attract attention!—cornering me instead.

Determined not to stand, I knew that he knew, and he knew that I knew that he knew, striking an impasse. He, intent on ogling a couple of fried-egg-sized breasts, and me, equally adamant: "no go, Joe."

When Brown finally ran out of small talk and CT grew bored with him, I confronted the standoff. "I can squat behind this fucking squash plant all day hope you're getting paid by the hour."

Another bare breast and bottom exposure could have landed me behind bars. My childhood friend, Pat Balentine, a city girl exec in a big box bank, rode up from North Carolina for a weekend. I treated her to Virginia's place for an afternoon of lounging around in spring fed pond water, nibbling chilled watermelon. As usual, Virginia and I hung out butt naked. After the sun dropped behind the cliffs striking elongated shadows and the mosquitos were out for blood , we packed up and darted for the car. Ptah, my new-found yellow dog jumped in the backseat and he, Pat, and I casually rode toward the Big Marrowbone. Halfway back, I glanced down suddenly to realize I was driving completely nude.

"Damn, Pat! What the hell! Why didn't you tell me I was naked?" I freaked.

"I just figured you did this all the time," she quipped.

It would have taken more than Daddy and Demeter to help me if I had ended up in the Cheatham County jail for indecent exposure, in the heart of righteous wing Christiandom.

Spontaneous adventures, spiritual as well as earthbound, built into the Big Marrowbone Valley were a big part of the allure.

Comical barn owls, white tailed deer families, nesting eagles, invasive wild turkey with no boundaries, magical blue heron with wings spanning the width of the creek and industrious dam building beaver all provided the daily bread of the Big Marrowbone Valley along side several eccentric neighbors. One bright spring morning, I sipped coffee on my front stoop, chatting with a potential new paramour on the phone.

"Wow, I'm looking at a horse up on the road that looks just like Trigger! Oh ... and ... damn, the man riding him looks just like Roy Rogers!"

Laughter rang out from the other end of the line. "No way! Are you sure you're just drinking coffee?"

Riding just to the other side of Roy Rogers and Trigger's great grandson was Randy Travis, my down-the-valley neighbor. Randy later told me that he bought the progeny of Trigger from Roy, and that Roy and Dale frequently visited and treasured the Marrowbone as much as we did.

I look back on those couple of fleeting years on the Big Marrowbone as the most joy-filled times of my life, a time when Mother Nature became the bond that held the once fragmented parts of my psyche for healing. Eating 90% from my own labors, proving I could wade waist deep in the creek during midwinter snowfall to replace the hose feed from the spring, or hunkering down under the floor of the guest cabin by the creek, with black widows scouting my every move to prime the pump feeding water to the main house, fertilized my budding best self.

I segued from a posh pampered princess lifestyle to a primitive piece of land that pried every ounce of male muscle I could muster. After the bruising ego-leveling, my masculine and feminine natures begged for mending and blending in harmony with my soul's voice. The Big Marrowbone was the quintessential repair shop.

Every minute of every challenge mingled my masculine and feminine,and merged the redneck with the princess. The princess flourished for six years in a stately home with full time help. She didn't shop for groceries, drive the boys to school or gas up her own car, polishing her to a high sheen. The fossilized, pre-Mississippian ritual grounds of the Marrowbone Valley breathed life back into the recalcitrant farm girl, a laborious yet glorious initiation.

If not for love and money, I likely would be there to this day.

# WITCH HAIR #15.

*The Tao is the One, from the One comes Yin and*
*Yang; from these two, creative energy; from energy,*
*ten thousand things; the forms of all creation. All life*
*embodies the Yin and embraces the Yang, through their*
*union achieving harmony.*
*Tao Te Ching, Chapter 42*

With ten happy toes rooting in verdant valley soil, saving
heirloom seeds like my daddy used to on Cauble Road, the
spirit of the Marrowbone spirited me back to the days of my
childhood on the farm. A wide awake, healthy, vital, bored inner
girl sprang out of hiding, excited to express herself, with urges
to write, paint, dance or squander the day stalking snapshots of
country living. From fornicating turtles, to creek spanning Great
Blue Herons, to busy beaver erecting their architectural dams
along the creek, to Ptah, my yellow dog plucking blackberries
off the briery vines with his teeth, to boastworthy full moon
shots of the valley and daily documentation of my vegetable
bounty, I became compulsive about capturing the joy in each
day, so for the rest of my life, I could never, ever forget the gift
of being there.

The artistic expression I most feared nipped at my heels nagging me to pay attention.

My life long fascination of play-like, which Butch and I pronounced, 'plike', starting with 'let's plike you're Scott and I'm Smith', probably was my four year old director, and soul's itch to perform trying to be heard. It would take over forty years for me to listen. The raw exposure of acting was the one creative expression that froze me in my tracks.

I had undergone disintegration on nearly every possible level, personal, psychological, emotional and professional. It was time to ground my new life out of churning chaos and turn full face to my fears. Jungian Psychology says that chaos is the great game changer that precedes a shift in the paradigm, personal, regional or universal. I had dismantled every possible pattern, paragon, paradox, or precedent over the past five years, letting go of everything but my love for my boys and my rabbit. But the upheaval propelled me into an intimate relationship with my rambling unconscious causing dream disturbance. Every night, three or four confusing, complex dreams I was ill-equipped to decipher, haunted my joy time and I was not going to ever let joyfulness fall through the cracks again. I had to find a way to converse.

*Memories, Dreams and Reflections*, Dr. Carl Jung's autobiography, became my interpretive manual on the intricate languages of the mind. The conscious mind he considered the ego; the personal unconscious he called a reservoir for an overflowing conscious mind (mine was full), and the collective unconscious, where we all meet in One Mind, he mapped out as our mental terrain.

I desperately needed a translator to decode the dots and dashes of my nightly onslaught of jibber-jabber, owing to Jung's theory that neurosis is the unresolved tension between the conscious and the unconscious.

Once a month treks to Birmingham, Alabama to work with rock star Jungian analyst Nancy Qualls-Corbett, author of *The Sacred Prostitute: Eternal Aspects of the Feminine*, busted the seal on my mental underpinnings. I read aloud my dreams as I had recorded them in my journals and we'd poke around in my unconscious, picking up debris and sweeping out dusty corners for two hours on Friday evening and wake up and do it again for another two hours on Saturday morning. With Nancy's confident, regal intelligence and soft voice leading me down dark passages, I confronted my nemesis the cave monk, welcomed to the light my anima and animus, and dusted off my sexuality.

Jung's model of our psychological landscape paints the animus as the unconscious masculine side of a woman, and the anima as the unconscious feminine side of a man, both naturally occurring (in varying doses) parts of the human psyche. Since I was in the early stages of 'manning' my own publishing company, I needed to shore up my masculine, the logical, structured, analytical side, to muscle up financial stability. My intuitive, assertive, nurturing feminine had strong bones but needed muscle stretching and toning having flown from under the arm of a powerful male.

After a year of intense, gut-wrenching analyses, Dr. Qualls-Corbett admonished me to go out into the world and 'taste the wine of Dionysus.' To cap off years of monastic celibacy, meditation, yoga, vegan diet, chakra prying and out of body flying, she insisted I find a way to set aside the tools to tolerate life and simply celebrate being in life. Having never developed a discernible taste for wine, whether made by Dionysus or Chateau Lafitte, I swallowed my southern pride, faced my fear, and signed up for an acting class. Not with any purpose or intent to feast with Dionysus, the muse just happened to catwalk in the door.

Anima (I'll assign a metaphorical moniker) was late. Our newly clustered troupe was well into our first exercise when she breezed in wearing a clingy white tee and black biking shorts with a billowy vintage white crinoline pulled over them. I figured the crinoline had to have been added just before her entry. Otherwise, how the hell could she drive in that starchy haze? Her mane of chestnut ringlets framed a cover girl face, azure saucer eyes and one of those Meg Ryan smiles that deletes as it seduces. In all my years with gay BFFs, my lady parts were never aroused or my lips drawn to a kiss. Lips and lady parts simultaneously burst into applause.

As fate, or, as Nancy might say, Aphrodite, would arrange it, our coach set up a common motivation exercise, charging one student with conveying an intention to their partner no words, only eyes and minimal body language. After several rounds of failed intentions, he pivoted to Miss Anima, "you," then pointed at me, "and you!" seating us face-to-face, two feet apart, assigning her to choose an intention.

The Miss casually lowered her chin releasing a cascade of curls to veil her face, like one of the curly haired girls on the Clairol box, then slowly lifted her chin hinting just enough smile to dazzle with a couple of deep dimples.

No mistake, what I saw *was* seduction, but I didn't trust my adolescent animus not to project that he was being lured, as happens and has happened to the female gender for a thousand years, the male ego can make that shit up.

I held firm, volleying with a slow, exhaling lean in, testing eye contact with a snarky brow lift.

She countered with a subtle nip of her lower lip.

The instructor crouched closer to the stage monitoring the subtlety. In slow motion, I shifted my right hand to my neck, lowered my head, inching a few fingers downward.

She opened her crinoline-coated legs, gathered her knees together then threw back her head, taunting a scintillating smile to a full-throated laugh that did Lauren Bacall some justice.

"Seduction!" I blurted. "Your intention is seduction."

The fired-up coach adjusting his pants, stood with beads of sweat rolling down one side of his face and yelled,

"CUT!"

We continued the intentionality dance throughout our classes, requesting scenes together so we could meet up for rehearsals. Anima made a living as an actress and model in LA, stretching me to keep up with her. Although she was twelve years younger, she had the spunk to challenge me at every turn, confronting my wannabe actor, practicing alchemist and developing male,toward a comfort zone with risk. Her integrated, well-developed feminine intoxicated a part of me that I had yet to claim … and he required her.

We tantalized spring into summer, gardening, preparing dirt-to-dining dishes and occasionally auditioning together, once for *Hannah and Her Sisters*. Surprisingly I nailed the callback for Hannah, but the role ultimately went to a younger threesome of sisters, validating my concerns that landing even local theatre roles in my forties would be dicey.

Anima and I let off some of our seemingly off-limits sexual steam by dancing around town – while painstakingly dancing around sex. Our chemistry was obvious to all my friends, especially the gay ones, teasing about the wafting pheromones trailing in our wake. We finally confronted the dilemma of completely hetero sex and what to do with it all, then danced some more, until a sleepover, when the space finally opened for a lovely spontaneous kiss.

Sweet. Delicious. Youthful. Blissfully feminine, I was listing on the edge of everything.

With thirsty lips in toto, our bodies took the lead, enticing us toward the next, and the next … pirouetting our ballet to a decidedly anti-climatic completion. The capitulation itself became the orgasm that ended the romance, but not our friendship. After that pivotal night, our relationship was never the same, not as much fun without the flirting, and more and more we found ourselves to be more competitive than supportive.

Anima roused a dormant male that extolled rather than controlled, a quality of my slumbering self that had to be realized before my venture as a company owner. She later confided it was my feminine that captivated her, surprising, because I felt so male around her, easily falling into that role. The waltz with

Anima led me to believe that inherently I am bisexual, but then again, what is that but an ability or choice to love from the soul, bypassing gender?

It was a lovely dance. Personally transformative and alchemical, and I haven't kissed a woman since.

# WITCH HAIR #16.

*The meeting of two personalities is like the contact*
*of two chemical substances: if there is any reaction,*
*both are transformed.*
Carl Jung

Compulsive self-communicator that I am, I ruffled my own
feathers to figure out why my feathers got ruffled, whittling
myself down to a nub. Since the body-slam of '82, I've amassed
fifty-six volumes of blank art books scrawled in barely
decipherable self-talk. On a whim, I randomly picked up volume
ten, hoping for mirth, bracing for mayhem. Shameless, brazen
joy from the lean but green years on the Big Marrowbone sprang
from the scrawl, immortalizing another not-so-clandestine
midlife collision with the springtime of youth.

In two marriages, my feminine strength had been feared, leading
to physical overpowering, then mentored, lending imbalance
in power, but never had I felt fearlessly valued for my feminine
kinds. My Big Split ex recognized and freely fostered my
capabilities as a music executive and producer, but for the most
part, disdained the woman; my boys' father was simply terrified.

Still coloring outside the lines to feed the famine, I found myself in yet another acting class tango. Gender-opposite doppelganger to Miss Anima, Animus, Jr., popped in for an advanced class. Who better to buss new life into a bedraggled feminine and rivet a newly transformed masculine than a good-looking, talented male?

Animus, Jr., a local professional actor and protégé of longtime acting coach Ruth Sweet, signed up for a refresher class. No matter how long you'd been acting, working with Ruth blew the lid off another layer. Elated to be accepted into any class of Ruth's, at forty-two I resigned myself as the class senior citizen.

All the actors vied for scene work with Animus, Jr., not only because he was a big star in a smallish theatrical town consistently aired on a well-lauded PSA, but also because he was a gifted thespian. A generous actor, his intention was to energize the scene for the good of the whole, not to prop his ego or splay his training. I held back on the third row, content to observe good actors doing powerful work, never entertaining participation at their level. Ruth had other ideas, pairing the weakest with the strongest, and there I was in an impromptu cold read with *him … Streetcar Named Desire …* Stella and Stanley … one of their makeup scenes.

From the opening lines, when our eyes caught, there was little need to act. The energy between us was an electrically charged chemical combustion. I don't know if it was his skill at lifting a partner to his paradigm or if two souls were resuming roles already played, but we were Stella and Stanley.

Animus, Jr., with his perfectly imperfect mound of curly brunette locks, indigo eyes, pouty thick lips, and oh, so fresh movie ingénue countenance, mirrored a male counterpart to Anima. Laying aside gender, the only other variable was age: he was twenty-four years old!

I suppose you might call our romantic adventures over the next few months dating. He was uncannily fluid, and I, inherently clumsy, simply puppy-dogged his lead. Animus, Jr., a prototype of an uninhibited, preternaturally self-assured, confident male, developed in a petri dish of a functional loving home with a mother who encouraged all things creative and cultivated a capacity to adore. And to be adorable.

He turned me on to movies that kindled my curiosity about filmmaking, and I broadened his eclectic music palate. Always animated, Animus, Jr. would break into dance without provocation. While making me miso soup for breakfast, he put on some shit-kickin' music and taught me how to two-step.

"So how in hell did a New York-schooled actor learn two-step?" I yelled over way too country for me deer-dip, stumbling over too many feets.

"My mother taught me years ago. She also taught me how to tango!"

That was a fucking understatement!

Sometimes I couldn't decide if Animus, Jr. perpetually performed or was a paragon of innocence, but little escaped his keen observation or dampened his broad-minded reasoning.

He'd pick interesting or controversial articles from the morning paper to read aloud, initiating probing discussions on topics from politics to pop culture. If an insatiable curiosity is a prerequisite for anyone with a master plan to inhabit the creative arts, and, according to Einstein, a signpost of intelligence, Animus, Jr. was perhaps the most creative being I'd reckoned with.

Continually peppering me with challenging questions from our mutual interests in acting and music to planetary paradigms and metaphysics, I was staggered how anyone could be swarming with such broad knowledge in twenty-four years. He was attractive, brilliant, funny, unrestrained and just quirky enough to be provocative, but what won my heart was the way he venerated me as a woman without resorting to flattery.

Animus, Jr. moved into my tiny primitive—meaning no shower or toilet—guest cabin by the creek ostensibly for a month to finish a one-man play he was writing called *Desperate for Magic*. His title, a plea ripped from my feminine psyche, flashed on and off like a neon sign spitting in the dark: 'Middle Age Woman, Desperate for Magic' ... desperate for magic ... desperate for magic. One of those glorious, nasty epiphanies where I didn't realize I was aching until the balm of youth soothed the sore.

I offered little resistance to his open-hearted, wildly attentive infatuation. I did feel slightly shackled by the age difference, specifically how to explain to my boys that I was in a relationship with someone careening on their age and what I'd do if someone asked if I was his mother.

Good actors, sharply attuned to their surroundings, know when to create a scenario in their favor. Animus, Jr. made a play to get to know Garin by inviting him out to my kitchen for a spaghetti fiasco, just the two of them. When I walked in late that evening, they were still hanging at the table sucking Buds, raving rock-and-roll, with Led Zeppelin bouncing off the valley walls, oblivious to the axe murder scene in the kitchen. From the explosion of tomato sauce and shards of dead pasta plastered to my white floor with the dog and rabbit happily polishing their paws, it was clear who reaped the male bonding benefits.

Shannon pragmatically dismissed the whole affair with an eye roll and, "Jesus, Mom, that's a little embarrassing."

One cold rainy weekend morning, we were lounging in bed with CT hopping jealous, as rabbits are prone to be. He thumped his hind leg against the wood floor, thudding like a baseball hurled against the side of the house. If Animus, Jr. had Gucci loafers they would have been his prey. Animus, Jr., took on CTs daring glare, then leaned in to kiss, then softy bite, my lower lip, prolonging CTs agony. Then with no foreplay he yanked up my upper lip, leaning in to inspect my teeth. I felt like I was at the vet, did he have to be so insatiably curious about everything!

"Are those your real teeth?" he probed incredulously.

"Well, yeah, what do you mean, real?"

"Is that the way your teeth naturally grew in your mouth?" Interrogating like a prying dental student.

"Ye…sss."

"Well, that is incredible!" He, who flashed perfectly aligned, bright white twenty four year old teeth behind those enticing lips, "I had to wear braces for nearly three years to get these teeth."

Nothing seemed off-limits to his throbbing curiosity, especially sexually. Sired from the loins of the conservative South, where sex dialogue balked behind closed doors, I had to push myself past my own inhibitions and shame-induced reticence to join him.

After five years of baseball bat to pillow pounding and scrawling rage letters that practically incinerated themselves, I slowly lowered the flame on the dark pine tree house, priming me for a free spirit like Animus, Jr. I figured my better angels invited him in to rebuild my demolished sexual ego, refurbishing it into the open expression of feminine power, better known as *passion*. His well-balanced gender fluidity, freed him to channel both male and female qualities without threat to his ego. No wonder he was such a good actor!

Accomplished as he was as a performer, he surpassed himself in kissing. Until Animus, Jr., my scant romantic life and marriages had been bussed by few good kissers, and witches do appreciate kissing skills. Goes without saying, the chemical properties have to match up, but then dexterity has to kick in. From our first Stella and Stanley kiss in class, the former and the latter were intact. But because of the age disparity, I left all forward movement up to him. I'm glad I didn't know the word *cougar* at the time; certainly it would have been fair game to apply it. But the reality is we loved most everything about each other and were temporarily crazy compatible.

As with Anima, I especially loved how he, without a hint of judgment, challenged me to broaden my understanding of myself as he probed deeper to know me. Amid the dance of our romance, he adorned me with his presence, and like

Anima, at every turn, he asked about and was supportive of *my* creativity, excitedly pouring over my Marrowbone photographs, reading my stories out loud, scene practicing with me and of course, dancing, he always wanted to dance. Having spent the preponderance of my adult life nurturing and supporting the creative journey of others, an abandoned part of my soul was flattered out of hiding for the laying on of fresh tender hands.

My readiness to move forward, male and female two stepping toward the arms of forever love, playfully ministered by Anima and Animus, Jr. charmed and challenged my shadowed parts into the light of acceptance. I honor them for striking the original match under this book, and bow in deep recognition for rousing joy in the morning of becoming.

# WITCH HAIR #17.

*Fall seven times, get up eight, but no one will keep*
*you from lying there to process what happened.*
*Japanese Proverb*

The trickster lurked in smoke and mirrors. Betting on the 'come'
while living without income stirred the slinky prankster napping
in the shadows. While I lathered up creatively and frolicked
naked through the greens of the Marrowbone, so followed my
bank account. My publishing catalog, well-stocked with record-
ready Lewis Storey songs, was my financial ace in the hole, so I
needed songs sailing up the charts, quickly.

The Music Row trajectory toward authenticity suddenly back-
slid to inane twang, thanks to the rise of my horse-riding
Marrowbone neighbor, Randy Travis. I was treading the trend
of deer-dip music, having to earn money. But how hard could it
be to get a few Garth Brooks cuts to lend a support beam to my
newly-formed enterprise? Helpful, I'm sure, had I even seriously
listened to his music, instead of yet again squandering my time
continuing to mine talent of promising writer/artists. Outmoded
harbingers on life support, but I couldn't seem to pull the plug.

Instead of knocking on doors up and down the row racking up 'holds' to earn back money fast leaking out of my bank account, I behaved as if I still subsisted on corporate funding.

Bowen had a point.

I slid back into my comfort zone of developing songwriters into recording artists, having launched the careers of several successes. It was also my confidence zone, but my savings account moaned, so I pitched songs to the Garth Brooks camp, betting on the come in a high stakes roll. Interesting to note: a writer/artist I was developing for an exclusive contract got not one, not two, but six Garth Brooks cuts after I shuttered the company, all access to the wrong path barricaded.

I conceded earning money doing something that was reasonably fulfilling, if not blissful, instead of following a logical career path might be better suited to my emotional well-being. I was an awakened creative neophyte clamoring to express her self in any and every way, and ministering to songwriters was not my idea of a creative outlet. So cue the trickster: no country music windfalls.

Someone who loved me suggested I might want to consider a trade more suited to my current alignment, like counseling: advice on how to maneuver Music Row, structure verses and choruses, and how to lift a melody out of the doldrums. But how to tune in to the strains of the Universe was parceled out free of charge. Counseling didn't fit my creative needs by any stretch, and I eye-rolled from over in my blind corner, but it might replenish the coffers.

Exactly how I would manage it wasn't clear, necessitating a temporary detour after my bankbook cried "uncle" and I had to get an actual job. In 1989, I temporarily left Ptah, my dotted third eye, Egyptian wonder mutt, on the Marrowbone with a housesitter, dropped off my rabbit, CT to babysit my mother in Salisbury, and relocated for a few beats to Durham, North Carolina, when I was hired to help a longtime friend build an independent record label.

My cranky inner three-year-old squirmed with no creative outlet *and* no Marrowbone, so though the money restocked the till, it proved a challenging experiment.

Less than a year later, circling love found me, and for love, I surrendered my A&R gig, packed up Ptah and the truck, after CT flew back to the warren, and moved to Bev-er-ly … West Hollywood to be precise.

After an exhausting interview for an A&R position with the highly esteemed A&M independent label, lost in a stifling smog stupor, I made it to the bathroom just in time to retch all of my fed-up-with-the-music-business into the white bowl. If my brain didn't realize it was time to sever my long-tethered tenure, my gut certainly did.

A well-networked film business friend who knew I had been a meditation and yoga practitioner for a number of years rang to see if I might be open to teaching her to meditate. Elated at the idea of spreading the gospel according to Yogananda and life-enhancing techniques of inner practices, I started a meditation group for six West Coast women movers and shakers. That one capitulation to a casual invitation forever changed my life, and for Callie Khouri and Renée Armand, I am forever grateful.

Within eighteen months, my popular practice had evolved into its own form of spiritually-based psychotherapy. Not at all uncommon now, but in 1992, it must have been quite rare judging from the response. In my spare time, or because my partner traveled for a living and I seemed to have spare time, I decided to see if I could test up to a degree that allowed me to practice my model of healing under credentials of some sort.

In a couple of years I had a B.A. in Human Behavior from a local college geared toward Somatic, or holistic, Psychology. Soon after, I half-heartedly committed to masters-level work in an advanced program in Spiritual Psychology. The undergrad program whetted my thinking and writing skills and lit up my world with a writing mentor: diminutive eighty-year-old Dr. Benjamin Levine. His nurturing support stepped in where Anima and Animus, Jr. left off. My thirst for the right write for my beloved Professor propelled me through the four-year program in less than two years.

I continued to develop and expand my practice, working with actors, models, producers, rock singers, and the LGBT community, several of whom were HIV positive. A plethora of intriguing, challenging seekers with compelling inner narratives tacked me experientially toward a Master's.

The therapy model I practiced was based on my own inner journey, which Dr. Jung referred to as *individuation*, or the lifelong process of growing into wholeness. My personal exploration, along with my healer daddy's voice from the other side and exciting new experiential anger release techniques from Onsite Workshops, guided my approach to a living balanced protocol.

It worked. Within months, I had a wait list.

If not, in Joseph Campbell's words, 'following my bliss,' I was at least making money at what I had been, to the detriment of my bank account, doing altruistically with songwriters. Besides, I'm not convinced there was any bliss to be had in Los Angeles in those years; if there was, it was entitled to those better at it than I was.

I leaned into my inner life, which unlike the love that drew me to the land of lost souls, did not wear a blindfold. The extreme trust that it took to abandon the tranquility of the Marrowbone and relocate to Los Angeles, a choking miasma of chaotic energy cocooned in toxins and smog, tied me to the stake for a trial by fire, literally and figuratively

Mirroring my despondency, Ptah, lingered at the front door sad and displaced for hours, whining for a romp on the Marrowbone, pleading with actual tears to please go home. We were both repressed and depressed, with righteous reason. During our first few years in West Hollywood, we were jolted near senseless with a rumbling 6.7 earthquake, throngs of destructive race rioters torched buildings near our neighborhood, raging wildfires blazed out of control in Malibu, not to mention the whole Desert Storm fiasco, which I feared might ignite World War 3. All of the joy and light inherent in our Marrowbone days quickly spun into some of the darkest imaginable, with more yet to come.

As the Yin and Yang weaves in and out creating light within darkness and darkness within light, so was my new life. Leading meditation with groups of determined self-evolving women gave me the courage to keep putting one foot in front of the other, all the while reminding me that authentic love cannot be corralled.

At the height of all turmoil, while LA was barely breathing, my practice was thriving. Sensitive, aching souls searching for a glimmer of hope streamed in, evolving into ongoing women's groups, men's groups, and some weekend sweat lodges and workshops. We condensed into a tight knit community of open, loving people living in collective hope for a peaceful existence in an oh so troubled environment, without the gnarly transference of a guru, I remained a seeker walking along with my clients.

Because my spiritual sabbatical turned me inside out, without brag I was a more peaceful, more authentic human, because my fellow Angelenos were suffering, because I needed an income and because The Other supported my transformation, I had no recourse but to pay it forward as a springboard to higher consciousness, as had been done for me. I feel the same now in sharing a little how-to manna in the next few paragraphs, collapsed into bullet points for an easy self-administered analgesic.

Use as needed.

The *Recapitulation Process*, as I tagged it, blends measures of magic into life's pathos by cauterizing wounds taunted and antagonized when an emotional response to painful stimuli is impeded, creating a toxic dump of denial, shame or repression.

Simple, effective, and easier to swallow than harmful prescription drugs, recapturing past amnesias by breathing to where they hide in the subconscious releases blocked emotions that, with or without permission, color and contaminate daily choices and behavior.

Everything is energy. Love is energy. Love is everything.

Balanced energy is connected to the Source of all energy, whatever that might be; it feels good, whole and complete, like love.

Seven primary energy centers conduct all life force in the human body. Balance these centers and output is increased.

- First energy center is sexual, survival, and energies that ground you to the earth; located at the base of the spine, it is activated by the color RED.

- Second energy center, located between the top of the pubic bone and the navel, is emotional energy, activated by the color ORANGE.

- Third energy center, located at the solar plexus, is power, activated by the color of the sun or the sun's light.

- Fourth center, located at the sternum, is heart energy or love, activated by GREEN.

- Fifth center, located at the throat is the center of creativity and communication and is activated by the color BLUE.

- Sixth center, also called the Third Eye, is located on the forehead between the brows and is activated by a color varying from INDIGO BLUE TO PURPLE.

- The seventh center, called the Crown is where the soul enters and leaves the body and is activated with WHITE LIGHT and sits about a foot above the head.

These centers revolve in a clockwise direction and can be easily tested with a small crystal (energy conductor) on a string or chain.

Energy is life force streaming through all life forms both animate and inanimate from a constant Source that cannot be created or destroyed, only transferred.

*Energy flowing from Source is received downward through the crown as finer spiritual energies, which in turn propels the energy to the intuitive properties of the third eye. Intuition then informs the communication/creative energies at the throat, allowing understanding to open the heart center. Once the heart center is open, compassion and empathy create personal power, flowering the solar plexus. Inwardly enhanced personal power then allows the fragile emotional center to slowly develop a comfort zone, disengaging the ego, to allow feelings to flow freely. Once feelings are released to come and go without hindrance or judgment, the root center which houses survival, procreativity and connection to the earth, shifts from survival mode to creative mode and sends the balanced energy back up the flow system, creating homeostasis, or balance. Keeping the seven energy centers open is the goal of meditation.*

Deep dives, even randomly conceived, can release either snippets, or a tsunami of repressed emotions containing valuable information and insight into personal behaviors and choices. Sometimes the trail can be followed through smells, sounds, music, or through any of the proprioceptive senses, which are position or movement, or the sense of force or heaviness against skin, muscles and bones. Sexual perpetration recall can be triggered even when occurring in a preverbal state though proprioceptive recall. The body knows; the body remembers.

If I thought, "oh, that's why I do that" once, I traced it a thousand times to a little clump of dust hiding behind an open door, one more piece of the Dixie puzzle lying in wait.

Our groups began with color balancing the energy system, then in early work, immersing first into the emotional center, where the piles accumulate. To immerse is as simple as breathing until reaching a deeply meditative brain wave between alpha and theta, then visualizing a descent, down stair steps works, into the chosen center. As each center cleared, the focus moved to another center, usually the heart after the emotions, or the first center, if sexual abuse is uncovered. We continued descents for over nine years, clearing each energy center of congestion or clogged emotion. I facilitated the descents through guided meditation, but it's perfectly within reach to assist your own deep dives using the breathing technique below.

The technique below quickly bypasses the conscious mind, which may be suppressing recall:

*This breath combo is utilizing the Ujjai technique of allowing the breath to pass gently along the glottis creating a soft but audible sound with the mouth softly closed, the tongue tucked slightly against the roof of the mouth with the tip against the back of the front teeth. The breath seemingly is drawn in and out through the throat center but actually comes silently through the nose. Practice creates a co-existence between the breath and sound until soon neither is apparent.*

*Inhale to a count of three into the abdomen, a count of three into the chest, another count of three up through the top of the head, hold at the top of the head for a few beats until an energetic connection is felt, then exhale keeping the mouth closed to a count of nine.*

*Within twenty minutes of breathing in this way, an alpha or blissful state is reached. From there, the Universe awaits.*

*The recapitulation—or re-capturing suppressed emotional*
*history from traumatic early childhood experiences—naturally*
*emerges once a solid, trusting spiritual connection is in place.*

No matter the mode of coaxing, the ego is reluctant to release its
role as primary sentinel of protection without a spiritual base.
Elevating the stakes to its own survival, the ego fights hard to
maintain dominance over the soul. Meditation is the spoonful of
sugar that makes the medicine go down.

Relinquishing the rich array of shadowed feelings convinces
the ego that its role is less and less paramount to surviving the
earth experience. No doubt it can be a decidedly harrowing
process. As buried scenarios of abuse, boundary violations or
perpetrations are relived emotionally, the subsequent feelings
of fear, anger and rage are released, allowing the opposing
energy of love to fill the vacancy. Most self-seekers readily access
sadness, guilt or shame, but tend to divert around rather than
persist through anger and rage, the last hurdle. Rage release by
physically pounding a plastic ball bat against a pillow, screaming,
rolling or other movement to create a physical expression of
emotional content is instantly cathartic. It can also be helpful
to prime the pump with letter writing—a safer, mental form of
release—to trigger physical expression.

When I was able to view my work in West Hollywood in the
rearview, to see the outcome for the beautiful beings whose
paths I was honored to illumine, I knew there was one more
place I wanted to take the work.

I loved every minute of the ten-year practice. Several of the
groups stayed together for the duration. My original women's
group still gathers periodically, thirty years later, to meditate,

share, forage and bask in the deep unconditional sister love we cultivated. They remain a glorious group of women, still scattering love and light to all corners of the world!

In sharing my therapy prototype and aspects of my personal process, I'm submitting myself as a work in progress in the hope that some facet might leap out as inspiring or accessible. After returning to Nashville, I knew the one population that could thrive on these simple steps was the thousands imprisoned in ten by twelve cells. I volunteered—begged was more accurate— to teach meditation in a Maximum Security prison.

I have no idea if a process of this sort is now taught or readily available. Surely so—there are a bazillion books on meditation and emotional, psychological healing, but what if, just what if, you wanted to strike out on your own and give it a go with the backing support of an able therapist or guide? Hopefully this witch hair can serve as a primer.

While the ten years of my practice proved deeply validating and spiritually fulfilling, I was still ministering to psyches and souls, and mine was pouting. She yearned to be free to create on a road less traveled.

One, two, three, GO!

# WITCH HAIR #18.

*Refusal to believe until proof is given is a rational position; denial of all outside of our own limited experience is absurd*
*Annie Besant*

I despise cell phones. Not for the reason I despise flies, or pine trees, but because they're unhealthy, unholy, and unwise. Yet on Christmas Eve in 1994, as my love and I slowly snaked our way down the red ribbon side of a bad-tempered freeway, I clutched the baneful device, clunky and unwieldy, my life-line to death.

On the other end, almost a continent away in Nashville, my friend Dale Franklin, lay comatose fighting for every breath. Our witchy women tribe circled her bed in a hushed, dimly-lit room, softly singing her Home, lifting her soul to higher realms in perfect harmony. Ringing to say it was time for final goodbyes, a friend held the phone to Dale's ear so we could carry out one of our pre-arranged agreements. When she was ready to depart, I would assist her crossing.

Shaking, I paused to find the right words to caress my friend of twenty years into loosening her grasp on the rim of life.

"You can do it, Dale; it's exactly like we talked about. Just let go and leap."

Suddenly my words rang hollow, banal. We're talking about death, quitting life, not quitting a job, or a relationship, or smoking, but a face-to-face, toe-to-toe leap into humanity's greatest fear. My throat seized as a strangling wave of fear shivered through the phone line. Is this Dale's fear, or mine? The urgency of her struggle to let go of all she knows to be reality for some great, possibly mythical unknown, pierced my gut like surges of electrical currents. For an instant I glimpsed the freedom that awaited her, then winced as freedom spun into panic.

Confusion surged as my friend desperately clung to the edges of earth, knuckles turning white, stiffening fingers tiring, struggling to hold on and struggling to let go. Tears soaked the soft cashmere of my Christmas dress binding the woven wool to my heaving chest.

I took a few deep breaths searching for some center. In an instant, I relived birthing my sons. How the moment of deepest pain urged me to hold my breath and push.

Yes! That's it! "Dale, push! Push yourself out of your body, you can do it, Dale, PUSH!"

Whether Dale, one foot in and one foot out of pure consciousness, reminded me, I'm not sure, but I plummeted back to the holiness of our last time together. Golden October twilight streamed through the leaded glass windows of her barn house, bathing us in rainbow prisms. We snuggled by a crackling fire, arms and legs wrapped around each other. I studied Dale's soft face, ringed in vibrant brown curls, untouched by time at fifty-four, matching eyes untouched by death, not wanting to break my gaze for fear of forgetting every lovely nuance.

"Now," Dale began matter-of-factly, as if addressing her board of directors. "I want you to help me die, if that becomes necessary. I mean, if I chicken out or anything, remind me that I'm not afraid. I'm not afraid of death, but who knows how I might react when dying becomes the only choice I have in the moment. I don't want to carry over a carload of fear with me."

I nodded in agreement, a weak smile wrenching through a torrent of tears.

"And Dixie," Dale instructed, "we need to be able to know conclusively if indeed, I can consciously reach you and you can conclusively know it's me. I mean, beyond any shadow of doubt. How can we do that?"

"Yes," I agreed, "it has to be tangible, beyond doubt. Here's an idea, why don't you touch my check with an eagle feather, I'll definitely know it's you. Nobody but you would do that!"

"Perfect," she purred, her entire face held captive by a toothy smile. "When you feel the feather drawn across your cheek, stop and breathe so you'll open up to me. Got it?"

It took all the energy I could muster to tear myself from the rural barn house holding my Dale that fading fall evening, but I had to return to California. She'd seemed radiantly celestial since her terminal diagnosis of metastatic breast cancer, round two, six months back. A full-on six years after a double mastectomy followed by reconstruction, without chemo or radiation, advised when only a few nodes contained the contaminated cells, cancer had stalked her again. This go 'round claiming power over one of the most powerful women I'd ever known. Pulling out of her drive that night, refusing to acknowledge it might be the last time I'd see her face, denial drove me back to town.

Impatient freeway horns annoyed me out of my reverie with Dale, back to standstill Christmas Eve traffic, and my promise as her death coach.

My misty-eyed partner touched my arm. "We're almost there, my love."

"Dale, I have to hang up soon. It's time for you to go, too."

We finally arrived at the church where family waited inside, lifting their voices in ritual celebration of a holy child's birth.

I wondered if my final words were reaching Dale through a labyrinth of rising emotion. My voice labored through thick molasses, knowing my link to her might be forever disconnected when I hung up the heavy cell phone.

"I understand, Dale, I understand, my friend, how hard it is to let go." Hanging up the phone was a mere taste of just how daunting it must be for Dale to hang up on life.

"Goodbye, Dale. Let's let go together now, it's time for us to part, and for you to depart. Remember, ok? Remember our plan. I love you, Dale Franklin, I love you beyond this life into eternity."

A short time later, sitting numbly on the hard pew, vaguely aware of the choir singing, 'Silent night, holy night, all is calm, all is bright,' I whispered to my partner, "Dale's gone home," as I felt her swish past me when her soul flew into the vast unknown.

On a sad, bittersweet Christmas Day, I flew to Nashville and immediately drove out to Dale's eclectic barn home. Much had been left undone. Death was a work in progress. There were presents undelivered, cards written but not sent, lists partially checked off. Administrative disarray was not Dale. It was painfully obvious that death had the last word.

The charming barn, professionally decked and decorated, felt unbearably empty, other than her two dogs pining in the out shed, nothingness screamed out loud. Her ubiquitous spirit had departed. Shuddering at the inertness, I invited the dogs inside to keep me company. Their pitiful moist eyes mirrored my own as we mourned together.

For the next three days I puttered through fog, finishing up what Dale would want completed, especially some cards and a few half-wrapped gifts. I picked up one card to a mutual friend abandoned in mid sentence, called him to read what Dale wanted him to know, just how much his friendship in her six-month final waltz with life had truly meant to her. We cried together.

On my third and final night, exhausted from the weight of grief, the unending list of to-dos and my overwhelming sense of responsibility to get it all done, I crashed into bed before ten o'clock. I camped in the single bed in the guest room, so as not to disturb the energy in Dale's serene bedroom.

Some time in the night, jarred awake by the dogs barking excitedly, I stirred and groaned for silence. I tried to roll over and go back to sleep, but their voices were insistent. Am I in danger? Are they warning me?

My heart tumbled in my chest, pounding adrenaline throughout my body. Somebody's in the house! The public knew about Dale's death; her obituary was front-page news. Not only had she in earlier chapters been road manager for the New Riders of the Purple Sage, worked for Bill Graham at the Fillmore East in New York, been transportation director for Woodstock, but had founded the elite Leadership Music workshops in Nashville. Dale Franklin was a mover and shaker in the music community, widely recognized, beloved and respected, infamous for her disarmingly dulcet but fierce resolve to get it done.

I quickly concluded that her house was being robbed with me in it!

I froze. Face to the wall, convulsive fear racking my body. 'Breathe shallow.' 'Don't move a muscle.' Hoping against hope that the intruders would not consider the tiny guest room doubling as a laundry room bounty worthy.

Seconds later someone was in the room!

Standing by the bed!

'Don't move, just don't move, and they'll go away,' I was as close to actually praying as I had ever been.

Someone leaned over me, brushing my cheek with all the softness of heaven. The essence of an eagle feather swathed in silky strands of hair skimmed my left cheek.

"It's Dale," her voice lingered sweet and clear in my ear, her scent soaking the room.

My response startled me then, and does to this day. I was utterly terrified! After all our plotting and planning, I was petrified into paralysis. My face was still to the wall when Dale slipped into the bed beside me, spooning her being around my body.

"It's YOU! It's really you! You did it!" Words poured in a torrent of excitement, haunted by a tinge of fear. I was chagrined by the fear, hoping Dale didn't sense it.

"It's difficult for me to be here, Dixie, but I wanted to come. I promised. I wanted to show you that I could, that it's possible."

Momentarily stunned in wonder that I was actually carrying on a face-to-face conversation with someone who had crossed over, I strained for words. There were so many Universal questions to ask and all I could find was, "What's it like? Is it everything we believed it would be?"

"Everything and more. It's everything all at once." Dale's voice sounded resonant, present.

I felt her body shift on the bed. "I can't stay long, I don't have the power accrued yet."

"What do you mean? There's so much I want to know!"

"I'm new to this form. It's hard to keep my energy focused."

Dale. This was my Dale, here with me.

More than anything in that electric moment, I wanted to see her face, but was too frightened to turn. Did I think I might see some chilling ghostly apparition? I'm not sure, but what I did know was that lying beside me on the bed, Dale embodied wholeness, completeness, love without boundaries or borders … life plugged in to its perpetual Source.

With crystalline clarity, Dale wore the cloak of eternity while retaining her bodily characteristics and personality. Her hair had the same silky texture, her voice the same unique rasp, her scent the pure essence of Dale resonating to a field of bluebells. Every quality I knew to be Dale Franklin was omnipresent in the moment.

I felt the bed shift as she rose to leave. "I'm going now."

Summoning all available courage, I rolled over to see her face one last time. In awe and reverence, I clearly saw her slightly translucent image, intact, but different. Her arms, floating akimbo seemed long in proportion to the rest of her ethereal body form. Her legs appeared weak, undeveloped. Her movement was unsure, unsteady like an infant in development learning how to manage in a body.

That's it! Dale's parting gift sealed, the circle clicked. A newborn! Birth and death are one and the same, one no more powerful or frightening than the other, both simply an ordained part of an endless cycle … the circle of life.

I sat up in bed and watched as Dale vanished through the wall of her beloved barn home without a hint of emotional attachment or hesitation. She was on a mission to grow strong in her new existence, just as she had been on her earthly excursion. There was no gravitation pull to stay; she was simply and lovingly fulfilling her promise to me.

"Goodbye, Dale." My lip formed the words that filled the empty room, proving once and for all that love is more powerful than anything, even death.

# WITCH HAIR #19.

*You lay there fighting for each breath, while angels
hovered 'round your bed, with open arms like God's
own smile, they led you to the light. What a battle you
have won, and now your journey has begun to the
land where spirits fly, and your soul will never die.
So travel lightly in my heart, you and I will never part,
and far beyond this world we see, there's a place for
you and me.*
*Rodney Crowell from "Things I Wish I'd Said"*

Until a stroke felled my Mother in 1996, I dwelled in veiled
denial that she would always be around to cook up pinto beans
and cornbread for me, one of the many ways she doled out love.
The alluring smell of long simmering beans with a discretely
hidden hambone at the bottom of the pot let me know I was safe
in Mama's arms, the sustaining nutrient in my life.

Smoking was Mother's unyielding addiction from the time she
hit her teens. Her ache to quit was obvious, but her aging body
declined the invitation over and over again, until nicotine had
the final word. After a cerebral hemorrhage, months of physical

rehab attempted to retrain her brain to communicate with slack muscles, but nerve damage had taken most use of her left arm, a blessing it was not her right. None of the physical damage hindered Mama's quality of life like the shitstorm left in her brain. Signs of paranoia with auditory and visual hallucinations popped up in disjointed conversations, like whether or not there was a dog sitting on top of the refrigerator, and, true to psychological prognostications, her deepest wound crystalized into crazed obsession.

It was sexual.

Mother's innately positive countenance and warm personality skimmed a river of deep sadness. A melancholy lived just behind her sad brown eyes that I attributed to myriad experiences in her short childhood: an alcoholic, rage-oholic father, who today would have been diagnosed with a mental illness, the loss of her beloved mother she always proclaimed as 'the kindest, sweetest Mama any baby could ever have,' and the loss of her childhood to her mother's untimely, unexplained death.

It was a saga that would remain interred in onerous oblivion for over sixty years.

My sign up for membership in the blight of the boomers club, the gut-churning choice to relegate Mother's care to a nursing facility took nearly a year. Professional caregivers one after another fled shrieking after a few days of trying to tame the untamable. Her brain, tuned to shame and blame would not be dialed back to the center. To this day, I carry guilt that I had to trick Mama into a long-term care home. I schemed with her doctor to admit her to the hospital for observation until a suitable place could be found for her level of need.

Mama made me circle around the hospital block three times, her shaking hand mopping moist eyes. She knew. Even though her brain, wracked with painful memories and haunting reflections, refused her will, her heart knew she would never return to her comfortable subsidized apartment she had called home for fifteen years. She loved her eclectic community of many skintones and persuasions, caring for their needs as if they were family. She liked nothing better than toiling on her knees tending the slender strip of ground outside her window. Saucer-sized tomatoes, crunchy cukes, squash and green peppers magically appeared each summer, like it was a half-acre plot.

A young chaplain new to Rowan Hospital took to Mama right away, fractured brain and all. She called him her 'boyfriend.' As an introduction to his new town, the local paper did an extensive interview and he picked Mama as his favorite patient. They appeared hand in hand on the front page of the Salisbury Post, his long fingers, smooth and even, laced in her bent and knarled twigs, the old and the new, one on the way in and one on the way out, two souls owning their moment. Even with less than a functional brain, Mama managed to be the Polly Appleseed of love.

On the day of her transfer to the nursing care facility, I brushed Mama's thin wisps of hair, put some rose on her cheeks then carefully shaved her witch hairs, detesting that women had to solve such a bad shake as a lady beard, but intent on getting Mama's off her chin before she was moved.

After getting her settled into a tidy, clean room in a sparkling new facility just outside of town, three weeks of ordeal later, it was time to return to my practice in West Hollywood.

Extracting myself from my mama's fractured presence seemed cruel and inhuman. She stared at me so long and so hard that I heard her heart whisper what she could not.

"Don't leave me, my Girl, I won't see you again …"

I kissed her cheek and cupped her quivering chin.

"It's ok, Mama, I'll be back, I'll see you again soon. Your new place is so pretty; you'll be happy here, I just know you will. Billie is just a few miles away—she said to tell you she'd bring you a barbecue sandwich, and Dixie and Pat will come to see you too. I bet they'll bring you something good to eat. Ok, Mama, ok?"

A few months later, only hours after I'd arrived at a friend's in Washington, I got the dreaded too-late-to-be-anything-good call. Mama's condition had worsened, possibly another stroke, if I wanted to say goodbye, I'd better get there. Seattle, about as far away from North Carolina as a continental map will take you, has an outlying airport. Sharon Dougan, a fellow therapist and close mate of twenty-five years, raced us down the freeway, barely making it in time for me to grab a red-eye.

I spent the interminable flight begging, "Mama, you can't leave yet. I have to hold you one more time, I have to feel your heart beating against mine. I have to say all the things I wish I'd said. Please Mama, grab the edge and hold on until I get there."

A faint smile found Mama's ashen face, when I slipped into the hushed room nearly twenty-four hours later. Although her body had loosened its grip on her soul, she knew I was there.

I sat a two-day vigil by her bed, softly intermingling amends with flight instructions.

"I'm sorry, Mama, for every unnecessary lie I told you. The necessary ones, you knew anyway. The others? Just plain weakness when it came to boys."

The sliver of a smile again.

"You were there, Mama. You were always there. Even when I didn't deserve you being there, you never judged and you always loved me, no matter what. I hope I learned that from you, Mama. I hope it's inside me like it's inside you."

Every now and then a faint twitch of her mouth told me she was responding, it just couldn't get out.

"I'm here, Mama. You can cut loose now. Butch is good, I'm good, you done good, Mama. You can go. I'm sad, but it's OK to let go now."

I invited Mama's second-favorite Dixie, my ex-sister-in-law, Dixie Cauble, around to say goodbye. As Dixie and I sat on the bed jabbering away as we always did, I felt Mama's soul smiling, looked over and sure enough her thin blue lips stretched in a big smile. Mama's soul was in charge now.

Goodbye visits from the circle of my hometown mates, Mama's second brood commenced, before being joined by Shannon, her first grandson, who had driven down from Nashville. Mama's eyes lit up when she saw her Shannon.

Forty-nine years before, this woman had labored to push a tiny five-pound, three-ounce bundle into earth glow. Now, two months after her seventy-sixth birthday, it was my turn to reciprocate. The circle of life wraps around no greater honor than facilitating either.

Like birth, death has it stages as the soul is pulled back into the field of Pure Consciousness. The various stages are preceded by changes in the breath pattern—the last being Cheyne Stoking—characterized by a pattern of intermittent inhalations followed by a period of apnea when breathing temporarily halts. This phenomenon is a natural effect of the body's attempt to compensate for the changing carbon dioxide levels. I recognized the distinct patterning from my training as a Respiratory Therapist, my first real job.

Anyone who has ever sat vigil with death knows, it expedites on its own terms … like labor. The child arrives in its time, as long as it is not rushed along for convenience by drugs, and the soul exits in a letting go ballet with the body as organs go quiet, then shut down. Many times death is aided by drugs to alleviate gasping for air, but Mother masterfully conducted her exit on her own terms.

The next morning before darting out for a quick breakfast with Shannon, I told and retold what a loving, generous, kind mother she was.

"I can't speak for Butch, Mama, but I'm sorry if I didn't turn out as good as you'd planned me, but Mama, I know how to love. I know how to give my heart to those who can receive it, and even a few who can't, and that's you, Mama. That's what you showed me."

Her soul told me she wanted Shannon to read the Bible. Even hovering on the edge of life, she knew I was not the Bible reader.

"Shannon, she wants you to read something from the Bible," embarrassed not to be sure what that might be.

Shannon picked up her Bible and turned to the 23rd Psalm. "The Lord is my Shepherd, I shall not want ... though I walk through the valley of the shadow of death, I fear no evil, for thou art with me ..."

Miraculously, my analogy about birth and death being different ends of the same rope played out in the next minute. For months, her body, a skeletal frame with no living muscles attached, had not budged without assistance.

Suddenly, she lurched to an upright position on her bed, making my heart leap to my throat. Mama lifted both arms, one mostly paralyzed, to chest level. With elbows bent, her hands pointing straight up, she gripped her fist into determined balls then PUSHED her soul, through the top of her head, out of her body.

Shannon and I gasped, whoa-ing out loud, then breathed in the miracle surrounding us as her now omnipresent spirit filled the entire room.

"Mama! You did it!" I clapped, cheered and cried. "That was amazing, Mama!"

Her body then lowered itself back on to the bed and began to twitch slightly.

Fearful that she had changed her mind, "No, Mother, don't come back; you're free, fly, Mother, fly!"

And she did. We felt her spirit whisk out of the room. Daughter and grandson held each other as we collapsed into an eerie, empty reality. She was gone.

I had visualized myself conducting Mother's memorial service around the time of the pleading-with-her-to-stop-smoking period a few years before her stroke. Maintaining the illusion of control, I preferred having a plan in place, rather than being shocked into ineptitude. But nothing could have prepared me for the impending desolation of orphanhood.

Barely able to catch a breath between violent, body racking sobs, alternating between Mama running with my limp body comatose from bee stings and knowing I'd never smell her again, I still had a memorial service to arrange within two days before Shannon had to return to Nashville for work. Grateful that my roughed-out plan was in place, between convulsive shock chills where my legs would not stop shaking, I proceeded to pick out music, arrange her cremation, and for her beautiful young Chaplain boyfriend to take care of anything he thought might make Jesus and Mama smile. My most daunting task turned out to be hunting down and contacting what few family and friends she had left, hoping the local obit would fill in the blanks. I couldn't stand the thought of too many empty seats, when my mother deserved all the love she'd left behind streaming right back her way.

Moving through thick fog, half in and half out of my body, my mind shuffled the narrative, one minute thinking I had it together enough to pull off the service, the next wondering if people actually died from a broken heart.

Though I lay in inert exhaustion beyond lifting my arms or sucking in a satisfying breath, I couldn't seem to fall into sleep. Sometime during the long night, Mother appeared by my bed. Like Dale, her essence remained intact, her presence physical, as if I could reach out and touch her. Unlike Dale, I couldn't quite see her form, but I felt her, all of her, clear and whole, condensed into everything. Also, unlike Dale, there was no preordained intentionality giving the meeting content, but no doubt, it was Mama.

Her voice pealed around the room, strong, with more conviction than I had ever heard from her.

"It's time to stop cryin' now, you're gonna make yourself sick. I love you, my Girl …"

Again, just like that, she swooshed out of the room and was gone.

Mother's simple, authentic memorial service pretty much followed my preemptive planning visualized years earlier out of self-preservation. After some phone searching, no internet, that resulted in an unexpected trip to Kannapolis, I found a copy of Rodney Crowell's song, written for his dying father, that sang my heart, too.

More people than I could have imagined were not only still alive but managed to get themselves in the small funeral home chapel to say a heartfelt farewell to one beautiful, loving soul.

There were few empty seats.

Although confident with the content of the service, I felt weakened, unsteady on my feet when it came time to start. Visibly shaking, I mounted the podium, taking a few deep breaths to keep from bawling or falling. I had no idea how I was going to get through burying my own mama.

Her ashes sat in a simple box on an altar with my favorite photo when she was in her vital fifties, along with a laminated image of her with her boyfriend the Chaplain, surrounded by many versions of roses, which Mama loved.

I stood silent breathing in all the power I could muster in the moment. Then in a now or never turn when I finally glanced up from my notes, my eyes landed on an unexpected miracle.

The three beautiful women, who had individually lent shape and form to the woman I am, were sitting side by side on the third row. Not only had they never met each other, but I hadn't seen two of them in forty years and the other in over twenty.

Smith. Sister. Wilson.

The earth angels in my life, drawn together in loving support of an orphaned little sister, my mother's *second* most selfless act in her departed legacy of love.

The best was yet to come.

## WITCH HAIR #20.

We called him Garin figuring it would look good in lights someday. GARIN GAMBLE: simple, easy to remember, and pretty damn creative for a couple of twenty-one-year-old small town kids. From the start it was easy to see that he was destined for some kind of fame: he had the name, he had the edge, the sparkle, and the shine. By the time he was a year old, he managed to pull the right-tone pots and pans out of the lower cabinet, flip them over, strike the right spots with spoons in synchronized timing ... the first of many drum sets.

At eleven, Garin cobbled together his first rock band in my garage. By sixteen, he was playing professionally with a recording contract in the works for his band, but, alas, not with Garin. After being the creative catalyst for his groups garnering recognition and deals, Garin would be fired for not being present for his part of the bargain. He couldn't make it to rehearsals and showed up to gigs high.

Drugs and alcohol, the obvious issue, but suffering was the real issue.

Even seasoned skeptical musicians instantly recognized world-class playing in simple rock songs, seemingly casting him toward a world-class career. Coupled with a genius level IQ, rock star looks and charisma to match, Garin was unstoppable, arena-bound to all who heard him play.

I had grown immune to the many years of drug treatment programs and the inevitable relapses. After all, his genetic predisposition to addiction was apparent; both his maternal grandfather and paternal grandmother suffered from the disorder as well as his father.

Sadly, for ten years, I never delved deeper than addiction.

Then, after having recently bought a country getaway back on the Marrowbone, partly to assuage my unfinished business there, partly to escape Los Angeles, and partly to be near my first grand, a one a.m. phone call pierced the rural nighttime silence.

"Is this Mrs. Gamble?" A strange but sincere voice on the other end jarred me out of out a deep sleep.

Fearing the worst, I braced for another crisis. "Yeeesss ... What can I do for you?"

Officer Twana Chick, savior to many mentally ill on the streets of Nashville, calmly came back, "I have reason to believe your son Garin is suffering from mental illness."

Denial shattered.

A month or so later, the summer of 1997, just after Garin turned 27, my partner found him in the bathtub with a butcher knife to his throat. This life-crushing message followed years of fast-talking, manic behavior that we relegated to drug use. As a trained psychotherapist, I should have been able to see through to the brain illness, but as a Mom, denial fractured my reason.

My denial quickly scattered when we took him to Vanderbilt Psych and the intake Psychiatrist asked him what month it was.

"December," he answered. It was August.

When the official diagnosis came, the jolt of the giant fist thrust deep into my gut felled me to my knees on the kitchen floor, unable to breathe. For hours I laid there, curled in a fetal position writhing in pain at the loss of my hopes, dreams and goals for my beautiful, prodigious son.

Garin had a severe mental illness, Bi-Polar Disorder, compounded and complicated by Schizo-Affective Disorder, which meant he was psychotic.

He heard voices. They called him 'Breeze.'

Fuck a brain disorder. I would conquer it for him. I meditated, practiced yoga, consumed only organic food and believed in miracles. I was a strong, independent woman who could swing the bat at a challenge and at least make it to third. I could save my boy. I joined NAMI (National Alliance for the Mentally Ill), became an activist and spokesperson for the mentally ill, especially those on death row. The same year Garin was diagnosed, I made a film about a man who suffered from Schizophrenia and was executed for a crime he likely did not commit. I became a Volunteer Chaplain at a maximum-security prison, teaching meditation and working with the mentally ill.

I was voted 'Volunteer of the Year' by NAMI. I found Garin the best treatment center in the state and joined their Board of Directors. I desperately fought his illness with every ounce of life force in me, and when that life force waned, I fought on with one foot in the grave.

I wish I could look back and say everything I was doing for Garin helped him. It didn't. But it did help me survive the shock of the blow.

For several years before he entered halfway house care, Garin tried living in his own apartment under the daily care of a mental health community outreach program. This risky experiment imploded when he was abducted by crack dealers and held hostage. They supplied his raging brain with drugs while holding a gun to his head for his disability check. My partner and I cleaned up filth and drug residue and repaired smashed-in walls more times than compassionate, resilient hearts should endure. In spite of our valiant efforts and all that the frail, but good-hearted community mental health services could put forth, Garin did not get better. Even though half-heartedly compliant on his medication, he was hospitalized in deep psychosis, on average, four times a year.

After one hospitalization, still deeply traumatized and wildly psychotic, not unusual due to the ridiculously early insurance discharges, I couldn't reach Garin on the phone, nor was he in his apartment when I checked. After two days of Officer Chick and me calling, I finally found him in the city jail, charged with 'resisting arrest', a common charge for the mentally ill. I went to the jail to see what was going on. When Garin was brought to the glass partition, both arms were blackened from his wrist to shoulders from bashing blows from a police baton.

Sick to my stomach with rage, I held on to the chair to remain calm.

"What happened, Garin?"

"I was mad because I stay mad, so I took it out on my car. I killed the voices in my car with a metal chair, and the neighbors called the police. I didn't hear them knocking because after I killed the car, I could sleep. They kicked my door in, yelling and screaming while they beat me."

A lifelong activist for the mentally ill was born in that moment.

At each hospitalization we were told Garin's chances of coming back to the previous baseline were growing slimmer. Still, I refused to surrender my power and sure as hell not my hope or my passion for making it better for everyone.

Fortunately, Garin was among the lucky ones to be placed in halfway house living after hospitalizations. Unfortunately due to neighborhood resistance, halfway houses are usually located in transitional or downright dangerous parts of town. Once while walking back from a nearby convenience store, a teenager walked up behind him and pulled out a gun demanding money.

Garin, turned to face the boy, "Dude, look at me, do I look like I have any money? I live in a fucking halfway house and talk to people who aren't there, but shoot me if you need to."

Despite my insistence on being notified before any medication change, a well-meaning young Psych Resident pulled a switcheroo on Garin's meds, creating a massive brainstorm. At midnight in October '08, Garin walked out of the halfway house where he'd lived for two years, disappearing into a black hole.

After three days of rummaging East Nashville, checking hospitals, jails and ditches, I filed a missing person report, which became part of a national database. Days of dragnet dragged into weeks of ghastly online morgue searches for John Does.

For nine agonizing months, I had no inkling where Garin was or if he was still breathing.

Miraculously, in early June, a police officer in Santa Monica, California matched Garin with the report photo and called my cell number on the poster.

There sat Garin, right then, in the station, right next to him!

My elation flattened when the officer informed me since Garin had committed no crime, he couldn't be detained, not even overnight to allow me to get to Santa Monica. Nor would Garin agree to speak with me. He slipped back into the night to his newfound world of street living and methamphetamine use while I screamed myself hoarse at the fucking HIPAA Law and a criminal justice system that works to the detriment of the mentally ill and their families.

Undaunted, at least I knew Garin was no longer in Nashville. I'd find him. A mother *can* find her child—even in the darkest of corners a mother can find her child.

The morning I was schedule on a flight to LAX, I got a call from my friend Leann Barron, a mutual friend of the late Dale Franklin. Leann did not know Garin was missing or that I was about to embark on a possibly futile search.

"I have to tell you 'bout a dream I had last night," Leann gushed before I could interject that I had a plane to catch. "Dale came to see me! I mean she really was here, or at least it felt like she was beside my bed. When I asked what she was doing here she said, 'I came to help a friend find her son.' Isn't that the weirdest damn dream ever?" Leann prattled on as only my beautiful blue-eyed friend can.

"Lee, Garin is missing in Santa Monica and I'm on my way to the airport now to find him. Please send me Light … you AND Dale send me Light, ok?"

After a long flight, in hour two of pounding the streets of Santa Monica with my yoga master friend Lona along for support, it was time to call in the big guns.

"Ok, Dale, it's time to find Garin now."

With every step down the boulevard my emotions whiplashed, afraid I would find him then afraid I wouldn't. We slowly scoured another half block stopping to gaze at the look-alike sun-scorched faces.

"Lona! That's him, that's Garin!" I screamed pointing across the busy street.

He was ambling through the picturesque park surrounding the famous pier. I darted across Ocean Boulevard threading bumper-to-bumper traffic sprinting to him before he was sucked into the miasma of homelessness.

A mother knows her child when she sees him!

Bearded, deeply etched and browned by outside living, he dragged a filthy blanket behind him as he purposefully headed toward the beach.

Lona grabbed for my arm. "Dixie, that may not be him. Let's slow down!"

Could I be mistaken? So many homeless looked alike and it had been nearly a year. I scanned for a sure sign, then saw the simple blue tattoo on his left leg.

"Garin!"

As he turned a dim sparkle flashed from his dulled eyes, "Mom, you found me."

Owing to the skill and heart of the well-trained Santa Monica police, Garin was committed against his will to the intensive care ward at UCLA's Psych Hospital. For three weeks it was touch and go whether any facet of his radiant, creative being might surface again. Trapped in another dimension, a world I was not privy to understand, he barely spoke to me when I visited each day. Street life had aged him. Boyish good looks now were masked in layers of moment-to-moment survival. His teeth showed signs that meth had taken its toll. Even after a week of showers, the street stench lingered.

Garin showed no emotion toward me, seeming uncannily bemused by his ordeal. When he made it clear to his doctors that he would never go back to Tennessee, my heart sank yet again. He was an adult, in his mid-twenties, I had no sway or legal recourse over his choices, even though his brain was not functioning in a decision-making wave. About the only coherent statement coming from him the entire time he was hospitalized was that 'he was on his 'walkabout' to find his freedom.'

That I understood.

By the middle of his third week in the psych ward, Garin showed glimmers of returning to a modicum of reality. Tiny movements forward gave me hope, like him looking up one morning when I arrived, "Hi, Mom," before returning to his underworld. Although his illness coupled with street survival had seduced him to a dimension I struggled to comprehend, I knew my child was buried under the rubble.

I persevered with my shovel.

Perhaps for Garin, it was a world where the vastness of the blue Pacific filtered the inundating sensory and verbal input constantly assaulting his defenseless brain. Maybe it was simply the freedom he felt living unencumbered by reality while cocooned in nature.

In one of our few 'conversations,' I had to laugh when I asked him if he realized we were looking for him all those months.

"I saw my picture on the bulletin board of the Community Center when I would go in for a hamburger." he answered flatly.

"What did you think when you saw it?"

"I thought I wanted a burger."

Since he could only be discharged to a designated care facility, I found him yet another halfway house, this one managed by two men who nine years previous had been bi-polar meth addicts living on the street.

Hope soared. This could be the magic bullet!

A couple of hours before leaving him in the hands of the good goddess, Garin walked me to the rental car. Lightly touching my arm, he showed a hint of emotion.

"Mom, you've done it all ... you found me, you got me help ... a place to live, and you've done it all, Mom."

Imploring, he added, "... now just let go."

I boarded the plane in a thin veil of hope. By this time I knew never to entertain anything near an expectation.

Garin's indomitable voices whispered he would die if he stayed there. By midnight he was back on the street.

I returned to Santa Monica a month later, with no resolve other than to get identification somewhere on his person. If unable to speak for himself, he would not become a John Doe. I had a right to know when my son was no longer breathing.

I never found Garin. After two weeks of constantly searching the boardwalks and beaches, I filed a 'critical missing,' meaning the police would actively search for him due to dire health concerns.

Three months ... nothing.

His illness swallowed him, all traces of his presence vanished. The shadow world had pulled him under. I had no way of knowing if he was still breathing, or if I will never see the delightful being that was my son again. The brilliant, charismatic, talented, enlightened boy/man that I cherished more than life itself had vanished again.

If Garin still walked the earth, he stepped in silence.

Now I had to burrow deep for the peace and grace of acceptance to find a way to live in powerlessness without desperate despair. Nothing I could do would save my son from his walkabout through darkness. His last words clearly told me that I had 'done it all.' Yet, in claiming his own sense of freedom, distorted as I might judge his choice to be, Garin had given me freedom. My Greatest Teacher, we chose to walk this tragic path together and now we had come to an end. Was it THE end? I had no way of knowing, but as always, I expected a miracle.

What is the deepest instruction life affords for trusting a benevolent Universe if not the loss of a child? What is the commitment to dive inward to swim in the soul's waters if not to be a lifeline to hope for a highest good outcome? Garin's highest good may not return him alive and well to the fold if not the path his soul had chosen. It was not mine to question or subvert.

The hardest lesson of this lifetime slammed down around me.

Meditating in my purple velvet chair every morning was my pathway to acceptance of what is. One early morning after a fitful night, I had a vision. Garin was in the ocean, gasping for air went down then came up three times, then disappeared. Was this reality or a metaphor? My reinforced spiritual connection did not shield my trampled heart. Was his soul guiding him along a path of survival, or the opposite?

I realized the five years I dedicated to giving voice to my soul had everything to do with exactly what was happening in our trial. Without trust in the portent of the highest floors of the Universe gesturing for us to step on the elevator, I would not have survived the crushing blows to my heart.

I almost didn't.

A new spiritually based acupuncture healer in Nashville, Gil Ben Ami, was recommended by a friend as something I just might need. When Gil gently touched my wrist, silently gauging my pulses, he immediately glanced up.

"Why do you want to die?"

Of course that one question broke down all my spiritually contained composure, allowing my heart to bleed.

"Because my son is missing and I can find him from the other side. From there, I can help him."

"Come on back," Gil gently guided my arm.

I was on Gil's table every day for two weeks needling my heart meridian back to normalcy. Spiritualizing feelings inserts a dangerous plug the body may not survive. Not walking my talk was not going to fly.

Then one cold January morning in '07, my meditation took a different tack. Suddenly I was yelling to no one in the room. Demanding all the way across the country or the galaxy.

"Enough! It's time for you to come home, Garin! No more! We need you and we love you. You belong to the Universe second, you belong to us first, come home! It's time." Not a whispered affirmation, or silent petition but a fucking DEMAND.

An expected miracle!

It was a gray Saturday afternoon. My cellphone rang, unusual for the weekend. Holding my breath, I said hello to an unknown number and fate.

"Mom, Mom, it's me Garin, I'm done with my walkabout and I'm ready to come home. Will you help me come home?"

With the degree of his incapacitation held in the ethers, I had to instantly reply to a daunting problem, exactly how to get him back to Nashville. With no identification, mental decompensation and hygiene that would likely empty a plane, flying was not an option. Driving out to get him would take forty-eight hours, and driving back with him in psychosis might crash us both.

Garin was in San Diego, having ridden a bicycle from Venice Beach ... through the desert! He survived the insurmountable and unsurvivable and in a moment of lucidity after a hospitalization and long-acting psychotropic shot, borrowed a cell phone from a stranger on the street to call me. Through the frazzle and muddle of arcing brain waves, he remembered my number.

"Ok, Garin, listen to me closely. I want you to go to the bus terminal downtown. I will buy you a ticket on the next bus to Nashville, so get there as soon as you can. Friends of ours will meet you with some food money. All you have to do is get on the bus and rest. Except you must pay attention when the driver says you need to change buses, ok?"

Silence.

"Garin? You hearing me?"

"Yeah, Mom, go to the bus station and your friends will find me."

"Right. And Garin, DO NOT get off the bus except to change buses, got it?"

"Got it, Mom." The line went dead.

I knew the chances of him actually making it across the country to Nashville, without the voices growling varying instructions was a long shot, but our only shot.

The Universe, masterful orchestrator of living chessboards, had arranged that we bump into some former West Hollywood neighbors at our sanity retreat to Optimum Institute the previous month, and we just 'happened' to tell them about Garin's missing person status, and unlike me, I just 'happened' to ask for one of the male couples' contact.

"Garin has just called from San Diego and I've instructed him to the nearest Greyhound Terminal. He's walking so I'm not sure how long it will take him to get there," I blindly connected puzzle pieces. "The next bus for Nashville leaves at half past six, a ticket is bought and waiting for him to pick up—could you meet him there in the next hour and give him $50 cash? We'll repay you."

Our friends called back two agonizing hours later to say they gave Garin the money, along with a bag of sandwiches and water, a few clean shirts, socks, and underwear. They watched him board the bus for Nashville.

Relief from searing fear of never seeing my son alive again, untied a torrent of wet, heaving sobs. Garin was coming home. After nearly two years, Garin would be safe in the arms of his family.

The clock started ticking down on the forty-eight hour wait. With every passing hour I took on his voices.

"You will not win this one! My son is coming home. He will not abandon his intention to be with his family according to your will, but will fight your every command. His walkabout is done, you do not have to instruct or protect him, he will be in our safe hands."

The last two days of our horrendous ordeal stretched into one of the longest. Seconds became minutes, and minutes hours, then finally it was time to go to the bus station.

My heart felt as if it would bolt out of my chest in terrifying apprehension. Fear that he would not get off the bus.

Then, fear that he would.

The entire family gathered to welcome Garin home. Shannon, Roben, his wife, Lili and Ella, a babe in arms at the time, my partner and I, waiting in silence, each praying in our own way.

We held on to each other as one by one, the bus emptied. No Garin. The stragglers and the wheel chair bound made their way into the terminal. No Garin.

Just as I was about to either throw up or collapse, Shannon spotted him.

"Mom, there he is! He made it Mom, he made it!"

Not Garin, but a composite of his vocal parasites using him as host.

As we all ran to greet him, gathering tribe like around our own, defying anything or anyone to ever take him from us again, we collectively realized that only a shell of Garin had returned to us.

The voices held him captive.

Showing no emotion at seeing us, the facsimile of my son pulled a few street trinkets out of his pocket, treasures he'd collected for each of us. Though he couldn't connect emotionally or express feelings, he brought us gifts. I carry my random metal belt loop on my key chain to this day.

Garin returned to us 'Indian.' Certainly his deeply bronzed skin etched in filth could pass for Native. Dreadlocks reeking of street cascaded everywhere and his teeth … oh, I had to bite my tongue not to break down when I saw the gaping holes beautiful straight teeth used to fill … so many missing and broken teeth. Oh, no, not his perfect teeth!

It took only seconds to smell that Garin had likely not bathed for months, the stench congealing around as we jammed our faces into our coat sleeves. Germy Annie that I am, I couldn't fathom how the crud and putrescence was going to wash off anytime soon. Completely psychotic, the voices had the microphone, so Garin was in no condition to be taken anywhere but to a psych hospital. But the mental health system doesn't function in a comprehensive, linear manner that would allow a beloved family member in the throes of psychosis to simply be admitted to a psych ward. No. That is not the way it works at all. First he would need to be 'triaged' by a mental health team, then determined to be a danger to himself or others before the team would recommend he be sent to a hospital. Simply walking Garin into an ER could even be dangerous if he behaved in a way that threatened Security. No. Calling the police was not an option. Taking him to a hospital, not an option. Taking him home, risky on so many levels.

Shannon came up with our only apparent option: to take him to a motel room where he would help him get cleaned up and stay with him until he agreed to hospitalization. In the mean time, Garin remained an "Indian," far, far away from reality and from those who cherished him.

True to the debilitating conundrum families face, Garin did not qualify for involuntary admission to a psyche unit since he was not an immediate 'danger' to himself or others. We returned him to his old Mental Health Cooperative Case Management team and they got him back into a halfway house under mandatory medication.

For nearly a year, while my heart returned to its normal rhythm and my soul took a deep breath, it was not a forgone conclusion that Garin's sanity would return to anywhere near a normal baseline. Deep psychosis is like a giant clamshell closing in on normalcy, depending on the depth it may never part again.

Having been an accomplished fixer since the age of three when I determined it was my job to find the perfect tit for the runt piglet, I began putting my son back together one harrowing task at a time. First order was the dentist, where Garin lost seventeen teeth compliments of meth, street hygiene, or a combo. Then, in a manic episode before a new med regimen kicked in, he decided he could fly (I'm reckoning this part), jumped off a stone wall, badly fracturing his foot. Surgery was the next order of fixation. Still, my son was home. I could see his face and not worry if he was breathing. He was with us.

Physically, anyway.

By early 2008, Garin was finally able to live independently in subsidized housing, and we settled him into a lovely studio in a high rise overlooking Nashville's prized Centennial Park. He struggled mightily with drinking to shush the voices, but he was med-compliant and working with his Case Manager. We made sure he had an electric drum set in case he was ready to play again, a computer to stay in with the world and during those years he accumulated enough music to open a small record shop. On the surface, he was semi functional if not verbally or psychologically present, he was safe.

Garin had no hospitalizations from 2007 until September of 2012. Appropriately medicated, his violent mood swings settled into a unipolar depression, and his baseline returned to 50% of self. Shannon and I reveled in periodic flashes of Garin's vibrant, smart, charismatic personality. But he frequently spoke of not living much longer and admonished us not to mourn, as he'd be returning to a pure form where there was no suffering, reminding me of a talk we had after his first hospitalization.

"You know, Mom," he began, speaking slowly from the sedative effect of the psychotropic. "I chose all of this. I'm an impetuous spirit, and they warned me it might be too early for me to return, but I wanted to come through you this time. Don't despair, Mom. It's all good. Besides, they gave me two lifetimes to work it out."

I wanted to hear how dire Garin's adventurous 'walkabout' that nearly killed me but obviously grew him, turned out to be, mostly to understand how he survived it. Unmedicated as he was, he stayed in such a deep psychotic state that he either didn't remember, or didn't want to, but he did share a few harrowing clips along the years depending on how delicately I dug.

"I'm curious, Garin, how did you manage to buy a bus ticket to Los Angeles?"

"I saved up my disability stipends each week until I had the $200 to buy a ticket and a couple of burgers when I got there. I stashed my backpack in a bush near Love Circle because it had anthrax on it."

"So, how did you lose your front teeth, did you fall off your bike?"

"No, a guy knocked them out because I was preaching too loud on the street corner."

"And those washers we had to take out of your ears, what were they for?"

"So I couldn't hear the voices."

"Did it help? Did they go away?"

"No; that's when they told me to ride my bike to San Diego."

"Did they tell you to take the desert route, when the temperatures were nearly a hundred degrees?"

"Yes, the route by the windmills; I wanted to get power from the windmills."

"How did you survive a hundred and thirty five miles without food or water?"

"Well, sometimes I drank out of the irrigation ditches and sometimes I'd stop. Then people offered to buy me a burger and a Coke."

"How did you know where to stop?"

"Them. They told me everything to do to stay alive, except the Mexico thing; that was my idea."

"Mexico thing?" I really did not want to hear this one.

"I wanted to see Mexico while I was down there, so I decided to cross the border. That's when it happened, the Border Patrol called the police and the police told me I didn't need to be in Mexico. They put handcuffs on me at first, but then told me to get on my bike and ride back to San Diego."

I didn't know whether to bow in homage to the voices or the Border Patrol, but had Garin entered Tijuana no doubt, he would never have returned.

As soon as I allowed myself to sink into a still-churning vat of normal in 2008, my health crashed and I was more or less bed bound for several years, subsisting on HGTV, which was the only stimulus my brain could tolerate, and barely hopeful integrative doctor visits. Thyroid, adrenals, sinus surgery with reaction to the anesthesia, chronic fatigue, Epstein-Barr virus, nerve damage from mold sensitivity—you name it, I was diagnosed with it.

My body lived on the street with Garin, sleeping under scrub along the beach so as not to be attacked, my body endured arrests that gratefully resulted in mandatory hospital stays with long acting psychotropic injections, my body suffered gnawing hunger and riotous ridicule, my body rode that bike to San Diego and had not withstood the desert heat or the pesticide-laden drainage water, my body was tired and had to rest.

For three years.

I was advised by David Haase, my friend and genius Functional Medicine doctor, that I needed to get out of mold spore prone Nashville, which had morphed into a moldy dump after the massive 2010 flood in the city. In July of 2012, again we packed up the house and crossed the country, this time for the charming vintage beach town of Ventura. In full consideration of his obvious affinity for California, I carefully explained to Garin, whose primary emotional issue was and still is abandonment, that once we were settled we would come back for him if he wanted to join us.

Two months later, when Garin had not picked up his cell for several days, I called his Case Manager only to learn he was in Europe on his honeymoon for two weeks, and no, there was no one attending to Garin's meds. This is called falling through the cracks. No meds! Recipe for disaster.

My love flew back to Nashville to check on Garin's well being.

He found Garin lying lethargic and psychotic on a single mattress. His studio apartment was stripped bare of all food, furniture, TVs, a computer, his electric drums, video games and player, stacks of DVDs and CDs … the place was empty except for the mattress on the floor, no bedding.

Everything, all of his clothes, toiletries—even his teeth—had been thrown down a five-floor trash chute.

It was contaminated with anthrax.

After a three-week stay in psych, his father flew with him on a mind-bending flight to LA. Once in Ventura with us, he was again hospitalized as a danger to himself and was properly remedicated. After a few weeks, Garin's baseline elevated to a point that he could live in a good, well-managed Board and Care facility where his meds are administered and food and daily care is provided. The 21st Century answer to mental health care, Board and Care facilities are about as well done in California as anywhere in the country, but scarcity still leaves over twenty thousand mentally ill on the streets of Los Angeles alone.

Not only are those who suffer from severe and persistent mental illnesses marginalized, maligned, and generally mistreated by their communities, but a lumbering, dysfunctional system victimizes the mentally ill. They are by far the homeless population most likely to lose their life on the streets.

Not only did Garin not make it to the 'big show,' but he's unable to play drums on the high levels of psychotropic drugs necessary to keep his brain from stripping down the veils, and his hands shake from nerve damage, a common side effect.

It's time for my beautiful, prodigious son, Garin Gamble, whose name was created for lights, to be seen, be recognized, as one of many brave souls, the rock stars who pioneer an archaic system for the rest of us.

Garin told me not to despair, that he chose this lesson even after being advised that it was too early for him to inhabit a body. He chose me, and his soul took the leap. I choose him. Everyday, I choose him. He suffers as my hero, my courageous musician, who never made it to the airwaves or arenas. I mourn his dreams that faltered and fell into the abyss of mental illness. Every so often, perhaps too often, I cry. I cry for his loss, I cry for my loss and I cry for public understanding of an illness, a disease of the brain, genetically passed from generation to generation, assaulting some of our most gifted.

This is one story. There are thousands of Garins suffering on the streets. Please pause the next time you see a dirty, ragged homeless person, chattering randomly to no one there. Stop. Be still. Ask, 'are you ok? How about a burger?' Be present as your heart recalls my Garin. They are someone's son, brother, father, grandfather, uncle or friend. Somewhere, someone misses them and loves them without condition. Can you spare a few coins?

# WITCH HAIR #21.

*"If I was a sculptor ... but then again, no. Or a man who*
*makes potions in a traveling show, oh, I know it's not*
*much, but it's the best I can do. My gift is my song,*
*and this one's for you."*
*"Your Song" by Elton John/Bernie Taupin*

If souls are indeed given the gift of a huddle with their cosmic counterparts before incarnating, as Garin explained he did, then my choice for a mother was exemplary. Sheer genius! My lifetime with her was the gift that kept on giving.

When Mama's departure time came, my Love, a musician contracted to a world tour with Elton John, was halfway around the globe. Not only was he unable to be with me at her bedside, nor at her memorial, his grueling tour schedule isolated me on the island of California to belly-crawl through the grief process. Though I was a practicing therapist at the time, I had no concept of how to maneuver my aching heart through the exhausting pain and blistering sadness of losing Mama and being orphaned. The bowling ball crushing the middle of my chest hindered my ability to breathe, much less function. My instinct whispered to stray far away from my body to keep from imploding into fragments, while my trained self recognized the harm inherent in spiritualizing emotions, especially grief.

The only redeeming light in all the blackness following Mother's service was Elton's Hollywood Bowl performance on the night I returned. Elton paused before launching into "Your Song," softly noting to his adoring throngs that I'd had a tough week then dedicated the powerful ode to me. In that stung-by-life moment, his strong clear voice echoing through the starry Hollywood night lifted my soul, as if the artist's true talent went far beyond his musical gifts, reaching a healing hand straight into my heart. I love Elton's soul, and his simple act of generosity hastened my healing. I know it did.

The next Monday, I attempted to see clients, but couldn't contain my tears in the therapy room. The therapist had reframed into a muddled wet mess.

I had rented a charming copper miner's cottage in Bisbee, Arizona for several years, staying the hell out of LA as much as possible while my partner toured. Condensing my clients' sessions into two-week slots, I'd drive nine hours southeast where I'd sunbathe in unobstructed energy for two weeks. In Bisbee, I could purge my aura, breathe clean air, and take my muse out for needed exercise.

I never had to ply my yellow wonder dog, Ptah, for a road trip; he daydreamed of escaping LA as much as I did. As soon as he noticed me throwing a few bits in a bag, he'd leap in the back of the SUV and wait until we bolted to Bisbee.

Nestled six thousand feet in the Mule Mountains, population nine hundred or so on a warm day, the hamlet replaced the copper miners with world-class artists and creative hippie drop ins. Like our West Hollywood home, the early twenties cottage, byzantine blue trimmed in white gingerbread captured the vintage allure I loved. Facing wildly seductive vistas of rolling copper hills hovering around a picturesque village that mirrored western movie lot, on first sight, I knew my soul had found respite from the mayhem.

Away from the pressures of my practice and the kinetic energy of Sunset Boulevard, I dove deep down to the bottom of my grief.

Each morning, I collapsed into the hammock overlooking the B Mountain clutching my journal to nab the regurgitation. Cradled there in Mama's soft lap, I'd record every scrap I could resurrect of my life and times with Pauline Woodson Morgan Cauble, the woman I called Mother. Intermittently wailing like a hungry newborn for her comforting tit, then frantically scrawling away the searing pain each memory awoke, I wrote past exhaustion day after day for weeks, until one day my memories drew no more tears.

On the night before I planned to leave Bisbee, a last plea before surrendering to well-earned sleep, bargained with an empty room, "Mama, if I could just smell you one more time, just maybe I could go back to my life."

As she had done on the night her soul flew for home, sometime in the twilight hours, Mama stood by my bed. Gently rustling the sheet to get my attention, I had already been aroused by her scent. Like, Dale, her familiar personality remained intact, without a hint of emotional content. Also, like Dale, her energy conveyed a matter-of-fact quality: *You asked. I came.* A convivial bouquet of coffee and cigarettes curled around my body, like a warm Mama hug. I can't be sure how long she lingered or how to convey her communication, but the essence was: *It's time to heal.*

As the eastern sun stirred me out of a sound sleep, I could have sworn Mama was in the kitchen enjoying her morning cigarette and coffee. The cottage brimmed in Mama essence for several hours before she moved on to more pressing business.

Mother proved yet again that love survives everything, even death.

Still, her greatest gift was yet to come.

# WITCH HAIR #22.

*"You don't choose your family. They are God's gift to you as you are to them."*
*Archbishop Desmond Tutu*

Family secrets for rural Southern folk were akin to buried treasures with mellowed shame and innuendos hinting where to dig. In Mama's family, no one dared pick up a shovel lest the shunning annihilate the excavator. Denial held a sacred trust in the god-fearing, shame-based Bible belt. Closed mouths catch no flies and tight lips attract no lies, or some such nonsense.

In 2006, my phone rang stirring me out of an early autumn Sunday afternoon snooze, insisting I push through the fog to pick up.

"Hello?"

"Hi, is this Dixie Cauble?" chimed a sweet southern voice.

"Well, it's Dixie Cauble Gamble, how can I help you?" I tiptoed.

"My name is Sandra Starnes Mussen and I have reason to believe my father is your brother. Is this a good time to talk?"

"Are you kidding? Bring it on!" Diving headfirst into the receiver. "Yes, yes, yes, tell me what you know, or what you think you know, and how you located me in Nashville."

Sandra described how she found my ex-sister-in-law (hold on tight), Dixie, who became Dixie Cauble when she married my brother Butch Cauble. Dixie was still listed in the Salisbury phone book. Sandra contacted that Dixie thinking she was calling me, but that Dixie told her she was pretty sure she wanted Dixie Cauble Gamble.

"My daddy, Frank Reid Starnes, is the sweetest, kindest, most gentle man in the world," Sandra shared through audible tears. "For sixty-six of his sixty-nine years, he's longed to find his mother, to see her face one more time before he goes. I believe she was your mother also. Pauline Morgan Cauble, right?"

Contact! Life shifted.

Instantly, entombed shame pierced by light alchemized into pure gold.

Sandra told me her Daddy, along with his positive, warm, loving personality, carried a palpable sadness that broke her heart. Recently she had started searching online for lineage to his family as a birthday gift. She said Reid, as he was called, had vague flashbacks of a mother, but since he was less than three years old when adopted by the Starnes family, he had few actual memories.

"Two were clear, each heartbreaking," Sandra went on. "In one murky memory he was under a kitchen table crawling around trying to find leftover crumbs or scraps to eat. I feel bad telling you the other one."

"It's ok, Sandra, I'm ready to hear whatever you are ready to tell me."

"Daddy remembers being handed off to a strange woman. A car drove up with a man and a woman in it and his mother, or he thinks it was his mother, handed him to the woman, then she put him in the back seat alone. The car pulled away from the only people he knew to be love as he screamed and clawed at the back window. He was driven away … never to see his mother again."

Silence stormed like a thousand ghosts from the past.

This soul crushing scene, more than my heart could absorb, triggered a flashback to getting a copy of my original birth certificate for my driver's permit. As I scanned the document, I noticed the space for live births was filled with the number 2. Even as a 15 year old, I wondered how there could have been a baby before me if I was the oldest? I certainly wanted to question Mother at the time, but being strongly fortified in Southern don't ask/don't tell armor, I never sorted out the right time to bring it up. I made up that maybe she and Daddy had lost a child in miscarriage or death, or possibly that Mother's crippled and mentally disabled half-brother, whom she devotedly cared for and rescued as needed, was actually her son. Ultimately I decided any of those scenarios would be far too painful to resurrect and besides, if Mother wanted me to know, she'd tell me. I went on my merry self-absorbed way, twirling, cheering, shagging (dancing, remember?), and boy-crazing through my teens.

"Where did the Starnes live? Where was he taken?"

"Mr. and Mrs. Starnes lived on Highway 29, between Salisbury and China Grove." Sandra explained, as I visualized that stretch of highway where Jean was killed, wondering to myself, were they neighbors? Is that how Mother knew about the Starnes?"

"Where did your Dad spend his adult life?" Trying to fit fragmented puzzle pieces as we talked.

"We all lived in or around Monroe, North Carolina, and still do."

"Sandra, Monroe is about a two-hour car ride from Salisbury where our mother spent her whole life. How could it be that they lived two hours apart and never found each other again?"

"Well, they almost saw each other once in 1968. Out of the blue, Daddy got a call from Lessie Starnes, his adoptive mother, asking if he wanted to meet with his birth mother. On that very day they picked to come to Monroe, Daddy was struck down with a gall bladder attack and ended up in the hospital. Their reunion got canceled, then the lady that arranged the meeting between your Mom and Lessie got real sick, then Tom Starnes, Daddy's adoptive father died sometime later, and nothing ever transpired between any of them again."

Imagine the incredulity that struck me in that moment! I could only surmise that some Universal intervention could have thwarted that fateful meeting. Knowing Mama, guilt-racked as she probably was, she took the cancellation to mean Reid did not actually want to see her and she never got up the nerve to contact Lessie Starnes again.

Mama lost her son twice.

"Daddy figured your Mama gave up after he got sick and canceled, thinking maybe he wasn't really sick but just didn't want to see her ... or maybe the thought of seeing her made him sick," Sandra reckoned.

To this day it doesn't all quite mesh, but suffice it to say, mother and son had not laid eyes on each other since the day he was wrenched from her arms, screams fading in the dust as the car pulled out of sight.

Sandra's warm authenticity and familial heart pulled me close. Bound by questions, tears and a few tortures, we chatted for hours that Sunday. I asked if she had found Reid's father.

"All I know at this point is his name was Charlie Smith but I will keep working to fill in the blanks." Sandra's strong-willed determination was proof positive we were blood relatives.

In fear of losing connection with my promised new sibling, my entire body resisted hanging up the phone.

"I want to see my brother, Sandra!" Embarrassed that it came out sounding like a demand, I softened. "Is there a time we can meet soon?"

We made arrangements to meet in two weeks at a restaurant in Salisbury. If even a snippet of our mama was carried in her first-born, Mother was kissin' down miracles straight from where she and Jesus were hanging out.

Like a child counting the days waiting for a new sibling, my anticipatory elation ran wild. I can't begin to define it even now. Another brother! The enormity of the gift overwhelmed any perceived disparities or concerns, but oh, my sweet goddess, let him be a Democrat!

The faux 'meat-and-three' was dark and mostly vacated by the lunch crowd. My Love and I walked upstairs to a private room, me on shaky legs, him following behind with solid arms.

When he spotted us, my brother shifted out of his chair turning toward me, and right there, right in front of my eyes stood a male version of Mama. Same sad doe eyes, round face, thin lips, grey hair and stout frame. He was hers alright.

And he was mine now. "You look just like our mother!" I sobbed through a current of tears so powerful they must have mingled with Mama's dropping from heaven.

Reid and I slipped into each other's arms and hearts held in timelessness, our souls blending with every teardrop, erasing all the years dangling between us.

It was over. We were home.

Sandra, my new niece, was not only gentle and genuine, but a stunning beauty. Rich brown hair, blue eyes filled with dancing light and lovely alabaster skin, all trimmed in a tender spirit. Mama's endless bounties poured into all of us that afternoon. Family warmly picking up where we'd left off in another place and time was proof positive that love honors no boundaries.

Reid and I mined the heart of every minute, two kids determined to make up for the lost years. Wrenching ourselves away from each other as the sun lowered on our time that day was almost more than our hearts could endure. On the road trip back to Nashville, we kept calling each other, neither wanting to hang up. Reid's solid, no-nonsense wife of over fifty years, Bernice, later told me "Now I just thank I might be jealous if'n you two weren't brother and sister!"

The remaining Morgan tribe, mostly first cousins, threw several family reunions welcoming Reid back to the fold. We all naturally melded into a familial tribe. It tore at my heart, though, to see Reid kneel hopefully beside a great aunt or cousin, peppering them with questions, desperate to pry a shard of memory from his first three years of life. Reid's sweet face mutated into that of a sad, lost child scratching at the door of time, hoping to find his Mama on the other side. Heartbreakingly, no one was able to help him crack the door.

Mother's one remaining sister, my Aunt Dorothy, eighty-eight and tangling with senility, didn't give up much beyond gazing on his childlike face, proclaiming, "yep, I 'member you, you's just a little thang last time I saw ya."

An older second cousin recalled babysitting Reid a few times when Mother was working or out looking to find work, but could offer no details about him. That fragile little boy must have felt so abandoned by everyone he knew and loved. Out of sight, out of mind.

And Mama. Our sensitive, loving Mama, how did her tender heart survive handing over her flesh and blood to a virtual stranger? Maybe the Starnes weren't completely unknown to her. Someone put Mama and Mrs. Starnes together, but who? Aunt Dorothy? Ghosts don't give up all their answers and some haunt me still, and will for the rest of this life. While Garin was missing for nearly two years and I faced each day not knowing if he was hungry, hurt or no longer on the earth, tripping my heart into a cryptic, potentially dangerous rhythm, Mother knew her boy was alive, and possibly even knew where to find him in his early years, but since Reid was officially adopted, I suppose she was helplessly bound by law never to make contact or try to see him.

Fractures in a mother's beating heart, and passing on her painful legacy, I understood empirically.

Reid was the one comforting me as I delved into Mama's unfathomable heartbreak over the years. The *Sophie's Choice*, so to speak, that our mother faced: clutching her hungry child in unstable arms sinking into the quick sand of their poverty-stricken environment, or allowing him a warm, healthy home with two mature adults who had prayed on their knees for a child to come into their lives. How Mama summoned the courage, wading through the pernicious fumes of her childhood, to face the most arduous daunting decision a mother could make, I will never know. Formidable as it was, she faced the crucible and chose the well being of her child over herself. Surely an agony many unmarried women found themselves facing in those lean days, but not after bonding for nine months, and three years.

My mother, the woman who never quite rose above it all in my near-sighted eyes, was now my heroine. A constellation dawned from a shadowy past illuminating the bravest woman I'd ever known.

Reid, being Reid, always expressed nothing but gratitude, if not total admiration for his adoptive parents.

"They were good to me," his almost perpetual smile lighting his round face. "Good solid people, who loved Jesus and I think loved me. They were purty strict, of course, but they took good care of me. I was never hungry or cold, and I finished my schoolin', and even went to a trade school to learn machinery."

In that seminal moment, I wished Mother could have been sitting there listening to her son's assuring words.

Then again, maybe she was.

Over the next few years, a couple of our elder cousins either muscled the guts to face the gauntlet, or having become the bearers of the tattered yellow map, decided to help piece some of the puzzle together. No small concession from hardened conservative Lutheran farmers in the rural south, who still spit tobacco juice in a Coke bottle and, more often than not, bombed the N word.

The narrative, certain to be partly truth, partly fiction, came together something like this:

As soon as Mother approached legal working age, she was more or less kicked out of the house. In a small house over stuffed with a step-mother, two step-sisters, a young half-brother crippled by polio and several of her biological siblings all subsisting on her Daddy's meager rock quarry check, Mama ranked expendable. Stands to reason, she jumped at the chance to leave the sordid nest to live-in babysit for a widower named Charlie Lee Smith, who had just lost his wife in childbirth. Whether by guise of seventeen-year-old consent to forty-seven-year-old fawning, subtle ongoing seduction, overtly expressed entitlement, or god forbid by force … Mother was made pregnant.

Sandra and I supposed Charlie Smith, dark-haired, thin and handsome in the only photo she was able to find, left with two kids and baby, wanting nothing to do with yet another newborn, also kicked Mama to the curb. Not to completely disdain someone we never knew, Sandra later located a legally notarized paper where Mother absolved Mr. Smith of all parental responsibility for the lump sum of $225. She was again a teen on her own, carrying a son.

Since most available work in the sparse rural area of Rowan County was either domestic or field, and she didn't own a car, there was nowhere for Mother and her baby boy to go. She and Reid stayed with varying relatives, night-to night, none who comfortably supported themselves, let alone two other mouths.

A tribulation no teenager comes equipped to weather, yet Mother managed it for nine months and three years.

The reality that came crashing down around the nightmarish crucible to let her baby boy go was not fully traceable. Only Mother and Reid bore the survival burden. I can surmise it had to do with one of Reid's very few memories.

"I 'member crawlin' 'round under a kitchen table lookin' for scraps. I 'member tryin' to move shoes to find crumbs, I's hungry, Sis, I just 'member being so hungry."

Fade to black.

Nothing gave me more pleasure than being able to, in my own maternal way, steep some joy back into Reid's life, freeing that three-year-old boy with sad eyes matching his mama's, to laugh again. Since he rarely ventured outside Monroe, North Carolina except for Outer Banks fishing trips, it took me a while to convince my new bro to board a plane, for the first time ever, for Nashville. We chatted on the phone every Sunday, and each conversation I'd chip away at his fears. I think the only thing that finally convinced him to come was when I asked for help with a squirrel and bird war in my city garden. Like our mama, he was a tomato-growing guru and couldn't stand the thoughts of the squirrels and grackles getting the best of my juicy red "maters."

The melancholy blanketing Reid's blue eyes seemed to fade each time we saw each other. The more I was around him the more convinced I became that he epitomized our mother's innocent nature, innocent not being a word for Butch or me. For two people who spent a mere three years together, they looked out of their eyes with the same soft, loving gaze, and besides growing stuff, they glorified not just catching fish, but 'cleanin' and fryin' em up.' Neither Butch nor I could fathom doing either. Lawrence Welk and the Grand Ole Opry were their musical influences. Reid described huddling by the radio listening to the WSM Barn Dance on Saturday nights, especially if Connie Smith was singing, and Mama thought Porter and Dolly were rock stars. Butch and I gravitated more to the fringes of country.

Their souls exposed no edges, they were boundless, neither wore wounds as badges of honor or cast their pain against others. Both carried ancient souls who understood and accepted life's pitfalls as nothing but temporary detours, this mother and son.

How delightful it was for me to have Reid in the home of country music! Having been a part of Music Row for many years, I saw the shadow side of the business, so after abdicating my role, I never looked back. Reid's deep reverence for traditional country music curbed my cynicism. Showing him around the County Music Hall of Fame not only muffled my tendency to loudly exhale, but schooled me on the artists I had all but ignored. Watching Reid's eyes light up as we happened on Webb Pierce's bat shit crazy, bull-horned Caddy convertible blew my tarnished heart wide open. His baby blues widened with wonderment rippling across his face at the very same vehicle we all used to poke fun at as Webb glided it up and down Music Row, after his star paled.

Reid's innocent way of being in the world brought much needed wonderment into my sphere. His mending was my amending.

On the last night of our Nashville visit, I had planned a full on Reid surprise. After treating him to a good meal, we pointed the car toward Briley Parkway. About halfway down the boulevard, I asked Reid if he could guess where we might be headed.

"Well, I can't say for sure, Sis, but I can say one thing for sure, I'm hopin' it's toward the Grand Ole Opry!" Finally the three-year-old boy came front and center, jumping up and down in unbridled delight.

Both my Love and I knew many of the artists appearing that night: Ricky Skaggs and The Whites, Marty Stuart and the Superlatives … and yes, Connie Smith! Introducing my Reid to everyone, especially Miss Connie, was big bounty. His cherub face lit up like a child at Christmas, and shy he wasn't. He carried on with Connie like she was a neighbor leaning up behind him in the church pew, thanking him for the ripe maters he'd dropped off. I boasted about his musical knowledge, and as Mama would say his *gall* in approaching Opry Royalty.

I snapped copious posed and candid shots of Reid with all the stars, then created a memory book for him. These indelible moments and the gift of his unfettered, unconditional love are forever pasted in my heart, sealed in unending joy.

Pauline Morgan Cauble's unfathomable anguish generated proportional mirth for three unsuspecting siblings, Frank Reid Starnes, Butch Cauble and me.

Tears fall in irrepressible gratitude to Sandra Starnes Mussen, my niece, The Fixer.

# WITCH HAIR #23.

*There is a Divine Law of justice and fairness upon which we can rely. That which is our own cannot be kept from us.*
*From my 1988 journal*

This is a tale of two brothers, one new, one old. My old brother and I were childhood playmates, boarding school companions who had each other's back, and unconditional worshipers of one sweet Mama. We generally enfolded each other in all the love and respect dirt-eating siblings with disjointed parenting could grasp. In genetic distribution, Butch got the addictive gene and I got the control chromosome. I brought home better-than-average grades with little effort, while Butch struggled then slid into below-average zones, though he was the brainer by far. Our parents' divorce disrupted the developing boy, heaping the role of man of the house on the shoulders of a child.

Butch's entire life became a perfect storm of blooming brilliance versus ravenous cravings.

At the age of twelve, my brother, a mechanical genius, built a car out of found junk after a neighbor offered him a rusted out chassis rotting in weeds behind his barn. Collecting four discarded tires from someone's yard, Butch then got a friend to drive him to a junk yard where he pulled an old motor, tinkered with it until it purred, then siphoned gas from Mother's car. Early one Saturday morning, I heard the roaring va-rummm of the car-like contrivance springing to life.

On the driver's side, Butch bolted in a donated bucket seat, on the passenger side he turned a bucket upside down. With no dashboard or starter, he touched wires together to crank the contraption. He managed to install a found steering wheel, which mostly wanted to go straight, turning not an option.

One Saturday Billie Mecimore, a regular at the farm place, dropped out for a visit. Mama, Butch, and I had moved back to our family home after lawyers sorted it out with Daddy, for my last two years of high school. My junior year I lived in Yadkinville with Wilson, so it was Mother and Butch at home.

Billie yee-hawed riding shotgun on the bucket, barreling-ass through the cow pasture. Eyes wild, legs flying up in the air with every unavoidable rock, Billie whooped and hooted, hanging on for dear life.

Butch had welded a metal handle of sorts where a dash might be so as not to eject his passengers in the first thirty seconds of the thrill ride. Billie, clinging with both hands shouting "Goddamn Fuckin'A!" at the top of her teenage lungs, tweaked the cows' natural serenity into wary curiosity. The almost motorcar was barely steerable, so avoiding anything ahead once it got going wasn't an option. As I sat on the fence taking in the spectacle, the thing plowed through a line of massive cow patties flinging cow shit up in the air from both sides! The contrivance with no

windshield tracked cow patties like a heat seeking missile.
I bailed off the fence escaping a colossal shit-splattering!
When Butch finally coasted the smoking monster to a stop,
cow poop dripped down their faces, as they wiped it off their
mouths, hysterically laughing their asses off. And that is exactly
why Butch never could shame the princess into a whirl on the
slop bucket!

Before he could legally drive, my baby brother was sucked into
the undertow of alcohol. The supply came easily, through cash
for working on neighbor's vehicles, or he'd ask to be paid with a
six-pack. By sixteen, he rolled cars end over end, barely
escaping DUI tickets, or sometimes not. It was rough for Butch
with no influential male figure in his life. His pals were older
men who were not the best of father figures. At seventeen, he
joined the Navy to escape a brewing shitstorm rapidly closing in
on disaster.

After I poured my listless brother into a rehab center near
Nashville some ten years past his Navy stint, he managed his
life without alcohol, and periodically without cigarettes, for the
next twenty years. From my perspective, I wouldn't exactly call
it sober living, but perhaps his brand of clean living. By then,
Butch's passion had switched to vehicles that fly. He piloted a
plane by sixteen and true to his modus got his pilot's license
somewhere along the way. He parlayed his mechanical genius
onward and upward to the highest realms of aviation, landing
a coveted gig as Chief Engineer for Chuck Yeager's Glamorous
Glen P-51.

Quality of life and sanity prevailed. Butch seemed to be at the
top of his game: in love with his planes, his motorcycles, his dog
and his wife, mostly in that order.

Then on September 6, 2001, I got one of those calls from Butch's wife, Jane (yes, my brother married a Dixie, then a Jane) you never want to think about. Butch was riding second seat behind his pilot friend, flying the Glamorous Glen to Chuck Yeager's retirement party in Ohio.

After take off, Butch, as he said, "in protection of my own ass." questioned the pilot if the radiator coolant door had been opened. The pilot responded, 'yes, it was open.'

This particular maneuver must be applied or the motor will overheat, a no-brainer in vintage plane aeronautics.

"The plane was in top-notch condition, or my ass would not have been in it," my brother later quipped. Thirty minutes later and ten thousand feet in the air, the motor started spewing smoke. Butch knew the plane better than he knew Jane, so he never panicked. He doesn't know the meaning of the word. Barking check engine orders from the rear seat, Butch followed the list down, then spotting a flame around the motor, he asked the pilot to pull the canopy, which he finally did.

The Glen sputtered to silence, wouldn't restart, then the treasured antique flying legend facsimile caught fire and began losing altitude.

"We have to bail," Butch shouted, tapping the pilot several times on the shoulder, who was still desperately trying to restart the plane.

Leaning forward Butch clearly saw the air coolant indictor switched to, CLOSED.

My brother is nothing if not measured and sure in dangerous circumstances, not only from a lifetime of practice, but Viking instinct thrives in perilous places. Whether racing dirt bikes or turning airplanes upside down for the fun of it, once with me in it, Butch flirted with the edge.

He kept his wits about him and again told the pilot, it was time to bail. Getting no response, he reached out, grabbed the pilot by his flight coat collar, unbelted and ejected him out of the sinking ship. Note that P-51s are flown in parachuted gear. Butch tried to follow, but by this point the plane was pitching and his feet were caught. Thinking fast, he deployed his chute, which jerked him out of the plane, sending him flying through the air at one hundred fifty miles per hour! When Butch sailed past the tail wing, his right arm connected, slashing his forearm to the bone, nearly severing his arm.

Miraculously, the pilot's chute caught in tree branches, dangling him thirty feet up. Butch's chute did the opposite and was compressed by tree branches so his ground impact was feet first fast, causing compression fractures in three places in his spine.

The Mooresville, North Carolina Rescue Squad was dispatched when farmers in a nearby field spotted the smoking plane, watched it descend, then crash in a fiery explosion. No one comprehended anyone surviving. When the first responders arrived to find the pilot dangling in the trees, they burst into applause. But when they spotted my bloodied brother lying nearby, they leaped into their skillset, administered first aid, then rushed him to the nearest medical center. A quick assessment had him transferred to a better-equipped trauma facility, back to Salisbury sirens blasting.

Butch's injuries were excruciatingly painful. Repeatedly dosed with morphine, not only did he sink into a deep post traumatic depression from losing the Glen, but after twenty years of sobriety, his substance dependency reignited by the powerful opiates, shifted the trajectory of his life from an upward to a downward descent.

The legal settlement of the near catastrophic event, several years in the making, resulted in my brother's truth losing in the end. It was the pilot's word against his. When it came to the knowledge of what a motor does or does not do, Butch's expertise was legendary. The sad saga not only crashed Butch's beloved plane but his sobriety, resulting in screaming nightmares and mental anguish from PTSD. He never disclosed the actual financial settlement he agreed to, only lamenting it wasn't commensurate with his suffering. In my view, no amount of money could have balanced the scales of justice for him.

The capstone on this pyramid is the sad fact that from the young age of twelve and beyond, I had an emotionally unavailable brother. As the years progressed, I missed out on so much of his life and times, either by living in Nashville or Los Angeles, or his unavailability. My choices to leave Salisbury wreaked havoc with Butch's still inflamed abandonment bruises, provoking him not to speak to me for many years. I missed him terribly. I missed his wry sense of humor followed by a liquid laugh, his accessible knowing of so much non-trivia, stuff I could never grasp. I longed for the respect he generously offered to his big sister. So many facets of Butch, I missed. But the heart of my sibling had not been open since he entered his tumultuous teens and surrendered compassion and empathy, neither of which he afforded himself, to Jack Daniels. Addiction severs emotional connections that fertilize relationships while fortifying the persona with a false sense of power to mask the shame.

Addiction anniliates intimacy. Period.

The 12 Step program can be a powerful took for many, as it persuades the ego to let go to the Higher Self or "greater power" realms, clearing narcissistic tendencies.

Butch never reached. Never surrendered.

When Frank Reid Starnes entered my life in 2006, I was allotted the gift of a brother my heart had craved since entering adulthood. Reid gifted all that Butch could not, and so much more.

Butch, a gun-toting collector, with warm regards for gun makers, the NRA, and the whole (in my opinion) perverted interpretation of the 2nd Amendment stands firm on his ground. Reid may have owned a hunting rifle, but I'd doubt if he ever killed anything more evolved than a tomato or turnip. Butch, although apolitical in an 'all politicians are crooks' sort of way, is a mildly conservative deep-south non voter, who certainly leans more right than left. Much to my ecstatic relief, Reid was a rare breed in the 21st Century … a vocal Southern Democrat!

While a vehement George W. Bush backbiter, my new bro was a social moderate, owing to his rural upbringing. Like our mother, Reid managed to bind to his personal understanding of the Bible in the most natural of ways, simply by living it. He mowed the churchyard every week, whether in 104 degree blistering heat or screaming knee pain. Mama too, had a wacky right knee, and well crap, so do I. But politically Reid passionately leaned left, never bothering to hide his opinion in the face of opposition.

Reid and I verbally high-fived when Bush rode on back to Texas, and rejoiced in Obama's historic election, damn sure we were on the right side of history. We chatted for hours about seeds, both exalting heirlooms. Reid lovingly packaged tiny seeds of rare heirloom tomatoes, mailing them in 'I love you, Sis' Hallmark cards. Every season, he painstakingly worked three large garden plots, remembering to the last slip how many tomatoes plants he set out each year, proudly proclaiming 'exactly sixty-two.' He and his Bernice canned hundreds of quarts of everything that could be put in a jar. Gathering bushels of pecans from his neighbor's orchard, a backbreaking task, he and Bernice spent weeks shelling, then storing them in their freezer. Whatever was preserved in the freezer or on their pantry shelf belonged to everyone.

Each Christmas, Reid carefully packed a gift box brimming with ten quart bags of pecans, canned tomatoes, fig preserves, pepper jelly and little surprises he'd sneak in the weighty, expensive-to-ship box and managed to have it arrive before Christmas Day. Not only was I his Sis, and he adored me, but his love testified in word and deed, which neither Butch nor my father, constrained by addiction, had been able to do.

Reid freely allotted love, without agenda or condition.

It is indeed within the realm of possibility that some of the clarity between us existed *because* we lacked childhood history, but mostly I believe it was about gratitude and appreciation. Grateful to have blood family in his life after sixty-six years and appreciative of the easy camaraderie and companionship we shared from the moment we first walked into each other's arms. Reid was no half-brother, or half anything. It incensed me when anyone referred to him as such. At first sight, he granted me full brother-ship and anointed me with his love and unbridled generosity. With all my heart and soul, I felt the same way.

In late July of 2015, while packing for a car trip to Crestone, Colorado for the month, my landline, reserved for family and longwinded friends, blared twice, within twenty minutes of the other. The first caller, a Critical Care Doctor with the Intensive Care Unit at Duke Hospital, was calling to see if my brother was Butch Cauble, and if so, did he have a DNR, and if not, as his next of kin did I know his wishes. This brother of mine, with more lives than most cats, had defied death on numerous occasions, but this one rattled me deeply. Since the plane crash, following twenty years clean, once-a-year binges at holiday time had escalated into 'oh, shit, not again' chaos. That translates into when Butch would go into isolation, denying food and consuming only alcohol for weeks at a time, his disease picked up where it had left off. Stage 4.

Not starting from scratch can be deadly.

The young doctor on the other end of the line said "Mr. Cauble's liver enzymes are off the chart, he is devoid of electrolytes, and if he survives for the next 24 hours, well, we'll see then about the outcome."

I had warned Butch many times about standing way too close to the exit door. This time he already had one foot on the other side.

I dropped the receiver on the bed stunned with the reality that this time just might be the last time. I stared at nothing for a few minutes digesting the loss of my charismatic, kindhearted, wise, but deeply wounded brother, pondering what to do next.

Just as my hand reached to pick up the phone to call Reid, it rang.

"Hey Sis." The sadness seeping through the phone was palpable. My immediate thought, 'he already knows about Butch.'

"I was just about to call you, I've got some bad news about our brother," attempting to soften the blow.

"Well, Sis, I've got some bad news of my own, I've just been diagnosed with pancreatic cancer, and I only have three months to live. I thought I had a lot more livin' to do, Sis. I really did." Reid spoke in his soft, matter of fact way, but that bite of reality shredded my heart.

I held my breath in stunned silence until my heart restarted. My only two brothers were dying at the same time.

"No, Reid!" Denial was all that came in the moment. "How is this possible?"

He methodically explained about abdominal pain he'd been experiencing for well over a year, which the local docs all thought was 'something to do with his gall bladder' or 'maybe indigestion' recommending that he drink buckets of pink shit. A year later he had tumors everywhere, including on his liver.

No chemo recommended; only hospice.

My numbed mind couldn't take it all in. I staggered into the living room, sank into my Love's arms, exploding in heaving  sobs that felt like giving birth … too big to push out without screaming.

How could a benevolent Universe of infinite wisdom not only take my two brothers at once, but the brother most likely to step through the exit door was not the one who constantly flirted with death, but the one who wanted more than anything to live?

The spiritual injustice of that moment defied all sentient understanding.

I wept to a limp exhaustion, then sent both my brothers all the Light I could muster in the emotionally engorged moment. The one whose soul has not completed its mission for this internment will stay, and the full-filled soul will leave, I reasoned. Neither is in my control. But for all the Love that is, the unfairness seemed impossible to reconcile. It could be argued that Butch had a choice, but it was definite that Reid did not.

As I sat with shuttered eyes in desperate silence, straining to reach a comforting Voice, a vision lit up my third eye. Mother sat serenely, patiently waiting to see her son. But, which son? Almost afraid to see the rest of the vision, I began to open my eyes, then Reid and Mother were embracing just as Reid and I had done nine years previously. That was my only solace.

Finally, Mother and her beautiful son were reunited.

Always considerate of *my* well-being, Reid told me I needed to go on to Colorado since I'd paid for the house in advance.

"Besides, Sis, Sandra is helping me with the Gerson diet, and you never know, I might have a few years left to grow some more maters."

My Crestone visit was a bust in every way possible, including mold in my cherished prairie rental overlooking the Sangre de Cristo Mountains and Great Sand Dune National Park. Ten days into a fractured, dystopian visit, Sandra called to tell me I needed to come to North Carolina to say goodbye. The next day Bo, my trusty four-legged traveling companion and I despondently hit the long road for Ventura. I had a plane booked the following day.

I barely recall driving the truck or eating food or how I managed to unpack then repack for a funeral. The human heart is the body's strongest muscle, but mine, already under chronic strain with my son's mental illness, now felt under direct assault. Butch had been upgraded from guarded to critical and yet again, would live to step away from the exit door. Reid however, had no choice but to lean in.

As I had with Mother, I resorted to silence, beseeching the Universe to allow Reid to stay long enough for us to share a final hug. Initially he'd been offered three months, but was granted only three weeks. Once more, the injustice batted all reason past my ability to grasp.

As I entered Reid's softly lit man-cave in the basement of his simple but neat home, he was lying in his Barcalounger, skeletal after having lost seventy-five pounds in a few weeks. I knew there would be no more tomatoes in his life.

Bending down, I whispered, "my brother, I wish you didn't have to go, but what a perfect brother you are." My sadness dribbled on his heaving chest. "Thank you for loving me without fences, thank you for being the most beautiful human being I've ever known. We only had nine years together but we filled them up with enough love to last a lifetime. Thank you for all you are and all you gave to so many. Our Mama is waiting, Reid. Give her a hug for me too. I love you beyond life and death."

With his soul already listing to the other side, his voice was weak. "I love you, too, Sis. Thank you for welcoming me, and my family into your life. I'm so sorry we didn't have more time, but I'll see you on the other side. I'm not afraid, Sis, I'm not afraid."

I sat in vigil with Sandra and Bernice, for four days, as children, grandchildren and countless friends streamed by for a sad farewell, all in awe as we witnessed my brother's courageous dance with death. Courage spilled directly from his mother.

Suffering wasn't apparent until the last day, when we all decided he needed to go to the hospice center for stronger medication. As was his way, Reid decided otherwise, quietly slipping out of his body early the next morning.

He surrendered his body on Saturday, I'm betting, so Bernice could plan the traditional Southern wake for the next day, their church day. With little notice except word of mouth and their church bulletin, nearly four hundred people filed past Reid's casket. A tiny church membership with less than a hundred devoted disciples in a small rural township with sparsely scattered neighbors, yet there they all were, so many good people lined up to bid a final farewell to my brother.

Reid and I shared only nine short years, yet his impact on my life was immensely profound. I can only imagine the loss his life-long mates and close-bound family must endure.

During almost every phone call we'd shared in the summer months over the years, Reid would lament how rain seemed to find a way to slip around his neck of the woods. "Just down the road, they got two and one fifth inches," he'd moan. "Tomatoes do not like to be watered, they like their water straight from heaven."

Butch, now heavily leaning on a cane, for many years having partnered with our childhood friend Pat, appeared gaunt and gray, but alive. As the three of us walked from the car to Reid's graveside, Pat noticed the beauty of the day, "not a cloud in the sky" she said. As we all sat by the freshly dug hole in the earth with Reid's casket resting on a stand, suddenly a smattering of huge raindrops cascaded in a loud staccato rhythm on the plastic.

Everyone lifted their eyes simultaneously, smiled knowingly … 'yep, there's Reid!'

# WITCH HAIR #24.

*"It is said that no one knows a nation until one has
been inside its prisons. A nation should not be judged
by how it treats its highest citizens, but its lowest ones."*
*Nelson Mandela*

My ten-year Transpersonal Psychology practice came to a
natural conclusion when my first grand girl announced her
impending arrival. Like a horse to the barn at the end of the
day, I pointed my nose back to Tennessee. We bought a six-acre
property next door to my left bereft with unfinished business,
still beloved, Big Marrowbone property. The post and beam
house constructed by a husband and wife team of amateur
builders was no one's idea of a dream house, but the property
itself was open and green, with a ready-to-plant garden plot.

Involuntarily spying from across the pasture separating our
two properties in the first Big Marrowbone house, I'd been
frequently bombarded by the courageous 'contractor' couple
screaming and hurling more than insults. Unlike my that house
which was built closer to the road, this house sat about thirty
feet off a raised bank over the Big Marrowbone Creek, just what
I wanted.

Half-heartedly I had mentioned to the feuding couple, "if you ever want to sell this house, if and when you ever get it built, I'd love to be the first to know."

Fast-forward ten years, drowning in the smoggy chaos of Los Angeles and I get a call from my former neighbor reminding me of my offer. I said, yes … sight unseen!

Ptah and I had grieved for the Marrowbone the entire time we lived in West Hollywood. A deep sadness bordering on despondency felt ever-present, as if my soul yearned to return to complete a thought interrupted in mid-sentence. My first-born grand triggered our return, completing the exhale my soul needed.

Six months later, when Elizabeth Jane Gamble made her entrance, the instant our eyes connected, I knew some part and particle of her spirit, had returned. The eyes staring straight into mine were my mother's soulful brown eyes.

Even highly pragmatic Shannon remarked, "Wow, Mom, look at that! Her eyes *are* Grandma Cauble's eyes!"

Needless to say, Lili infused our entire family with some sticky, gooey love, circling us closer as a family, while opening all of our hearts to embrace each other at a decidedly less judgmental, more unconditional level. Nine years later, Ella Grace Gamble followed Lili in just to reconnect with her. I know that, I just know that.

It was in this newly simmering love soup that Garin suffered his devastating complete mental break after my Love found him in the bathtub with a butcher knife to his neck. Nothing in our collective lives was ever the same.

Unlike many who suffer, Garin was fortunate to have received a clear diagnosis during his first psych ward stay. Our emotionally shattered, vulnerable family turned to NAMI (National Alliance on Mental Illness), a support, education and advocacy non-profit for some direly needed education.

All of the above was happening simultaneously with the State of Tennessee gearing up for the first state-sanctioned execution in forty years. Here we were, facing a less than hopeful prognosis for Garin's functionality, when a headline appeared proclaiming a severely mentally ill man suffering from childhood trauma-induced brain damage *and* paranoid schizophrenia would be the first in line to die.

An activist heart beats hard in my chest, so I got involved in the case and fought for the better part of that year to save Robert Glen Coe's life. I was also fighting for my son's life. The harrowing circumstances of this case were not only legally suspect since Robert's confession, at a time when he was not medicated, was the *only* evidence in the legal dossier that he had raped and murdered a local child in west Tennessee. True to many such cases, a brain-damaged man suffering from a major mental illness, was interrogated by police for nine hours. A confession was written out for him, which he signed, after a promise he would be take home, with a stop for ice cream on the way. Facts, right there in black and white! After devouring transcripts of the entire case and consulting with his post conviction attorneys, nothing about the arrest or case resembled justice having been served, and Robert was about to be killed!

Not only was I existing in a state of shock and denial about Garin's diagnosis, I couldn't imagine a scenario where Robert would actually be executed. After all, he was so obviously mentally ill that he had cut his own throat after not receiving his lithium. He also told his appeal lawyers he wanted them to prove him innocent, not crazy, in spite of the fact that he couldn't remember the child's name that he confessed to killing.

One of the questions Robert asked the Chaplain before being taken to the death chamber, "Can I still eat my catfish (his requested last meal) after they kill me?" would alone establish the veracity of his disordered brain!

Robert was executed, considered legal homicide, in April of 2000. During that sleepless night after he was murdered, I frantically scribbled out a rant on the horrific miscarriage of justice, which eventually worked itself into a short film. It was my first experience as a writer/director. *Out Beyond Right and Wrong*, painting in graphic detail the actual last fifteen minutes of Robert's life, went on to play many film festivals, winning top prize in several.

After nearly ten years, I had shuttered my LA practice, freeing me for our Marrowbone return, to be a present and accounted for Gran, and to create, to make documentaries that mattered. Robert's case and my proximity to the injustices of incarceration, especially for those who suffer from brain illnesses, made me realize that I truly missed teaching meditation and sowing soul growth seeds. What better place to do it than a maximum-security prison where human beings, predominately young African Americans, languished in six by ten foot cages ... too damn many wondering how they got there. Typically Christian preachers and their flock are the favored volunteer population granted access to the imprisoned. Of course, this could be due to the fact that they asked, and it is part of their ministry. It took an open minded, heart-centered prison Chaplain named Jerry Welborn to grant me access to teach meditation, a first in Tennesssee prisons. Only two inmates showed up for my first class, a thirty-five -year-old man incarcerated since seventeen and his 'cellie', a rapper who came along for the ride. I had little knowledge or interest in their crimes, but in the case of Rahim, my star pupil and his own success story, I am more than a proud mentor.

Rahim was serving a sentence of twenty-five to life for botching his first and only robbery. The plan had been to get a couple of hundred bucks' rent money demanded by his newly acquired father figure so he could remain as a couch guest and off the street. Rahim was an emotionally undeveloped seventeen year old, with a single mother, still searching for his identity. Few of my students actually had active fathers in their life; many never knew them at all, and unfortunately had desperate mothers who tried to control by physical abuse. I heard the same story over and over, and none of the men understood the emotionally overwrought, out-of-control coat hanger or leather strap beatings as unusual or undeserved. Beaten and shamed into submission, the boys floundered with no self-esteem and no personal identity, often resorting to gang lifestyles seeking both. Rahim was no exception, except he was not a gang member.

As their meditations progressed beyond vainly attempting to keep their eyes closed for twenty minutes, I used the same Recapitulation Process I had practiced previously and had the guys pen their personal narratives. When Rahim described the way his body shook as his street wise captor put a gun in his hand for the first time, I visualized a beautiful, thin framed, cornrowed young man filled with fear of his so-called father figure as well as the unknown of committing his first crime. His descriptive recall of the pivotal choice that ended life as he knew it, was gut wrenching. In vivid detail, Rahim described gripping the gun pointed upward toward the metal raftered ceiling of a convenience store. In a fear-driven moment, attempting to force the cashier to take him seriously, his shaky young hands pulled the trigger. The bullet struck a rafter and ricocheted downward into the belly of the middle-aged white man at the register. Rahim is black. The beloved family man died a month later of his injuries and Rahim was charged with first-degree murder.

Rahim's commitment to the personal process work and his leadership role in his cellblock brought many inmates flocking to the group, ready or not. In a few years the men began asking about yoga, hoping for an instructor. This inspired me to continue trudging through the dehumanizing protocol everyone had to endure to gain admission to the prison compound week after week. It was only after Garin's disappearance a few years later that I made the decision to save my personal energy in order to survive the unfathomable trauma of a missing child.

In 2015, after serving twenty-five years, Rahim was finally paroled after twenty of his mentors and friends, including me, had twice congregated before the skeptical and challenging parole board on his behalf. His prison penned book, *Unheard Voices*, speaks directly to kids vulnerable to falling prey to his same bad choices. At this writing, Rahim Buford is a highly successful social and criminal justice activist and Children's Defense Fund Organizer. To say that I am proud of this man is an understatement. Meditation gave him the skill set to defy all odds.

Four years into my volunteer tenure at Riverbend, Chaplain Welborn escorted me to Building 3, death row, to meet some of the men long forsaken by society, friends and family. I briefly met Daryl Holton, a wiry forty-five-year-old remarkably resembling Vincent Van Gogh. Daryl spent his days solving high algebra and calculus equations between reading dense law tomes. Smart, personable, insightful and funny, I liked Daryl immediately. Not only was I drawn to his clearly remarkable awareness for a man languishing in the death house, but from the get-go it was clear he had no appetite for small talk, opting straight for the essential truth of the conversation.

The first thing Daryl said to me when the Chaplain introduced us was, "yeah, I know who you are, you are one of those TCASK-ers." Nailed. Yes, I was an active member of the Tennessee Coalition to Abolish State Killing. Word traveled expediently, on death row. In that first meeting, I intentionally made it clear that I was not there as an activist, but as a potential friend.

Unlike nearly all of the ninety-two men languishing in death's limbo, Daryl immediately confessed his crime, walking into the local police station to report a 'homicide times four,' briefly adding, "the kids have been taken away from me and given back to me, taken away from me and given back to me enough."

Daryl Holton had enticed his three young boys and little girl to his uncle's repair garage, then shot them two at a time with a high-powered military rifle. Afterward, when he couldn't locate his wife, prostituting in a motel, to include her, instead of turning the gun on himself as planned, he reasoned it best that he live in order to explain what happened to his children.

Daryl's defense attorney encouraged an insanity defense, which is rarely successful in local homicides. From the moment that plan failed, Daryl decided to let the state do what he, in the end, chose not to do. He was reprimanded directly to prison carrying a sentence of death. He subsequently refused all appeal options, except one, which he wrote and filed him self based on ineffectual counsel. It was denied. When the state, having executed three men after Robert Glen Coe, handed an execution date to his attorney, Daryl severed all contact with post conviction counsel, thus ending heroic attempts on her part to postpone his well-laid plan to be murdered by the state. There would be no twenty-year appeals process for Daryl Holton.

After achieving his goal to be straight lined to the death chamber, Daryl, through Chaplain Welborn, requested me as his spiritual advisor, which took me totally by surprise. Raised fundamental Christian, Daryl surmised through the prison grapevine that I was what he called a Buddhist. I guess to a fundamental Christian someone who taught meditation and actively attempted to halt Tennessee's killing machine had to be a Buddhist. I took it as a compliment.

Over the next nine months, I visited with Daryl weekly. At first through a thick glass partition, then toward the end in the same room, with him shackled at his hands and feet with a correction officer positioned directly outside the door.

During our visits, we talked our way in and out of many stimulating subjects. Daryl's superior intellect challenged and fascinated me. I wanted to understand how a career Army Sargent, with a wife and four children he adored, suddenly snaps, launches into a homicidal rampage, killing his beautiful children: three boys, ages twelve, ten, and six, and their four-year-old half sister, a bi-racial child whom Daryl had adopted after his wife was impregnated during his deployment.

Intellectually centered conversation came easy with little avoidance of any subject except his case, but attempts on my part to kindle emotion were useless. After seven years of refusing a television, I convinced him to accept a prison-issued TV. Although little interested him besides news, he fell in with *Boston Legal*. I also was a fan, which eventually led me to sneaking in a few legal questions about his case, like how or why he decided on an insanity plea.

"Nobody in their right mind kills their kids," he was clear on that point. "My brain was in a fog of guilt and confusion when it became clear that my wife was no longer capable of caring for my children while I was stationed in Saudi. And it was imperative that I tell the truth as I knew the truth to be."

During one weekly visit, as he got more comfortable talking about his family, Daryl brought up his wife. I jumped at the chance for more information.

"Was she an addict?" I probed, even though the press had vaguely extended that information.

"Yes, and she became more and more dysfunctional," he explained. "I called home several times a week and on one call, my son answered the phone and said, 'Daddy, there's no milk.'"

"Well, tell Mommy to get in the car and go get some." He relayed this in a soft manner, as if speaking to his son in the moment.

I fought hard to keep tears at bay.

"My little boy started crying, telling me there was no gas," he slowly and carefully articulated this piece of the story completely void of emotion, not even a crack in his voice.

Daryl took a leave from Saudi to come back to Tennessee. His paychecks were deposited directly to his wife, so he knew something was terribly wrong.

After this scenario repeated several times, the Army gave Daryl an honorable discharge to go home and care for his children. Although the couple had legally divorced in 1996, Daryl continued taking his disintegrating wife back again and again, "for the sake of keeping the family together."

Daryl fought to hang on to his role of single parent, driving the children to school, keeping a tidy home and decent food on the table. The couple's long history of custody wrangling finally came to a head when social services stepped in after being alerted by his wife. For Daryl, the loss of his children was the last gasping breath of his family.

Confronted with finality, a profound sense of hopelessness triggered Daryl's genetic propensity for clinical depressive disorder. Army records show that during early enlistment, he'd been an inpatient at the VA hospital thirty days for major depression, anxiety and suicidal ideation, and was diagnosed with severe depression on discharge.

Toward the end of Daryl's ticking time, I purposely tried to sway our conversations toward death and spirituality. I felt a deepening sense of responsibility to give my mentally and emotionally troubled charge, and cared-for friend, the spiritual security he needed to face death. We talked about Buddhism vs. Christianity. He disdained the failings of the Christian and Catholic Church to evolve and educate the faithful and promptly abandoned his mother's fundamental church when he enlisted. Daryl spoke of developing a sense of inner faith, which quickly eluded him when hopelessness set in—my words, not his.

Of course Daryl knew I was an anti-death penalty activist and willingly talked with me about the failings of the criminal justice system and the fallacy of the death penalty. He did not believe that capital punishment deterred criminal behavior, but adamantly supported it for his particular crime. Daryl chose his carefully considered insanity defense because he truly believed, at the time of the crime, he was devoid of a rational thinking process, and said more than once, "Who in their right mind kills their own children."

My friend and ward disavowed currently suffering from any form of mental illness, although his obsessive-compulsive tendencies were obvious, and a court-ordered psychiatric evaluation determined Daryl suffered from a complex form of PTSD and clinical depression. I spotted his OCD our first couple visits. From outside his cell I could see that everything had to be lined up in perfect order inside. I noticed how he could not begin our conversation until he was seated on the floor, in direct eye sight of the pie flap opening, with his pad, pencil and books neatly arranged around him. In his taped confession, Daryl explained in detail how he told the children they were going to their Uncle's garage for a surprise, thinking that because it was near Christmas, it was likely the children would imagine it to be about a present. He took the two older boys in first, lining one behind the other, telling them to close their eyes and "don't peek." He lowered himself to one knee for perfect aim, shot the boys through the heart, then added a bullet to their head.

After carrying their bodies to a corner, carefully covering them with a blue tarp, he brought in the younger boy and little girl, who according to his confession suspected nothing. That part I had trouble comprehending. Those babies had to have known their brothers were not still in the room.

I knew all of this about Daryl Holton and completely concurred—no one in his right mind does this!

Unbelievably, as if meeting up with any close friend, our conversations were easy and spontaneous, with me feeling like I had to jog to keep up. My goal was to support Daryl's soul toward openness for redemption in the only way I knew how, and that was to listen to him.

Several months before he was killed, his attorney contacted me with the distressing news that Daryl had chosen electrocution as the means to carry out his sentence.

"Dixie, you've got to talk him out of this!" Kelly Gleason, his post conviction attorney cried. Like me, Kelly truly cared for Daryl. "There is so much that can go wrong; that chair has not been used in forty seven years!"

When I asked Daryl why he chose the electric chair, without a hint of fear or emotion he explained that he believed it was a far less painful and 'more expedient' death.

"Less chance of something going wrong, as soon as that first 2,000 volts hits the brain, the heart stops and induces unconsciousness. After twenty seconds, the cycle is repeated if necessary," he expounded, way too matter-of-factly.

I fully felt the weight of the responsibility I had rather casually committed to. I had to fight back nausea before I could speak. Wanting to carefully cull my words abiding by Kelly's pleading, instead, I stumbled and fell.

"But with lethal injection, you are also rendered unconscious with sodium thiopental before the pancer-onium bromide and potassium chloride are injected," I vainly argued, tripping over 'pancuronium,' which Daryl immediately corrected.

I knew I had struck out, because the fallibility of that protocol at that time in 2007 was all over the news, and court cases were being filed to halt the use of the lethal cocktail.

I had failed Kelly. And worse, I was failing Daryl.

More and more I grew concerned that he did not have a Christian advisor, fearing that in the end, he would turn back to the comfort of his childhood Savior and I wouldn't be able to support him.

Even with full recognition of his borderline mental illness, I could venerate Daryl's soul. By now, I understood some of the whys, without in any way condoning his actions. I found myself not only respecting his choices since being convicted but incredulously, feeling compassion for a child killer.

By May, two other execution dates had been rescinded because of the Governor's three-month moratorium to study the death penalty protocol.

September 12, 2007 was the next date issued.

My soul felt pressured to give a walking dead man the spiritual infusion needed to step toward death with as much inner peace as possible. It was difficult to experience his portrayal by the media as a monster. Daryl Holton was by no means a monster. He was a fellow human being who reached his own breaking point too late to intervene cognitively on his own behalf.

In the three months preceding Daryl's move to the death chamber, I reluctantly followed his lead, speaking about anything other than death. At this point, I had tried many times to talk about meditation and the concept of going inward for the solace and peace the soul craves, but he was too cerebrally centered to grab the bait. In the end, I decided to keep the energy positive, allowing everything to be on Daryl's terms and simply listen. There would be no spiritual proselytizing imparted.

During his last sixteen hours, while we visited every few hours through the glass partition of the death chamber holding cell, Daryl kept the conversation light. His demeanor suggested he might be waiting on dinner to be served, not waiting to have 2,000 volts of electricity blasted through his brain. He seemed calm and at peace, normal for Daryl. I fought hard to remain in that place with him.

His peace consoled me until 11:00 that evening, just sixty minutes before his execution, when I was allowed to sit outside his holding cell. Twelve feet away, in our clear view, three tubes snaked through the concrete wall normally used to carry the deadly cocktail. A thick metal door with a glass viewing partition waited beside the ominous tube device. Just beyond the door sat the horrendous killing chair.

Summoning all my inner strength, I reminded myself that I'd prepared all of my life to be here, with this human being, at this moment or I wouldn't have arrived.

But was I enough?

Daryl paced inside the cell like a caged animal, compulsively tossing Chex Party Mix, his request in lieu of a last meal, into his mouth, one piece at a time. An officer pulled a chair up to the bars so Daryl and I could speak privately, but just as I sat down, the phone provided for final goodbyes, rang like a sudden scream.

When I heard him say, "Hi, Mom," I stood up to leave, but he motioned me to stay. Witnessing a man, a man about to be murdered, attempt to find any possible words to console his sweet, kind, distraught mother, whom I adored, was beyond my endurance. Tears sprang to my eyes, but there was no way I could allow myself to break down in front of him, so I turned away briefly to compose. Inhaling each breath with purpose, I reminded myself over and over we are never given more than we can handle.

"I am enough. I am enough."

I grasped in that moment that Daryl needed me physically there as a buffer for *his* emotions. His anguish was palpable. I understood his vaguely veiled desperation to hang up the phone before he broke down. True to form for Daryl, he kept his feelings completely compartmentalized.

"I love you, too, Mom. Now, don't cry. I'm ok. I love you." Nobody needs to hear a son trying to console his mother when he knows he is about to be killed.

Daryl, his anxiety seeping through his pores, told me he couldn't wait to see his children. Attempting to calm and support him, I suggested he visualize his kids waiting for him.

As he paced wildly and popped party mix pieces, horrified, I became an eyewitness to Daryl's unraveling.

In our final twenty minutes, at long last, he talked about each child, their personalities, their likes and dislikes, and he brought up Crystal, his wife, whom he obviously still deeply loved. In the end, just as he professed all along, Daryl's focus truly was on his family.

I don't recall much more of our last few minutes, but I wasn't praying with him and was aware of a deficit. I wondered if it might calm him.

When the officer told me it was time to leave, I looked Daryl in the eyes, held his gaze and bowed slightly with my hands in a prayer pose and said, "Namaste, Daryl. I behold the Light in you and when you are in that place in you and I am in that place in me, we are One. We have our Oneness and I thank you for that, Daryl."

Daryl returned my Namaste and as I turned to walk out, Chaplain Welborn walked in and asked Daryl if he wanted the Lord's Prayer.

"Yes," he replied.

My shoulders slacked in relief that my friend could be comforted by what was familiar to his child self, a little boy who clearly was panicked beyond comprehension.

"Our Father, who art in Heaven, hallowed be Thy name ... forgive us our trespasses as we forgive those ..." the good Chaplain prayed, beautifully embodying his Methodist minister self. I dawdled toward the door, taking in the prayer for myself also.

Neither Chaplain Welborn nor I chose to witness the actual electrocution of a human being we cared about. In fact, Daryl had been emphatic that he did not want me in the viewing gallery, as I had assured him I had no interest in watching him die. We sat quietly outside the death chamber, each calling on a spiritual compass to guide us through.

An endless thirty minutes had passed when all the lights dimmed slightly and we heard a soft whirring noise.

"They are killing him right now," Chaplain Welborn whispered. I felt a lurch in my soul of the wrongness of the death penalty for any crime. No matter how heinous, was there not room for redemption and forgiveness? To calm my shaking insides, I breathed into meditation hoping also to, in some way, help support Daryl's soul to the other side.

Daryl was pronounced dead at 12:17, then Chaplain Welborn and I walked arm in arm supporting four shaky legs back through the barbed gates. Suddenly Daryl was directly above our heads, his Whole Being beaming us a message ...

"I'm free."

"Daryl's here! Do you feel him?" I shook the Chaplain's arm, "he's whole, and he's free to see his children."

I later heard from the Warden, as well as from the witnessing media, that Daryl had a heaving breath-robbing panic attack and couldn't get an inhalation, as he was being strapped into the chair. The viewing curtain had to be closed while he composed himself by breathing into a paper bag. When the Warden asked for last words, it was difficult for him to speak from lack of breath, but he mumbled the words, "I do." I took this to solidify his commitment to his wife and family beyond all frailties, wounds and addictions.

I drove over to an adjacent field where hundreds of TCASK activists were prayerfully protesting Daryl's execution. I walked into my friend Stacy Rector's arms and allowed myself for the first time to collapse into uncontrollable sobs. I cried not just for Daryl Holton, or Robert Glen Coe or Phillip Workman or Gregory Thompson, but all lives taken under the pretense of 'legal homicide.' Killing is killing is killing.

A few years later, I was asked to write a chapter on the intersection of mental illness and the death penalty for *Tennessee's New Abolitionist, The Fight to End the Death Penalty in the Volunteer State*, a compilation textbook designed as a teaching tool for college level education. Here's my closing paragraph:

*Our humanity is challenged as long as the death penalty exists. Such an institution confounds our sense of spiritual purpose, regardless of religious affiliation or belief system. Understanding the legal plight of the most maligned and vulnerable among us and comprehending how our judicial system subjects them to victimization and stigma will lead to a collective resistance to a flawed system. Only when we pull our heads out of the sand and recognize what is happening to those we are spiritually mandated to protect will we truly evolve as human beings. The death penalty and certainly the execution of the mentally ill challenges us to claim our spiritual birthright in a way that little else can. It challenges us to stand still, look at injustice, and take the time to understand how it affects us all. From a spiritual perspective, if there is a higher purpose for capital punishment, it is to grant us the lesson of forgiveness. There is not a higher principle in any religion than forgiveness, and the existence of the death penalty robs humanity of the opportunity to forgive those who are hardest to forgive.*

To this day, I live with the uncertainty that I gave Daryl what he needed to facilitate his soul's returning.

I am enough. I am enough.

# WITCH HAIR #25.

In his eminent equation, $E=mc^2$, Albert Einstein's theory of relativity teaches that matter and energy can be converted into each other. Energy and matter are interchangeable.

Light to dark, dark to light, yin to yang, dualistic principles of the Universe embed one atom at a time in all matter. Apply *focused* energy, as in meditation, a *passive* form, or passion, an *active* form, and voila, matter, or manifestation, materializes. My theory is The Other are able to visit in exactly this manner. Dr. Einstein and other Quantum and Theoretical Physicists, like my man, Brian Greene in *The Hidden Reality*, have theorized the concept of multi-universes and parallel realms or worlds, what I have referred to as 'the upper floors', is exactly what I demonstrated in my body-free travels. Einstein's theory of "many interacting worlds" suggests that parallel worlds not only exist, but interact with ours, as Dale proved when she returned in spirit form three days after exiting her body. Two thousand years ago, the Master Christ quite famously accomplished a similar feat. Atoms, free of bodily confines, lightweight and far less dense than when bound in physical form, are freed to unobstructed travel.

I experienced this same awareness with my cousin Jean, in my first job as a Respiratory Therapist resuscitating coded patients, with my mother twice after her departure from body, of course, with Dale, then with Daryl Holton after his execution. Pure Consciousness in the form of an atom is free to manifest physically when energy is applied. Like thinking about someone, your phone rings and there they are!

As students we learned that a molecule consists of two or more atoms bound together. Remember when Dale told me that she couldn't stay long because she had not accrued enough energy?

And when Mother appeared by my bed, I felt her, but could barely define an outline of her etheric body. Was the plan Dale and I had to connect her death the intention that amped her return in a way that I could see her new form? Was that why her communication took on a more visual quality?

If an urge to explore realms outside of physical reality becomes inspiration, then personal energy must be meted into a less consolidated state. This concept is the outcome of focused meditation, lessening the density of our energy field.

As a result, we become lighter, more refined, more defined and considerably more divine beings walking the earth, leaving a softer footprint and fewer scars in our wake.

This was exactly our collective intention on August 16 and 17, 1987, when our creative tribe gathered at Virginia Team's beautiful spring fed pond, surrounded by meticulously manicured landscape splitting towering bluffs, for the Harmonic Convergence. This was the term assigned to one of the world's first globally synchronized meditation events, which closely coincided with an exceptionally rare alignment the earth's Solar System.

On that cosmically auspicious weekend, eight planets aligned in a rarely seen configuration Astrologers called a Grand Trine. Exactly how rare is debatable, but at the time the idea of gathering to meditate, bake ourselves crispy in a sweltering sweat lodge, nosh together, swat hungry mosquitos, and brave assaulting heat and humidity for two days drew us all right in. As was the unstated custom on Music Row in the '80s, we were all social friends as well as creative cohorts. We adored each other and our resident psychic Hillary Ellers, who traveled from Atlanta to commune with us.

Dale Franklin, then head of a new organization formed to foster musical diversity called The Nashville Music Association (NMA), proudly revealed her new breasts, beautifully fashioned following breast cancer surgery. John D and Susan Loudermilk, whom Dale had introduced me to several years previous ranked as two of my favorite people on the planet. John D, who transitioned in 2016 at the age of 82, was, and still reigns as one of the most iconic, eccentric and successful songwriters of the 20th Century. His unparalleled genius penned "Tobacco Road," "Then You Can Tell Me Goodbye," "Indian Reservation," and countless other hits in so many diverse genres. "Tobacco Road" alone has been recorded over 250 times!

My friend and mirroring soul Rodney Crowell and his wife at the time Rosanne Cash brought their adorable young daughters Chelsea, Caitlin and Hannah. Both Rosanne and Rodney were well on their way to legendary status as songwriters, artists and producers. Pam Rose and Mary Ann Kennedy, coupled artistically and personally at that time, hanging out in the country charts often, joined us, as well as Virginia Team her lady-love, and, if I remember correctly, that lady-love's mother. The ubiquitous Virginia Team, who more than personified the term 'wild woman,' led the mama earth charge and I led the spiritual mojo for the gathering.

There may be a few participants I've grown amnesiac about, but everyone present was purposefully chosen, and magic sweetened every moment of our time together. Hours-long meditation sessions, clustered crystal burial, cooking over an open fire, sleeping in hammocks strung between trees, many of us butt naked, like Woodstock, it was a happening that won't ever be successfully repeated.

We prepared the sweat lodge by bending twigs and limbs to an upside down bowl shape then blanketed the skeleton with thick artist canvas, positioning the sacred hut conveniently between two cool flowing streams. Virginia built a roaring fire heating the lava rocks to be placed in a dug out bowl in the center of the lodge. We passed a wooden bowl filled with creek water and wild sage to splatter on the hot rocks, creating ego-melting steam. Of course we all decided nirvana would descend in the intense, unbearable heat and if nirvana hovers in a near unconscious state, I suppose we were all successful.

Especially Rosanne.

We'd been sweltering to a collective swoon about a half hour when Rose suddenly stumbled out the canvas flap in a pale faint, collapsing in the cool stream.

Chelsea, their youngest, scampered over to her near unconscious mother holding one bright orange Cheeto, "Want a Cheeto? You'll feel better."

On Sunday morning Rodney made the necessary decision to kill a copperhead that was slithering about the camp. We collectively questioned whether taking a life was proper spiritual etiquette on such a beneficed occasion, but the venomous reptile was four feet long and curious children and dogs were present. In keeping with Native practices, Hillary and Rodney skinned the beautifully stamped, venomous serpent, then displayed the skin in some ritualistic manner that I don't quite recall.

At day's end, we built a roaring bonfire by the pond, as if August heat in Tennessee needed supplementation, then each of us contributed a creative offering to the sanctified convergence by performing something uncharacteristic or out of our wheelhouse. In other words, gifted songwriters couldn't pick up a guitar and sing a song, but had to veer in another direction. I recall Susan Loudermilk drawing the perfectly imperfect Zen Circle, not completely out of her sphere, since Susan pretty much is a born Buddha. Virginia decided that the handsomely burning ceremonial fire was her creative contribution and we let it pass, as we usually did with Virginia's recalcitrance. I read a Rumi poem then danced around the fire in an exotic leopard print onesy. Sexuality was not completely out of my reach, but dancing qualified.

The Harmonic Convergence dismantled walls. Whether ego-fortified creative consternation, body shame, spiritual chagrin or childhood hauntings, walls tumbled.

We parted our auspicious gathering more congruent with ourselves each other, and the Universe, motivated to affect a more peaceful earth. I can safely say we have all maintained that spirit. We held hope for the futures of Chelsea, Caitlin, Hannah, Shannon, Garin, and all children who deserved to inherit a peaceful, verdant, breathable world. We drove down Little Marrowbone Road convinced that the worldwide gathering of millions of conscious seekers would usher in a new world order with peace in the wake.

Our innocent intentionality for world peace, presided over by our better angels prevailed that glorious weekend in more ways than we realized at the time.

Indeed, validating our innermost convictions, twenty-six months later, on November 9, 1989, the Berlin Wall fell.

The Cold War had begun to thaw all across Eastern Europe when the Chairman of East Berlin's Communist Party announced a transition in his city's relationship with the West. At midnight he granted citizens that had been trapped behind the pernicious wall access to the Western part of Berlin. Thousands of East Berliners, who for years had been living sequestered from the democratic West, fled to freedom, ending forty years of division between the capitalist west and the communist east. Each of us gathered at the Convergence that weekend was convinced the planetary peace meditation brought The Wall crumbing down.

Walls felled. Walls erected.

Many years later, Mary Ann Kennedy, Pam Rose and Randy Sharp wrote a seminal song on the subject:

*Some walls are made of stone*
*Sometimes we build our own*
*Some walls stand for years*
*Some wash away with tears*
*Some walls are built on pride*
*Some keep the child inside*
*Some walls are built in fear that*
*Love let go will disappear ...*

*If there is any hope for love at all*
*Some walls must fall.*

Thirty years and several pendulum fluctuations later, gyrating between dark and light, depending on political sway and conscious perspective, the planet is suspended in a socio-political-religious fulcrum world wide. Referred to in colorful expletives, from the descent of the Anti-Christ to the Second Coming, the United States of America holds her collective breath as the pendulum quivers near an extreme right.

Politics at the time of our Convergence seemed inconsequential compared to protecting and holding sacrosanct the beautiful ball we'd hitched a ride on. Many in our tribe were riding the crest of a pinnacling career while chasing the light of personal and spiritual consciousness. Rodney and I met regularly for lunch to discuss the latest Alice Bailey tome. Dense and witheringly hard to absorb, we needed tandem minds to slog through the viscosity. Our circle of friends thrived on being awake, striving for continuity while deep diving into our wounds.

Many of us gathered all those years ago at the Harmonic Convergence, along with other globally cognizant denizens have now, unfathomably, become the Resistance.

As in life, the repetitious vacillation of the planetary pendulum between the dark and light, even to bipolar extremes, is paramount to finding our way back to the elusive center. The shifting paradigm, not exclusive to America, manifests in myriad ways worldwide.

The good news is the cosmic metronome cannot indefinitely suspend in an extreme polarity. Gravity naturally lulls it back down to a gravitational center. In the meanwhile, what are we to do with this unsettling experience that many consider to be America's most challenging crisis in modern history?

Of course we resist. But also, we can opt for the mindfulness that extremes can create possibility for bounteous levels of transformation and healing. A near-death experience for democracy around the world will serve to strengthen the conviction of the masses that freedom to love whom it pleases us to love, to make healthy choices for ourselves and families, to vote our convictions, to openly speak an opinion, and to live in a state of conscious freedom, must always prevail. Consider that the dark underbelly of a racist, sexist, bigoted, fear-based culture languishing in a shallow grave has now been unearthed. A collective well-aimed inclusivity ethic will eventually pierce the ignorance. The Civil Rights Act did not dissuade Southern myopia that dark skin was inferior to light skin. Nor did Women's Suffrage and the Voting Rights Act protect women from objectification, sexism, and wage disparity.

The showdown between light and dark wages internally for humanity, therefore externally for the planet, as healing expresses in stages from the inside out.

Just as personal festering wounds must be laid open for healing, so it goes for a nation's addictions, dependencies, codependencies, abuses and denials. We as a nation thought we had at least begun to soothe the scars of slavery, the systemic oppression of brown skin cultures, and the shame it cast on our collective society when we elected, in a landslide, our first African American president. The shocking 2016 presidential election swiftly exposed our denial.

The pendulum swings.

As global citizens, when we collectively render ourselves less and less dense, penetrating darkness with the healing light of awareness, so goes our beautiful planet.

# WITCH HAIR #26.

From my first preschool glimpse of Ayer's Rock, renamed Uluru when the rightful ownership was returned to the Aboriginals of Australia, I was captivated, vowing someday to go half way around the world to Alice Springs to understand why.

That plan came to fruition some forty years later during a worldwide rock tour with the Elton John band. My Love had been invited to be a member by one Binky Poodleclip some years before, and when the tour headed to New Zealand and Oz, I accepted an invite to tag along. The tour started in Perth, on the western coast, right about where San Diego might sit on our map. Extraordinary beaches stretching long and wide, created vast vistas dotted with only a few beach goers. The Indian Ocean wrapped around the sprouting city, which at that time in the mid '90s seemed to be lifted out of the '50s. The nearest major city to Perth is Adelaide, over 2,000 miles to the east. Elton was and still is beloved in Oz, so it seemed most of the city showed up en masse for his concerts.

When the band left the continent for Japan, I stayed behind to visit Monkey Mia, a remote adventure destination 900km north of Perth in the Shark Bay Marine Park, a World Heritage site. I wanted to be up close and personal with the wild dolphin there. A friendly pod of bottlenose regularly swim in to the shore to interact with those they wish to know. There are two ways to get to Monkey Mia: rent a car and drive or, unbeknownst to me at the time, there is a private flight service.

My first obstacle was the look on the rental car manager's face when he found out I was taking his car to Monkey Mia.

"We don't allow our cars in uncharted territories where we cannot get them back should something go wrong," the no-worries, bright-eyed manager explained.

"What about insurance for the trip?" I wondered, exposing good ol' American naivety.

"There is no way to insure a car that cannot be returned to Perth, should something go amiss," he explained the Aussie way, with unbowed patience.

The willful child who would not keep on clothes that my body didn't appreciate sprang forth.

"What if I sign a release form saying I'll pay for the car should it not make it back?" I bargained, wanting to go be with the dolphin. The cost of a barely used car, which I could ill afford, was not going to deter.

I popped by a local natural food store to buy a large styrofoam, cooler, the only nasty kind available, and stocked up on enough salads, lettuces, eggs, water and munchies to last a week, just in case the car had other ideas and intentions than mine. Barely fifty miles outside of Perth I was virtually alone on a two lane road stretching north into nowhere through ochre colored desert dotted with scrub, lizards and little else, other than petrol shacks. The tiny stations, mostly frequented by lorry drivers who guzzled bright orange smelly hot dogs and cold, piss-smelling Budweiser, were few and far between making it necessary to pay attention to the petrol gauge.

No GPS in those times, so I relied on a map the aghast rental car dude insisted that I keep in front of me at all times. Shortly, I could see why. A hundred or so kilometers in, I ran out of road and ended up in a village with no road signs, not even a stop sign. Pulling along the side of a now dirt path, I sat there staring at the map wondering where I had gone so wrong. A car going in the opposite direction pulled along side me. An almost handsome bloke rolled down his window.

"Ye al rioght?" he grinned knowingly.

"Yeah, but I seem to be missing some road." I smiled back.

He explained that the road, indeed, ended at the village and the only way to get north toward Sharks Bay was to follow him.

I could hear my sweet mama's voice admonishing that this was nobody's fault but my own as I turned the car around to follow him into the roadless unknown. After five or so kilometers of orange, dusty almost paths, a narrow, paved two-lane appeared out of nowhere. Relieved, I rolled down the window and shouted a hearty "thank you," to which he returned, "no worries, mate, stay safe."

You gotta love the Aussies.

A wildfire roaring too close to the roadside for my comfort blanketed the entire area in a thick choking smoke for longer than I care to recall, conjuring up images of a burned out vehicle I might be destined to own. Finally reaching Monkey Mia well after lights out, the encampment napped, shut down and pitch black except what my car headlamps illuminated, making it appear primitive and uninviting. Maybe I had been duped by the beck and call of the friendly wild dolphin? Nonetheless exhilarated but exhausted, I found my little metal trailer by the number I was given on the phone when I booked reservations, Number 7, a good start since that was my cosmic number. Spartan, but clean, with full facilities; it was not my usual princess accommodation, but I was way too tired to pout.

With first light I leapt to the nearest window, yanked up the cheap blinds, and happy danced at the sight! The clearest turquoise water imaginable surrounded the peninsula, well padded with micro crystals of sparkling white beach spilling over into rust-red sand dunes. No wonder the dolphin, the dugongs, whales and turtles studied by National Geographic laid claim to these magical fingers pointing into the Indian Ocean. Sharks Bay was an unspoiled paradise!

A note in the trailer suggested the dolphin usually arrived at 10 a.m. but there were no guarantees. By that time twenty to thirty dolphin-lovers waited under the watchful eye of a uniformed World Heritage Site minder. Everyone squinted at the impossibly bright turquoise waters, hoping to spot a fin. Twenty minutes later, no fins. Had I really driven over five hundred and thirty nine miles, risking owning a decaying-in-the-outback rental for naught? Then the people pod burst into applause and there they were! Before our eyes appeared a school of about twelve happy shining waiting-to-make-new-friends dolphin! Larger bulls, medium sized female cows and a few calves made up the blue pod.

Of course, like me, the dolphin groupies wanted to wade in the water with the pod but rules were strict and emphatically enforced. You first had to be chosen and then you could hold a bucket to hand them a fish if you wanted an up close and personal encounter. After impatiently waiting for longer than patently impatient people do, finally the park ranger motioned for me to enter the water. Before he could get the bucket of fish in my hands, a female swam straight for me, intently, as if she recognized me. She rolled part way out of the water, turning one huge round blue fading to black eye, the most unique eye I'd ever stared into, directly up to meet my gaze signaling, 'good to see you again, mate.' She lovingly wrapped her dorsal fin around my leg, not moving but anchoring herself to me, staring straight into my soul with that one brilliant eye. Tears welled as I recognized the enormity and antiquity of her soul radiating through her eye. Time stood still as we honored our recognition and something that felt like Universal love for each other, cocooned in a spiritual exchange. When the conversation seemed complete, I bent over to her holding a fish. She continued to stare for a minute or so, then gently raised her head, grasping the fish in her mouth. When I looked up the people pod on the beach burst into applause as they, too, wiped tears.

"That's Margaret," the park ranger volunteered. "I've never seen her be so bold with anyone. Usually she hangs back and waits until last, then all she is interested in is grabbing her fish and heading out straight away."

"I think Margaret and I have a past," I smiled through cloudy eyes.

Apparently he didn't—he shrugged it off.

Margaret and I repeated our encounter every morning for three days. Word got out that there was an American Margaret-magnet in the people pod, so each morning I was chosen to wade in to see if Margaret was still interested in hanging out. By now, the Nat Geo scientific observers came to check out our morning dance. Each time as my dual eyes connected with her singular round eye, my soul gained entrance to a realm beyond the now, into a vortex of past, present and future simultaneously. Like a deep meditation, and much like the podium I gazed into while visiting with The Other on the vessel, in Margaret's eye everything seemed simultaneously posited in one space in time, like a microcosm of all time and space in existence.

When Margaret and I weren't communing, I explored swaths of the 1,500 kilometers of white shell and sand beaches, marveling how anything so breathtaking could have thrived without being blighted by throngs of tourists. The brochures explained Monkey Mia had only been a World Heritage Site since 1991 and this was 1995, so indeed, the pristine virginity of the environment remained in situ.

Time came for me to drive back to Perth for a planned flight to Alice Springs and Uluru but I was hooked beyond rationality. I couldn't imagine leaving Margaret. I called my Love somewhere in Asia sobbing incoherently about a dolphin named Margaret that I couldn't leave. Expecting that he would attempt to lull me into rational behavior, I prepared defensively, instead, he insisted I stay.

"Well, if you have a dolphin you need hang with longer, then by all means change your flight to Alice; no one is making you go but you."

What planet did this man come from anyway?

The next morning, tripping over a spectrum of emotions, I managed to pack the car and silently bid Margaret a sad so long as I walked her shore one last time.

Checking the map to see if there was possibly a more scenic route south, I saw where I could hug the coast for a hundred kilometers or so. Making a Lucy Ricardo-like choice to grab a few more vistas along the tantalizing turquoise waters, I turned west to find myself not on a road at all, but a dusty trail. If the rental car risked rusting-out abandonment on the northbound approach, the south bound meant my skeleton would accompany it. My turnoff must have been opted somewhere after Dongara but instead of taking Highway 1 (highway is sorely misleading), I was on a dirt path through the most mind numbingly beautiful environment I had even surveyed ...

and I was alone, achingly alone.

The entirety of the experience was speaking so clearly to my soul it never occurred to me to turn back, although it did occur to me that I had not passed another car for two hours. Now I was hearing not only my mother's voice admonishing this choice was mine and mine alone, intermingling with the rental car dude's voice reminding me of the cost of an abandoned car. Never mind, I reasoned; by the time this car is found I'd be long since past putting the price of a car on my Amex.

Every few kilometers traversed at the blazing speed of forty at best, the car carried me into vista after vista of wild, untouched beaches adorned with natural wonders so elemental and ancient that it seemed impossible to take in the astounding beauty with only two eyes. I was compelled to stay the course. Like meeting Margaret, the unblemished beauty was why I was here in this magical moment, completely alone.

It dawned on me as the sun dropped closer and closer to the darkening water, that I was still kicking red dust behind me on a narrow path that would hardly allow another car to pass if I encountered one. I was munching out of the cooler, but my body needed real food soon. Then, as if a mirage of some sort, I spotted a monolith carved into a head resembling an Easter Island head, except obviously male and balding. 'Ahhh, some sort of hippie bed and breakfast, my stomach told me, maybe I'll at least find a bowl of granola'.

I swung in, following the drive for a half-kilometer or so when it opened into a clearing dotted with small cottages strategically scattered around a larger structure that appeared to be occupied. In fact, they all looked occupied. There were two cars in front of one of the cottages, but nothing to suggest a bed and breakfast. What was most apparent as I unfolded from the car was the energy of the place. I found myself wondering if I had ventured into a coven of the darkest entities I had ever confronted, but figured it was probably my plummeting blood sugar talking. I was hungry enough to manipulate myself into believing that my sensitized body, having cosmically communed with Margaret then lifted yet again into the high vibration of the untamed Australian coastline, was in reality readjusting to a more normal energy. Or at least my growling belly hoped so.

I knocked on several doors, "is anybody here?" Feeling eyes following me, I was being noticed and watched, but heard nothing and saw no one. I tried a few more hellos, to no avail. By now, I'm getting an edgy, pissed-off feeling, signaling the blood sugar hangries had taken over.

"Hey, I know you're in there; I just want to see if I can purchase some food for the rest of my trip," hoping the famished pilgrim tone might at least cause one of the doors to part. Nothing. Reasoning, if that's what you could call it at this point, that I was being observed anyway, I nosed around the silent empty ground for a bit, then stumbled upon one of those copper plaques that might note a grave. The same balding man was etched on the plaque with an inscription that in essence said he was the head honcho of this progressively alarming, bizarre-sounding commune. My inner Lucy, wanted to grab my camera out of the car and snap the inscription, thinking nobody would believe what it said. Wish I'd let Lucy lose, so I'd have the wording to offer, but suffice it to say it sounded like a guru I'd never wanted to be in a cave with.

I got the hell out of there.

Of course when I got back on the trail, all I could think of was, what if there are women and children or young girls being held hundreds of miles from nowhere against their will, or being brainwashed into zombies or sex slaves? But I was far too lacking in blood sugar to be brave. I just wanted to make it to the nearest petrol shack for one of those bright orange smelly dogs, then to be on my way to Alice Springs the next morning.

# WITCH HAIR #27.

Alice Springs, widely recognized as the Aboriginal seat of the country, is an oasis nestled in a tableland of remote, endless nothingness. Halfway between Adelaide and Darwin, best traversed by plane or the infamous Ghan train, sweet little Alice is the pulsing heart of the magical island continent.

My childhood fascination, dancing through the glossy pages of National Geographic, formed the intention of visiting Ayer's Rock, renamed Uluru, after having been rightfully returned to the Aboriginals as their primary sacred site in 1993. The massive ochre rock, created over 600 million years was deemed sacred by the first dwellers more than 10,000 years ago. At 3.6 kms long and 1.9 kms wide, with a circumference of 9.4 kms it is the second biggest monolith in the country. To walk the circumference was my goal in visiting the Alice.

After landing at one of the cutest airports imaginable, with an Aboriginal dot-painted plane on the tarmac, I again had to remind myself to drive on the opposite side of the street as I followed the only road into the tiny westernized desert town. Laid out in a plus sign stretching four or five blocks on each prong, the original clapboard storefronts painted in various earth tones gave the entire town a Warner movie-set charm. The feminine feel, despite the rustic exterior of the village, delighted me into out-loud laughter and a behind-the-steering-wheel happy dance. Instantly I was back in 1950s American cowboy culture with an artistic twist, except no horses apparent on the hitching posts. For me, I was not in Alice, but I WAS Alice in a Wonderland!

Love at first sight.

As I strolled along the busy, yet not tourist-laden, sidewalks, lulled by the haunting strains of a didgeridoo echoing down the street, I felt drawn to explore the dozens of art galleries. Clearly Aboriginal dot art was the economic driver in this creative hamlet in the middle of a vast continent. The first gallery I drifted into, Mbantua, was nearly my last. As if moving in a dream, I found myself standing in front of paintings so raw, so authentic, so overflowing with spirit that my soul trembled, sending teardrops gliding down my cheeks. The deep purple and ochre painting in front of me depicted what looked to be breasts with softly curving lines drawn across them. I began to sense stories flowing from those lines; women's voices that spoke in a language not accessible to my brain but nonetheless gently penetrating my heart. Without words, ancient stories passed through generations of women teaching the *dreamings* of their tribal culture, seeped into my being.

"Hiya, Mate, everythin al'roight?" The male voice beside me sounded blocks away.

Embarrassed, I realized I was sobbing not particularly quietly in the middle of the gallery.

"The painting is speaking to me in stories. I want to be able to understand them. How can I understand what they are saying?" I choked.

"Well, Mate, I reckon you might have to be Aboriginal to do that," a smiling, slightly balding, mustached middle-aged man explained without the slightest judgment of my emotional display. "That there is an Ada Bird, one of my best painters, who like the great Emily Kngwarreye only started painting as very old woman."

Tim Jennings, the affable gallery owner with presence and charm surpassing even the typical Aussie's, felt like a new old friend from 'hiya mate.' I lassoed him with non-stop banter about the spiritually compelling art that for me surpassed anything I'd seen at the Met or the Musée d'Orsay. The unrefined, almost crudely colorful paintings, birthed by some of the most ancient souls currently inhabiting the planet, encased me in a timeless state as I slowly absorbed the *dreamings*, or what my intuition sensed they might mean.

Four hours and several thousand dollars later, I managed to drag myself away, with three cherished Ada Bird masterpieces rolled up in hand. This purchase would be the first of many and would lead to one of the most exciting adventures of my life—not only filming a documentary deep in the Utopian out bush, but also hold my honor at being invited to participate in a sacred ritual never before experienced by a white woman. The cost of this art was nothing compared to the life-changing events it would set in motion.

As incredible as my introduction to the art had been, there was much more magic to be mined as Uluru tugged at my soul.

The nearly five hour drive from Alice to Uluru, a straight shot sticking to the Stuart Highway, could be called boring were it not so esoterically compelling. It was the ultimate excursion, opening my eyes to the incredible diversity of the outback's moonlike landscapes. No scenic pull-offs needed in the flattened desert, the vistas stretched as far as my sight could carry me.

If you take away the open vista magnificence of the out bush, a roadhouse, which I used for a toilet stop, was about the extent of anything to talk about except the camel camp. The plentiful road kill, usually 'roos' as the locals say, was broken up by a camel carcass, inescapable by sheer size. As I pondered the dead camel, and wondered how the car survived the impact, I spotted a wooden board with 'Camel Rides' scrawled in white hand lettering. Why that intrigued me I can't imagine, but I turned off on the long dirt road and ended up at a corral full of not particularly friendly-looking beasts. A camel wrangler looking like a cowboy rolled in paprika pulled off his battered western hat, slapped it against his leg releasing a puff of red dust, then ambled over to the car. Two piercing blue eyes sparkled through a parched, road-mapped face.

"Can I help ye, Mate?" More words followed but I had stumbled and fell on his thick Aussie accent and was more or less in the thrall of his rugged good looks.

Was it the face that prompted me to stammer, "I'd like to hear about your camping trips into the bush," pointing to the menu of options on a crudely painted sign tacked to the office.

Handsome Camel-boy went on to explain there were weekend trips, week-long trips and a three-week trip. For some reason (the blue eyes) I jumped on the three-week trip, probing about cost and the most important aspect to me ... food. Neither sounded within my reach. Even though glamping under the Southern Cross sounded charming, grilled kangaroo steaks not so much.

"If I moight pass along some camel sense," Camel-boy grinned, "I'd say take the hour long ride in Alice, then decide 'bout your trip, Mate."

Inwardly thanking Blue Eyes for saving me from my robust feminine, I pointed the rental through the swirling red dust back to the Stuart Highway, an iconic explorers highway that runs from the tip top of the country, south to Port Augusta, on a straight shot to Uluru.

The first ochre monolith stretching above the desert scrub was the Olgas or Kata Tjuta, a group of large domed rock formations peaking out of the desert before the magnificent Uluru, and is often mistaken for the latter.

Like the dot paintings, my first glimpse fleeced my breath and turned on the Oz eye-water. This rock occupied some particle of my DNA and I bowed to the sacredness. For the Anangu people, it's not a rock, but a living, breathing altar where the spirits of their ancestral family come to commune and continue to reside. Highly sacrosanct for the Aboriginals, a part and particle of them lying dormant in me was awakened on first sight and as with the paintings, my soul had come home.

Outfitted in what I considered to be proper walking shoes, dressed for desert heat, plenty of bottled water and camera in hand, I was ready for my trek around the 10k circumference of nature's powerful megalith. Checking in at the Uluru-

Kata Tjuta Cultural Centre was mandatory in order to learn the dos and don'ts of the three-to-four hour journey.

An Anangu guide was optional, but I chose instead to be briefed by a female guide on the 'men's business' and 'women's business' rules of the rock, as well as the spiritual defamation of *climbing* the rock, which of course I had no intention of doing.

"Men's Business, no lookie, Women's Business, ok", the lovely young guide explained. "Sign tell you, Men's Business, Women's Business, ok?"

"Ok, got it!" Anxious to begin I hugged her and off I trekked. Since their language has no word for please or thank you, and most find them offensive, as they imply ownership or are seen as begging, I let my huge grin convey my delight.

Putting the four-hour adventure into words is analogous to clarifying the past, present, future incident of the podium experience when out of my body, I'm hard pressed not to sound like a New Age neophyte or someone who missed the chance to be a permanent cave dweller in India. Nonetheless, my expensive walking shoes connected with the red sand and my soul led the way. I must have been pounding along about 30 minutes when the first concavely carved-by-time indentation displayed a warning sign: Men's Business. Damn if there wasn't a powerful urge to look! Impulsively I tried to sneak a peek to see what would happen, but my neck would not budge. I couldn't turn my head, as if someone had placed palms on either side of my head over my ears, preventing my head from turning until I moved past the site. I jerked around checking behind me to see who the hell had grabbed my head. I heard distant giggles turning into a raucous hee-haw that kind of pissed me off, although not enough to keep from putting one foot in front of the other.

No doubt for me, the cosmic veils were decidedly thinner in Oz.

I noticed the change in vibration of the next site minutes before arriving, softer energy curled in an open, airy fragrance. This sacred area marked 'Women's Business' was a receptacle for a small underground spring pushing through just enough moisture to allow the area to be dotted with fragrant green saplings. Verdant. Women. A lush, leafy oasis in a thirsty desert. Just as with the paintings, not only did I feel a Song of the Siren call to linger, but captive in the pervasive female mystique, the veils grew thinner still. Far away I could faintly hear the repetitive singsong rhythms of women's voices, though not within reach of my comprehension.

The next leg of the walk-around was the major portion of the blistering south-facing length of the rock. Interestingly, this was the only area I ran into what looked to be tourists. Lots of Nikons flopping around necks and loud chatter did not suggest that sacredness was noted or acknowledged. I felt invaded and protective of the rock. The next sites were near the western curve. This time I wasn't even curious about the Men's Business site, either that or I wasn't up for getting my neck wrenched again. There were several smaller women's sites, equally compelling and heart expanding, but not as moist and green as the first site.

There are myriad ways to meditate, and certainly this walk was one. As in sitting meditation time shifts senses to oneness, but the rock's massive vortex had been created by tens of thousands of years of designated divine distinction creating an immersive field of force that seemed to control my will, which my sweet mama would say was impossible. As I hiked, swatting thirsty black flies fighting each other to sip from my nose and mouth, any sense of the personal self dimmed. Every atom in my body shifted into a higher purposed self, old and adept, new and dilettantish in the same breath. The only brain-train thought not derailed by omnipotence was that my life would never be the same.

I recalled the guide telling me there would be a waterfall, some benches, and shade for rest on the north face of the rock. I was ready. But not quite ready for what was to come first. With my Pollyanna face to the journey, I nearly tripped over a visitor lumbering across my path. A giant goanna. I had never met a lizard of this size, or any lizard larger than those that scamper between cracks in the sidewalk. The fierce creature looked like someone attempted to shrink a dinosaur but gave up before it was a shy little creature darting about under stones. The reptile exceeded my five feet four inches, not that I measured him/her, with considerable girth.

Typical me would have gone into a head mash-up about toxicity and teeth and aggressiveness but when I stopped, she stopped. Much like Margaret, my dolphin mate, she opened her round eye, blinked then snared me in a frozen stare. Having no inclination to step over her, I surrendered. After what must have been five minutes or so, as with Margaret, there was communication, which I felt hapless to decipher. The goanna seemed eager to transit some sort of message, that one eye glinting agitation as we became wrapped in our mutual standoff. She wanted me to understand something I was too dense to take in. I assigned a feminine gender to the lizard because of a docile, non- aggressive countenance. Colorful and yet still blending with the desert landscape, she was a beauty. A little scary, but a real looker.

Hot and sweating profusely, I apologized for my denseness and indicated that I was ready, willing and able to receive the message she offered. For several more minutes we both held our respective stances, me scared shitless to move a muscle, she, unflappable with that piercing eye with the snake-like slit. She slowly blinked again, like a camera shutter opening and closing, and instantly a sepia-toned vision was right there in my third eye. A group of primitive buildings with dark and light skinned children laughing and playing next to a stream, appeared for several seconds. The vision, scored to a distinct sound of dots and dashes ticking in the background, reminded me of nothing I'd ever seen. I had no idea what the flash meant, but I nodded as if to say, 'ok, got it.'

The lizard then softened her gaze and her body
shifted into lumbering movement. Lifting my camera, I furiously snapped until she grew bored, then trudged off to the other side. I slipped into a happy dance, I think I had just dallied with the Dalai Lama.

After my jig, I realized how much my aching body needed a respite from black flies and heat prostration, not to mention the perplexing lizard. The flies were so tenacious I found myself wishing I had purchased one of the silly hats with netting to cover your face. The more I sweated and my nose dripped from the dust, the more desperate the black scavengers were to slurp on my face.

The inviting negative ions of a waterfall announced the
last major Uluru landmark. Parched tourists huddled in the

spray, before finishing the arduous walk. A rushing rivulet had carved a deep downspout, sending a cascade of water over the rusty rock forming a turquoise estuary below. I wanted nothing more than to rip off my dusty clothes, and sink my body neck deep in the cooling pool. I didn't see anyone else consoling themselves from the heat and flies, so assumed dipping in the waterfall reservoir was also a desecration. I opted for a bench where I painfully unlaced my shoes to massage my numbed, crimson feet and took some deep breaths. Damn, I thought, not many folks dialogue with a mini dinosaur that is potentially toxic and can easily take off both legs with one bite. If Margaret reflected the light of the yang was the riveting reptile the dark yin?

I completed my spiritually exhilarating, bodily exhausting walk-about anxious to ask about the goanna encounter. The guide seemed surprised the goanna had stopped to linger.

"Goanna now you totem," was all she gave up through a couple of twinkling dark eyes.

Aching from the distance, the bitchy black flies and heat, my body was cranky. I swallowed sustenance from one of the restaurants, figuring if food had to be shipped half way across the desert to be rendered palpable, then it wasn't. As in Monkey Mia, lodging varied between a double wide and a Four Star Hotel. As long as I could get my body in a prone position, I didn't care and opted for the trailer.

Capturing the rising sun as it kisses the stupendous red rock is a photographer's dream. The first light coupling in the hush of the desert did not disappoint. As it scaled the horizon, the hoisting sun lit up Mother Nature's masterpiece like a spontaneous mountain wildfire. Forty years later, I stood knee deep in awe, inhabiting the exact image of the rock I'd seen in Nat Geo as a child. Unfortunately, hundreds of others with Uluru *dreamings* furiously clicked away behind their advanced Nikon lenses, seemingly oblivious to the sublime beauty and spiritual magnificence unfolding before them. I grabbed my definitive shot, but the shooting frenzy seemed to denigrate one of earth's mighty alters.

On the uneventful drive back to the Alice, a few kilometers outside of town I noticed a historic marker pointing left to the Alice Springs Telegraph Station Historical Reserve. On impulse, I turned into a narrow, blacktopped road ending in a car park. Paths led from the lot to a group of primitive stacked rock buildings with shiny tin roofs. As soon as I opened the car door, I heard the insistent ticking of the telegraph broadcasting around the property, as if still desperately communicating with the rest of the world. The waning light was perfect for grabbing a few photos, but as soon as I sunk into it, a young uniformed guide announced closing time. I decided to return the next morning before my flight to Cairns to find out if the dots and dashes I heard in the vignette flashed by the goanna were indeed related to *these* dots and dashes.

I arranged an early wake up call, hoping for a soak in the history and living antiquity of the station. Browsing with an elder, I learned why Alice Springs has a lady name. The settlement was named after the popular Mrs. Alice Todd, the wife of Charles Todd who convinced the Australian government to spend the $250,000 to construct the overland telegraph as a repeater station. Repeaters boosted signal for relaying messages both urgent and mundane from other parts of the world, and served to keep Oz in the loop. Bouncing dots and dashes were relayed from Asia to Darwin then to Alice where the signal was re-charged to send it down to Adelaide. I reckoned that the picturesque milieu chosen by Mr. Todd had to do with the clear stream flowing beneath the towering McDonnell Ranges, and his assumption that it supplied year round water. The basically self-sufficient station survived on dry goods and other provisions arriving once a year by camel from Adelaide, but thrived locally with a sustainable vegetable garden and cattle from their own stock. The station offered comfortable, relative to the time of 1872, spacious family quarters for the Stationmaster, policemen's quarters, stables for horses, lots for camels, various sheds for buggys and the blacksmith, as well as a kitchen building and dining hall.

As I moseyed around, the unrelenting ticking of the telegraph becoming almost as irritating as the ubiquitous flies, apparently having followed me from Uluru.

The long dining table having been neatly set with the tin plates and cups, the original stove (or a replica) reigning over the kitchen and neatly made beds in the family quarters looked as if a ship had beamed up the inhabitants. A clever contraption rigged to shoo flies away from open mouths jarred me to another culture's sad reality. A long pole extending from the veranda to the large fan over the table had to be jockeyed in constant motion. In one of the many compelling photos, a young native boy toiled in stifling heat, distractedly pumping the lever protruding through an open window. The child's skeletal frame looked as if it could easily be hoisted by the weight of the long shaft. The systematic piracy of native lands for white people's purposes mirrored America's inhumane treatment of its

Native tribes, as did the indentured servitude of gentle brown-skinned people.

At the end of my enlightening tour with the Aboriginal Elder who lectured the entire place back to life with a smiling pride in his heritage, we routed through to a bookstore and trinket shop. A small paperback book called *Alice … on the Line* stood out from the stacks of historic books about the Overland.

I devoured the beautifully voiced narrative on a two-hour flight to Cairns, neglecting to even observe the sky view of the luscious out back of Australia. The personal account by Doris Bradshaw Blackwell, daughter of Thomas Bradshaw, the first Stationmaster to bring his children to live in the wilds of the bush in 1899, had me alternately laughing hysterically, quietly wiping tears and feeling for all the world like I could have been there.

As I read, I began to understand the image transferred by the Lady Lizard. The vision of light and dark skinned children playing by a stream spilled from the story as Doris revived her teenage years spent with her brothers and sisters as the first white children to live at the station. Doris's unconditional love for the Arrernte people was palpable, as each vividly recalled visual imprinted my being. The pages danced before me with the same clear vision shared by the goanna. I vowed to adapt the rare autobiographical account into a film script so that the outside world could experience not only the hardships of the Overland Telegraph, but also the interrelationship of the Bradshaw children with the Arrernte, testimonials otherwise undocumented for that time period.

Fast-forward ten years, and my respect for, obsession with, the Utopian painters, their spiritual *dreamings*, their struggles with the modern way of life and cultural losses have chiseled into my soul ... and bank account. I've amassed quite a collection of small and medium pieces by the artists that I most admire. I hosted Tim Jennings, who brought canvases to Nashville for viewings and lectures, several times in an effort to shine Utopian Art's light in my corner of the world. Tim has long since been my hero for his love of the Arrernte-Alyawarra people and the ultimate respect he affords as business partners and beloved friends. His procurement of the paintings is a most unusual story: every fortnight Tim drives a four wheel drive SUV deep into the bush to the myriad Out Stations of Utopia to drop off rolled canvases, always painted black, along with acrylics and brushes. Two weeks later, he makes the twelve hour trek back to the bush, in summer a mind-melting 42 degrees C, to appraise and purchase the pieces from the artists. Both men and women paint for Tim, but for me, the women's work is soul-searing.

In 2007, I assembled a small crew to trek into the Utopian out bush to document Tim's work with the artists.

Kathy Conkwright, my film partner at the time, David Dare Parker, Australia's Walkley Award winning photojournalist, and I spent three days visiting the various Out Stations and *sorry camps* to capture Tim's thriving, life-bettering business with his painters. Skeptical at first that the undereducated, innocent women could easily be taken advantage of in their business transactions, I soon came to understand Tim's affection, respect, and compassion for the women. I also came to appreciate his ongoing intention to educate himself on the spiritual underpinnings and inspirations of the artists and their *dreamings*. Against daunting odds with the inherent addictions and *humbuggings*—men absconding the art income to gamble and buy booze—Tim's striving was and is not only to elevate the personal lives and well being of the talented women but to support and preserve their ancient culture and way of life, one quickly disappearing from the earth.

It was at a women's *sorry camp*, referring to a group of women having escaped deep into the bush far away from the men, to mourn a death, that our little crew became the first white people allowed to film a *corroboree*. A corroboree is a highly sacred ritual involving singing, dancing and dreamtime connection, their form of meditation.

I was shocked when one of Kathy's favorite artists, Mary Morton, who speaks a bit of English, said, "you come to dance," motioning for me to be painted so I could participate with her and a dozen other women in their sacred women's corroboree. So pumped that I shook from anticipation, I tore my tee over my head for my breasts to be painted, then sat down on a blanket in only my leggings and shoes. As if on silent cue, the women started softly humming, and drumming with sticks on found pieces of wood or plastic.

The distinctive feminine lines, in the shape of sagging breasts, drawn by Ada Bird on the first painting I purchased from Mbantua were gently painted in white on the chests of a few of the other women by their silver haired elder artist, one of Tim's rockstar painters. Mary sat directly in front of me transforming my bare chest into a sacred art piece. Although certainly immersed in the sanctity of the ceremony, I could hardly escape the expressions on the faces of the long-breasted women as they checked out Mary's brush floating over on two small fleshy pancakes. They did a respectable job at stifling giggles, then the chanting began. Unbelievably, it was the same sing-song rhythm I had heard while standing in front of my Ada Bird's Women's Ceremony painting ten years earlier. The highly contagious, identifiable melody must have been cellular memory. There it was again.

The catchy rhythm and sing-song chant, accompanied by women and children clapping or beating sticks on cans, stole me to a timeless place where we were all one family, one tribe. A constant flow of tears dampened my freshly painted breasts, as an umbrella of unconditional love for these women, my sisters on the path, the witches of their culture, overtook my senses.

Joining in on the familiar melody, I grew one with the women, our souls simultaneously focusing through the same lens.

La la, lalala, de la la, de la la, an exquisite simplistic chanting melody rode on the desert winds as we sang.

After a time, minutes or an hour, I don't know, Mary floated off the blanket like a teenager, broke into a wild dance and I'm telling you, that old woman—maybe seventy-five at the time— could move. The corroboree dance is about slip-sliding bare feet through the red sand making indentations that imitate kangaroo tracks, while singing in rhythm with the movements. Didn't look hard at all. Then Mary motioned for me to come dance with her. I quickly became "flat-chested white-girl dancing," and the giggles were no longer stifled. Didn't faze me in the least. I was lost in another world, in another place in time.

At the end of the ceremony, a glowing Mary, looking like a teenager, hugging a besotted me, whispering in my ear, "you one of us."

Indeed, Mary, indeed.

The *sorry camps* were horrendous environments rubbish heaps to a germaphobic princess. A dozen or more rusted out dead cars littered the area, surpassed in number only by packs of emaciated dogs in various stages of starvation. A coughing woman, looking to be in her nineties, lay curled on a bare rusted bedspring waiting for death to come. Filthy mattresses matted in layered dog poop were strewn under humpies constructed from bent twigs and tattered tarps. The humpies haphazardly cobbled together to protect from the sun and wind, functioned as living quarters for the women, children and dogs. The squalor was hard to take, but the ritual was a life-affirming experience that has continued giving over the years.

The indigenous live off an arid land so any watering hole or *bore*, as they are called when outfitted with a windmill to pump the water, is for drinking and cooking, not bathing. Being one challenged to acclimatize to unhygienic situations, embarrassingly I held my breath when in close proximity to the women and children. When I was sitting on the blanket during the corroboree, the nauseating stench, a cross between fresh dog poop and three-day-old road kill, threatened a fit of out-of-control retching. It was only by hyper-focusing in the moment that I avoided a full on puke-fest. As our SUV pulled the art trailer out of the camp blending into a deep red sunset, everyone stared aghast at me, holding noses and gagging.

Finally David Dare Parker found some baby wipes in his gig bag and said, "here, Mate, how's about a clean up?"

"Fine, I will wipe down, but I'm not ready to lose my paint job!"

In one *sorry camp*, which looked like it could be the home of choice for several of the well-known women art makers, we filmed a stumbling starving puppy desperately lapping acrylic paint. At one of the Out Stations, which is a permanent settlement, we captured a young boy who had assembled pieces of a drum set in an abandoned car, banging away like John Bonham at Wembley Stadium. The younger children chased lizards, baby kangaroos—I was hoping not for dinner—and tossed a deflating basketball through a makeshift hoop nailed to a tree as exuberantly as if they were in a shiny gym.

A primitive existence for these women and children living in the starkest conditions imaginable pulsed with an innocent, palpable joy. The children were playful and happy, the women smiling and content; only the emaciated dogs reflected the direness of a culture in the throes of death.

My adventure into the bush with Tim, Kathy and David, with Tim's daughter along as cook, was one of the highlights of this lifetime, rarified along with seeing the faces of my newborn boys and grand girls and meeting the love of my life. My Aboriginal sister, Mary Morton, changed the trajectory of my life when she extended a hand to participate in their Women's Ceremony and be the white girl dancing.

One with them, I am.

*Epilogue:*

Sadly and unfathomably the Australian producer for our documentary, *Utopian Art: A Bridge Across Time* and my script, *Alice on the Line,* the venerable Paul Smith, passed away suddenly of a massive heart attack during negotiations for production deals and distribution for the projects. Shortly after Paul's death, my son Garin disappeared for nearly two years, subsequently followed by my health crash. A mighty shadow clustered around one of the most profound spiritual/creative ventures of this life …

within that shadow lives all possibilities.

## WITCH HAIR #28.

As is true with sentient beings, houses imbue light and dark.
As a very young child I loved being in my Aunt Edna and Uncle
Strick's serene home. Newly built, warm, and well-appointed
with heirlooms, it was far more inviting than our 100-year-old,
austere farmhouse. One whiff of a slop bucket or an outdoor
toilet could send a redneck princess running for the door. I'm
guessing that was the main reason at two years old, I squalled—
my mama loved this word—begging to go home with them when
they visited, "They won't take me, they won't take me!"

The harbinger-of-bad-things-to-come house squatting among
pine trees next to an EMF-belching radio station assaulted
my six-year-old senses on first entry. To this moment, I recall
the darkness of that strange little house that I begged not to
move into.

My devoted young mother, finally mustering the courage to
escape the bends and abuses of alcoholism, had no clue the task
ahead was more than she was equipped to handle. Raising a
second-grader and kindergartener while holding down a second-
shift job at the VA Hospital was in itself challenging, even with

my daddy as somewhat of a backup. Now as a single parent armed with only a defeating experience for coping, financially or emotionally, Mama again tumbled in to a rabbit hole. Buried beneath this new burden was her lacerated heart, left battered and bleeding when forced to wrench herself from a child she loved because she couldn't afford to feed him. With this miasma of my mother's shadow in tow, we left the farm for the house in the acrid pines.

In those days there was no set protocol for finding sitters except word of mouth or newspaper ads. Forced to leave under threat, Mother was desperate to find someone willing to be at the house when we got home from school, and stay until she came home near midnight. Hoping she'd solved her dilemma, Mother rented one of the two miniscule bedrooms to my newly-married first cousin and her husband, in their early 20s and expecting a baby. It seemed like a workable solution for all concerned, but me. Sorry Mama, but I hated it all.

My cousin's husband was an opportunistic child predator. The disturbing details, involving an erect penis touching me through pajamas, have long since been excavated and eliminated, but suffice it to say, there is no harmless way of violating the boundaries of a seven year old.

I don't recall telling my mother anything about it, but somehow I suspect my pregnant cousin knew her husband was not a safe bet around children and moved out in short order, damningly, not before forever changing the life of one, or possibly more, innocents. Forty years later their first-born girl contacted me to say she believed that she'd been sexually violated by her father. I believed her and told her so and why. Her mother did not believe either one of us. Although I pointed my cousin toward many sexual healing therapies and modalities, sadly to this day she suffers from copious chronic health issues that have her nearly bed-bound.

The next live-in sitter situation was another newlywed duo, the nineteen-year-old son of Mother's best friend and his fifteen-year-old bride. What could possibly go wrong here, right? Another unstable groom with no idea what a boundary might be, coupled to a developing child desperate for affection, blew into on our lives in a gale of misery. Emotionally crippled teenagers, they splayed their sex life around the entire house with repeated fights and loud make-up sex, oblivious to innocent children caught in the wake of their dysfunction. Bless my mother that she heard me when I told her I didn't like them, and double bless my old daddy, who must have sensed the implosion of life on his children. At the end of the school year, he came pleading for Mother to come home with him. After a minor Christmas tree fire at the farmhouse, he had refurbished and modernized the kitchen and moved the toilet inside. We had an actual bathroom, no more pooping in the johnny house. Mother capitulated to his charms as she had many times over the years, before finally surrendering to the inevitable.

The live-in sitter debacle lasted less than a year, but the internalized wound of stolen innocence and shattered sexual boundaries haunted my life, losing its grip only after years of personal reconnaissance. Once sexual perimeters are violated and innocence retracted, repeat infractions come calling, magnetically attracted on a thread of prematurely awakened sexuality. One in three women is likely a misnomer. It is rare for any woman of my generation not to remember at least one perpetration.

Naturally, the breach of my innocence was not the fault of the sad little house in the pines, but a familial lineage passed from grandmother to mother to daughter. The circumstances of Mother's first impregnation ultimately resulting in the gift of my cherished new older brother were never resolved, perhaps even by her. Mother had no sense of where to plant her boundaries or if, indeed, she was entitled to any, so had no way to foster mine, tragically making Mother an unconscious instigator.

As I have noted in an earlier Witch Hair, Jungian Psychology was a palpable presence in my passage to healing. Dr. Jung purposed houses in dreams as metaphorical images, representative of containers for the self, or unconscious expression of personal identity. Jungian Psychology is rich with archetypal houses, the various rooms mirroring various emotions or complexes.

Long before the Tiny House rage, I craved a small cottage preferably on a hill with expansive views, facing South for maximum light. After moving to Los Angeles in 1990, realizing I held my breath in the kinetic mayhem, I rented a Victorian getaway cottage in Bisbee, Arizona. Just one day away through the Arizona desert, the drive gave me plenty of decompression space. Hilltop views scrolled across a picturesque dell, spilling into copper colored mountains and feeding my passion for writing. Creativity was alive and well in Bisbee, home to many artists of all genres and an inspired milieu for soul rescuing.

While my Love toured the world, I spent three years driving back and forth, splitting the months between my AZ writing haven and my LA therapy practice. I bid a sad farewell to the copper miner's cottage high on the hill to accommodate big life changes, but I never lost my yearnings to hunker alone in a tiny space to suss out what kind of write might live there.

Fifteen years later another hippy-hued art colony, this one bearing a spiritual pedigree, popped up on my radar. Crestone, Colorado is home to twenty-four spiritual-meditation centers ranging from Buddhist to Tibetan, a Carmelite monastery, several Hindu ashrams, five Zen Centers and various spin-offs of each. Nesting eleven thousand feet up in the Sangre de Cristo Mountains, it was the spiritual big sister to Bisbee.

Since there is no place better than Colorado in August, I tagged along with my Love for a music festival he was headlining there. Crestone, decidedly a destination spot, is cloistered in the foothills at the end of an eight-mile winding road off blue highway 17 in Southeastern Colorado. One way in, one way out, you're never lost, at least geographically, when in Crestone.

Echoing beings and houses, swatches of land also emit discernable energies, even for the uninitiated. Native dwellers dowsed certain spots for ritual altars and thousands of years later those same spots support cathedrals and spiritual centers. As we neared the welcome kiosk a discernable shift caught my attention.

I grabbed my Love by the arm like an excited child, "Do you feel that?"

"Feel what?" Smiling with a familiar, 'oh, no' tone.

Spiritually smitten and soaked in the diversity of the festival, I was already half in love with the iconic little village. The next morning, we were breakfasting at the aptly named, Bliss Café, an enchanting prairie cottage winked at me from the back page of a local real estate mag. The date was August 9, my birthday.

"Babe, check out this amazing little house! Let's go take a look, out of curiosity, nothing else ... I promise!"

"Please don't tell me I'm going to have to buy you a house in the middle of nowhere for your birthday," lamented my know-me-better-than-anyone-else Love, mostly not kidding.

I wrangled the realtor and an hour later was introduced to the Heatherbrae house, a two-story aqua lady, hand-built by female designers. Rising from the isolated splendor of a massive open prairie called the Baca Grants, she stole my heart. A couple of talented, intuitive women built their off- grid masterpiece on the Golden Ratio, a special number found by deducting a complicated mathematical formula based on 1.618, considered a divine proportion or esthetically pleasing number. I have no concept of how this applies to constructing a house, but the end result was irrepressible magic. Intentionally or not, the brilliant women created a piece of art, a personal temple rivaling a Rembrandt.

The isolated lot, embraced by 14,500-foot peaks of the Sangre de Cristo Mountains to both the South and West, and the graceful San Juan Mountain range to the North and East, displayed a spectacular 360-degree view of some of Mother Nature's finest towering earth altars.

Body, mind and spirit in tandem, I fell in lust with the cottage. The skillfully hand-carved, built-in everything, including couch and beds, reminded me of the interior of a sailboat. The U banquette, forged from one massive tree with the trunk supporting the table slab, easily seated six. To collect maximum solar energy, the placement of multiple banks of windows and a solar porch allowed for not only constantly streaming light, but jaw-dropping views.

My soul whispered, 'home.'

Making an offer on the house might have been a no-brainer had my partner also fallen in love. He did not. In spite of the awe- inspiring vistas he more or less disdained the whole 'isolated, dilapidated, detritus' that was Crestone. For me, purchasing a Rembrandt for a mere $90,000 at least deserved to be investigated.

Closer examination, coupled with my partners pragmatism kindled a year of angst-ridden vacillation on a buy the house/ don't buy the house emotional roller coaster. A home inspection revealed numerous costly repairs, including a new solar system and replacement of many of the hand-carved windows. As my mind eddied and churned, the little beauty ended up being auctioned off online. I idled in front of my computer, a caldron of uncertainty wallowing in, to bid or not to bid.

My Love was the one to finally admonish: "Just press enter, if the house is yours, you'll win the bid!"

During my trek around Uluru my neck froze to prevent even a peek into *Men's Business*, now my trembling finger froze on the send button. I could not seem to enter my bid and the house sold to the only other bidder. After some emotional pattering, I righted my focus to 'when a will prevails, a way will evolve' and Mama's willful little hussy took over. A few weeks later I located the winning bidder by calling the Saguache County Seat. A woman my age had purchased my Rembrandt as investment property! Yes, she would love to rent it to me for six months as soon as she finished $40,000 in repairs to a house she bought for $93,000. I have never been more in love with my partner in life than in that moment!

I didn't own a mountain-ready vehicle, so I invested in a relic Chevy Tahoe with four wheel drive and low mileage, just in case mice moved in as they are prone to do in Crestone. Many years before, Ptah, my constant traveling companion to Bisbee, sent Bo to ride shotgun in my life. Bo seemed to love Colorado as much as I did, especially the elk herds. He'd whine at the window until I let him poke his head out as herds of thirty to forty elk filed in front of us. It was a long-ass two day car trek from Southern California to Southern Colorado, a feat my Love wasn't happy to see me tackle, but our pass through the magnificent Four Corners Region and the glory ride through the open majesty of Southern Colorado reduced the trip to mostly cell phone snap ecstasy. The scenic panorama massaged the tired out of the backbreaking drive.

The prairie cottage far surpassed all my head-in-the-clouds projections. I added only a few personal pieces of furniture and accouterments and a cozy nest was mine. Most afternoons, I spent at my upstairs desk extracting journal ideas for *Witch Hairs* under the watchful spell of the mighty Sangres. Vigilant Bo kept sentinel on the deck hoping for an elk herd or better still a mountain lion to amble through the prairie grass. Friends came calling in a steady flow, so I took time to hike the stunning trails share photography expeditions in the wildflower-laden alpine meadows. The North Crestone Trail, one of the finest hiking trails in Colorado, hugs a rapid-running creek dotted with accessible waterfalls. On one afternoon hike Bo spotted a herd of calmly curious mountain goats perched high on the cliffs above us. I snapped long shots while he tried in vain to communicate. The handsome Bo, a delicious confection of retriever, chow and whatever, unconditionally loved all creatures, so nature's offspring in the wild ventured in close when we hiked together.

Crestone is the only spiritual community in the country that boasts two Stupas, which are Buddhist shrines used as repositories for venerated monk's ashes. Nine thousand feet up the mountain on a dirt road called Spirit Highway, the Big Stupa stands as regal custodian of the vast prairie. Monks and other practitioners intensified their meditation by coursing the circumference of the base until bypassing the mind. As I circled the big Stupa, Bo dutifully followed, meditating behind me.

I took full advantage of the proximity to the Zen Centers and hiked several times to the unusual Ziggurat, a spiral-shaped structure modeled on the temples of ancient Babylon. Placed as it was in the middle of an open prairie, it seemed more demonstrative of a donation from a passing space vehicle than Mesopotamian antiquity. Along with the picturesque Great Sand Dunes National Park, which I could see from my deck, the shrines around the area attracted seekers from all around the world.

The attractive diversity of the audience at the music festival was mirrored at the Bliss Café, one of two good places to get healthy organic food. In addition to tasty locally sourced meat and veggies, the Bliss served a potpourri of colorful characters: a six-and-a-half-feet-tall Rasta dude, with knotted dreads that added another foot of height, scintillating fresh-faced Tibetan Monks decked maroon and saffron robes, dusty chain smoking cattle wranglers, vibrant earth women, mamas and quality of life acclimatized children, along with steady steams of hikers, climbers and seekers. Crestone was a living microcosm of cross culturalism.

In early June I awoke to a summer snowstorm blanketing the region with seven inches in one hour. As a pioneering prairie novice, grasping the necessity of sweeping snow accumulation off the solar panels to maintain energy banking, I felt dutifully efficient and self-sustaining, but the reality of gouging a half foot of frozen crystals off my heat source while my feet froze in non-mountain foot wear was social media fodder.

The sun's tango with snow-capped peaks as it drifted behind the mighty Sangre range whispered me out of the house every afternoon streaming oh-my-gods behind me. Snuggling all but eyes and nose under my down comforter in my hand carved bed, sitting eye-level with the sky, communing with the Milky Way and bits of my own DNA, kept me from having to fire up the wood stove at night.

All things considered, I grew pretty damn confident that I was cut out to be a mountain woman scribe.

Yet I had now been in Crestone for six weeks and had only managed to generate twenty pages of *Witch Hairs*, falling far short of my projections and sales pitch to my Love. Here, it occurs to me, either as excuse or self-rationalization, I have neglected to mention that my first month in the house was spent with a solo carpenter tediously completing the costly refurbishing project. Pounding hammers, shrill saws and spewing dust pounded the sanctum and my psyche. The owner, who'd promised the project would be completed by my arrival, was more sanctimonious about the protracted work than I appreciated, but hey, I occupied my birthday dream house; what could go wrong?

At long last, when silence descended, I was finally able to fully immerse in this project, BOOM! Unbelievable! My computer crashed, potentially wiping *Witch Hairs*. I was not only unable to continue writing, but doubled over in panic, not knowing if my work could be recovered. The nearest computer expert was three hours away, in Colorado Springs, so reluctantly, Bo and I made yet another exhausting drive back to Ventura for a new hard drive.

Two weeks later, new innards for my computer and mounting trepidation on both our parts, Bo and I gassed up the Tahoe for our return to utopia. Pesky visions of being stranded in the scorching desert in July buzzed about like Australian black flies.

I swatted.

This brings up one of the complex challenges of trusting intuition. Is it my fear that the car won't make it, and if so will feeling my fear manifest what I fear, or is my Higher Self giving me fair warning, 'my dear One, the car won't make it'?

What gloriously relevant vacillations.

Bo and I drove out of Ventura on a late July Sunday morning. We'd made it a full thirty minutes to Santa Clarita when the car made a groaning noise taking off from a light. My intuition was pretty clear about turning around, but I called my Love, my earthbound guidance, to ask what to do. Alas, he's in Norway. While I'm ranting away about the growling noise and the blistering heat, I'm pulled over for talking on a cellphone. $100 ticket. Lucky me; it could have been $500 without the tears and an explanation that defied congruence to the baffled cop. My Love advised me to "be easy on take off."

The aged Tahoe purred along all the way to Needles, reputed to be the hottest place in the country in summer. No arguments from me; it was an inferno. I turned off for gas and after a fillup, big blue bomb declined to start. The Shell woman person says, "Just let'er sit, Hon, it's 116; they don't like the heat either." I let'er sit for five minutes, she starts perfectly, and off I drive toward Kingman. All gas stations should hire women, and the stretch of I-40 between Needles and Kingman is no man's land, unfit for even rattlesnakes.

About half way to Kingman with cruise control on, the tank-like SUV launched into a lurch fit, coughing and making racket like an eighty-year-old chain smoker. I wrestled it to the side of the freeway, checked the GPS and I'm in the only stretch on I-40 where there is nothing but baked rattlesnakes for fifty miles. Here I recall saying to my Love, 'what if that fucker stops somewhere between Needles and Kingman?' I'm pretty sure I heard Siri say, 'Oh shit!' A desperate glance at the thermometer on the mirror and it's screaming 118. I maintained enough composure, albeit with visibly shaking hands and knees to hit 911, detailing my location. To which, the unflappable operator apathetically replied, "Well, Ma'am, we'll try to get an officer there sometime soon."

"No!" I screeched, "You must be far more positive than that! It's 118 degrees, I won't last long out here, nor will my 13-year-old dog!"

I called Honey in Norway, where by now it was 3:00 a.m. to tell him where I was in case he needed to find our bones.

My Honey, my Love, my Angel, got on the phone and located his keyboard player, John Jarvis, living in Bullrun City, about forty miles away, and gave him my location in case 911 forgot about me.

Meanwhile, I'm wilting fast, my tee is soaked through and Bo is looking at me like, "Ok, Humanperson, this is where you do something, right?"

I tried restarting the car and it sorta-kinda leapfrogged along at about 5 mph, racketing Bo all over the back. We had limped about a half a mile on the shoulder, when I spotted something glinting in the sun. "Oh, my goddess and all the angels of mercy, don't let that be a mirage!" A weigh station sign declared itself to be a half-mile away. Open! It says open! Oh, please don't be lying; they lie, they lie, please, not this time.

Thirty scalding breath-robbing, heart-pounding, death-defying minutes later, the Tahoe groaned up a ramp at the open weigh station, just as a patrol car pulled up behind. Bo and I, both soppy, addled and scared, dripped sweat into the station where two young officers took a few beats to look up. After finding my ability to inhale again and getting Bo into a small back office with a tiny window air conditioner, I dialed AAA. I have no real understanding of why this took three hours other than the border town issue, Needles is in California and Kingman is in Arizona. We were literally in the middle of nofuckingwhere. Finally I got a call back from the AAA dispatcher assuring me the tow truck driver would be calling in forty one to sixty seven minutes. I dung you not.

Two sweltering, it's 84 degrees IN the station, hours later Tow Truck Dude rang to ask if my dog would fit in his truck. "Dude, it's a dog not a horse!" He again assures me he'll be there in sixty-one minutes. I lost all sense of decorum and begged for mercy. That put him arriving at 9:00. Bo and I had now been in the semi-cooled weigh station for six arduous, nerve-racking hours with nothing to eat but energy bars for me; he, of course, was well fed.

Meanwhile, my hero, piano virtuoso, John Jarvis, had called several times to check on us, promising he's on the way, but is a desert hour away. I ask the officer and his sidekick where best to have the car towed, back to Needles, to Kingman, or perhaps to the rim of the Grand Canyon?

At 9:01 p.m., this time good to his word, Tow Truck Dude arrives right on time. I stepped out into the now 108-degree desert, as he blundered out of his massive truck, proudly blazing 'Steve's Towing' across the door.

Offering a sweaty hand, "Hi Steve, I'm Dixie ..."

"I'm Shimmy," Tow Truck Jimmy slurred, clasping mine with a clammy palm. A cloud of alcohol stink wafted around my head as he swayed my way. Holy shit, he's drunk! Tow Truck Dude is soused!

I trounced back in the station, disabled of what little patience I might usually claim, "I'm not going anywhere with this dude, he's fucking drunk!"

Policeman, "Seriously? I'll go talk to him."

I stayed put with my head in my iPad trying to figure out where to tow the Tahoe, Bo and myself. I checked outside and there's Shimmy, squatting handcuffed on the curb in the 106 degree heat. Mother Theresa Complex kicks in, I asked the station cop, "please take him some cold water."

My knight in shining armor, one of the best piano players in the country, galloped up in a cooled down Prius, alongside his brother Steve, in his matching Prius. They started reloading my Love's instruments, which I'm attempting to get to Colorado for his performances, in my Joad-family-packed ailing SUV. At 10 p.m. the desert pulsed heat so sizzling that I'm light headed, hovering on fainting, and beyond rank smelling.

The remote weigh station did not have a budget for a breathalyzer kit, so Tow Truck Shimmy, now momentarily out of handcuffs, struggles to touch his nose and walk a parking lot line while we waited on the Arizona Highway Patrol to deliver a kit. I couldn't watch; I truly felt sorry for the Dude.

The dual Prius chariots were successfully loaded (good thing there was two of them), and at long last Bo and I, safe with our piano playing rescue team, were bound for Lake Havasu, for the closest and reportedly the best mechanic in the area, according to Tow Truck Shimmy, anyway.

Our Prius caravan arrived in the Red Neck Riviera of Lake Havasu, home of the London Bridge, at 11:00 p.m. AAA, which my friend, Pam Rose, suggested should drop one A, informed me the Tahoe made it, towed by Steve himself sometime after midnight. I know not whether Tow Truck Shimmy spent the rest of the night sleeping it off in jail, or his bed. I hoped for the latter because the mechanic he recommended rocked.

Two nights and days in a furnace, where I had to carry Bo to potty to not blister his pads, two catalytic converters, one fuel pump and $1,700 later, not counting food and hotel, we were back on I-40, shooting for Gallup.

Three hours and a bit over halfway to Gallup suddenly the steering falls loose and lax, like steering a boat on placid water or a car on slick ice. Denial lasted until I tested it out by kid steering it around and the wheels barely turned. FUCK! I called on both Higher Selves to report the steering issue, one now in Germany and the other on higher floors, to help me pilot the cumbersome vehicle. I circled the blue bastard in more light than my average plane flight and pressed on to Gallup. Bo and I crashed at a pet friendly Sleep Inn. The next morning I googled, 'shitty steering in a Chevy Tahoe that really should be at the bottom of a canyon' and read, "dangerous, if it breaks, you can't steer the car."

I GPS the shipwreck to a Pep Boys in Gallup, where pundits suggested without a definitive diagnosis, pittman arm, idler arm and a coupler, none of which they had in stock. Anyway, one young Native shyly informed me, their air compressor was broken so they couldn't put the car on a lift to further diagnose or repair it, and someone might be coming to fix it an hour ago. I opted to take my chances and drive on to Albuquerque for a Chevy dealer, dropped it off, then googled to find a pet friendly Best Western, which turned out to be a kennel where dogs could bring their humans.

Got a bright and early call from Richard at the Chevy dealer. Without trying to sound like I know what I'm talking about, I'll just say the list of things wrong with the steering mechanism was staggering and would run, if all went well, tada! $1,700. See a pattern here?

My not-so-kind response to soft-spoken Richard: "I will Thelma and Louise that fucker off the nearest canyon before I spend another dime on it!"

"I don't blame you, Ma'am." And with that I was off to Taos, then on to Crestone, beseeching everyone in the entire Cosmos who could tune in to help me steer.

Turning into the now-greened property, glowing in lavender bee-balm, at first sight watery eyes, rinsed the surge of detritus from the besieged trip back. The familiar joy at being at the foot of my mountains rushed over me and I let a thousand miles of pent-up stress roll as I unpacked the suffering car. Exhausted in every way a human could be, I fell into bed at 7:00, soothed by the dark silence. Some hours of deep sleep later, I was roused by voices and strains of rock music. Was I dreaming? How could it be, when in the Grants section of the Baca Grand, the structures within sound range were an uninhabited yurt and teepee? Half asleep, I struggled upright in my expansive view bed as it occurred to me that maybe the stress of the past five days had rustled up some of the same kind of voices Garin hears. But then half-mast eyes caught the eerie glow of a fire, striking a match of fear that even in my present state, I was forced to go outside and check out. A bonfire. A dozen or more revelers and a bonfire. A prairie grass fire was and is Crestone's living nightmare. Summer fires are strictly verboten, there's one way in and one way out. What was happening?

With the morning sun, I could see my new neighbors three lots away, a rickety RV pulled backward into the lot and a white growing tent setup. The illegal legal marijuana growers had started moving in on the easily purchased cheap lots in the Grants.

Time for me to go.

As the sun faded to Fall dim, and winter's shadow lurked, so did the inevitable shadow side of my love affair with Crestone and the house.

The next year, willful fixer that I am, I took one more stab at renting the sweet house for the month of August. My Love and I had barely settled in bed when we both were startled by noxious fumes wafting out the vents and had to frighteningly escape for a room at the Bliss Hotel. It was mold, my health nemesis that can be a dangerous stalker. No way to be in a mold proliferated house. With August booked a year in advance, I was attempting to ride out my final three weeks hopscotching around to various available rooms, when I got a call from my niece, Sandra Mussen, that my brother Reid would not be around three months as we were told, I had only days to get there to say goodbye.

The curtain fell on my love affair with Crestone, Colorado.

For thousands of years spiritual pilgrims like myself have been drawn to places of high energy to meditate, to soul search, to pray, to create, recreate and to recover redemption and atonement. But what I had to discover hidden in the grassy prairie adorning the mighty mountains was that spiritual muscle amplifies not just the light, but equally the shadow. I imagined my time in Crestone to be six months writing in the pure bliss of nirvana and scholarship of the Absolute. But my halcyon lay buried in the voice of the shadow and the experiences waiting for me there.

The pokey carpenter driving nails in my write, the death of a hard drive threatening these stories, the vehicle that seemed destined to descend to the bottom of a canyon—which I still drive—a landlady of dubious character nipping at my composure, and a stampede of illegal, legal pot growers poaching my peace, all served to subjugate my power to act or react. I'm human and did both.

But it's not about what happened in this or any of my light or dark Witch Hairs, the gleaning is in the insight, understanding and acceptance of the pitfalls put before me. I mined gold, not in the scintillating light, but in the dirt and dust balls hiding in the dark corners: the pratfalls and pitfalls, the devastation of addiction, mental illness, sexual perpetration, the death of my mother and the untimely loss of a newly found beloved brother. Vortexes like Crestone, Uluru and the great Utopia Region, serve as a sieve to mine the priceless gems by lifting each undergo, each suffer, each endure to a higher floor, an illumined floor with an expansive view.

With all my Fixer heart, I hope some part and particle of these stories, some of which have defied belief, have opened your eyes, deepened your breath, and lifted your spirit to a floor filled with unimpeded perception. Perhaps my personal view might be an invitation to step on the elevator and push the up button.

Gestated in the lofty eddies of the Sangre de Cristo Mountains, these Witch Hairs impregnated with the ancient genetic codes of the region, exalted my life to an ultimately challenging, frightening, exhilarating, out on a limb undertaking—the sharing of these words. Words once released cannot be taken back.

Rounding full circle to *The Other* and *The Five*, (the 'woo-woo' eyeroll zone), for thirty-five years I petitioned the Cosmos for one more glimpse, one more touch or even a swift bypass.

Amid gut churning vulnerability and doubt while pulling these chronicles from my journals, at long last, The Five revisited. Not in a meditative state as before, but in a walk through the door, 'we're here to give permission to share' sort of way. I trust The Five will have my back when the inherent shadow side of extracting these Witch Hairs descends.

And so it is that I stand on the edge of everything … with my Love.

## WITCH HAIR #29.

He said his name was John.

For nearly two years any John that ventured into my orbit was fodder for perusal, based on name only. Once I flew to San Diego to meet a potential *that* John. Was I chasing an apparition? Did I imagine telling him, it didn't matter who he was, "this is everything"?

The dusty corners, swept into piles and scooped into the trash bin, I declared myself ready for vibrant, healthy love to step in. Most therapeutic modalities had been tapped, and I had been baptized in the eddy of addiction and codependency, and was not pulled into the undertow. I felt love worthy for the first time in my adult life.

So where was the elusive John, who had descended on me from the Cosmos?

During the previously mentioned years after the Big Split, I took a leap of blind faith into a personal publishing venture after exiting Warner Bros and the corporate world. My friend Katy

Bee, former radio personality-music journalist, and I decided to create a stable of what would now be termed Americana artists for management. Lewis Storey was one of the artists.

One morning Katy showed up at the office with a Frets magazine in hand.

"Look at this beautiful guy", she gushed, "he's in a new band called the Desert Rose Band with Chris Hillman and Herb Pedersen, a classically trained musician with a music pedigree. You're good with men, you have to help me with this one!"

I glanced at the magazine.

BOOM!

Knees buckled, I'm kneeling on the office floor, head spinning wildly, nausea creeping in to my throat.

It was HIM!

I'd never been more certain of anything than when I looked at the way too young, sculpted face with a chin dimple shining back at me.

"Are you ok?" Katy laughed, oblivious.

"Yes, this photo reminded me of someone I've met before, but then I realize … perhaps not." Stumbling over myself as I lied out loud.

"Well, let's come up with a plan so I can meet him and maybe we can double-date sometime." A few months later, Katy had managed her own rendezvous with John Jorgenson, the Desert

Rose Band guitar wizard. She traveled to a DRB show in Copper Mountain Colorado, I'm guessing it was in 1987, where John passed her a cassette of a studio album he produced as a duet project with the California Queen of 'Colorful Hillbilly,' Rose Maddox, of the Maddox Brothers and Rose, circa 1930s -1950s.

"I really want you to hear this project," Katy insisted. "Rose Maddox is a California legend; she's 62 and John is 31, and they sound magical together!"

We listened, me mesmerized, not only by the clarity and innocence in the duets, but the enchanting dynamic between the two of them. They sounded as if they had been singing together for a hundred lifetimes.

"We have to get a deal for this project!" I shot, ignoring the fact that THE John was the producer and artist and what was I going to do with all that?

I decided a phone conversation was necessary to determine if the project was, indeed, free to be shopped to labels and if so, were Katy and I cleared to represent him. Expecting to knee buckle again when I heard his voice, I braced.

No need, it was a straight ahead business conversation in which he explained that at the moment a musician friend was representing the music, but if nothing firm developed, he would let me know.

Fair enough … and was that *really* the voice I heard in my out of body experience? A few doubts drifted in … so good, maybe he was Katy's prey after all and geezus, how old was he, twenty-one?

The Desert Rose Band's eponymous debut album had their first chart hit, "Ashes of Love," and were scheduled to play the venerable Station Inn. Katy laid out a strategy to conquer.

"Come with me to see the band, and I can introduce you to John Jorgenson after the show," she strategized. "Then we'll take him to breakfast the next morning … and I can drive him back to his hotel."

Thinking to myself, 'I don't even like that band.' Leonard Cohen himself could not have dragged me to the Station Inn that night if Katy had not been my business partner. There was simply no excuse short of the ER that would have sufficed. So I hid under a head obscuring cap, which I hardly resort to even on bad hair days, a Jack Webb belted overcoat, which I pulled out of the closet unworn, and wonkily managed somewhat incognito to the Station Inn.

Once my eyes, still behind sunglasses, adjusted to the darkened preshow room, I froze. HE was on stage tuning.

BOOM! Here it comes again … airy knees, trembling hands and sweaty palms, wrapped in wilting will. Jerking all doubt aside stood in the flesh the *being* who lowered his energy down to me and when I asked, "Who are you?" said, "well, I'm John." Wordlessly questioning my memory.

I numbly squirmed through a skilled if not thrilling set, except for virtuosic guitar playing, intricate sibling blend harmonies, and well-written country-ish songs.

Well, maybe a tad thrilling.

Afterward, Katy pushed us through the clusterfuck around John, introducing me as her business partner she'd been telling him about, who 'knows everyone in town.' I lamely poked a paw through my overwhelming overcoat and gamely croaked, 'hi,' careful to avoid eye contact, lest I lapse into the vapors again. John later confessed how underwhelmed he was with 'Cousin It,' her devouring costume, and pale personality.

As promised/threatened, Katy had arranged a breakfast meeting to discuss the *Johnny and Rose* recording. I dawdled, managing to be nearly thirty minutes late, which was not my usual business modus, further undermining Katy's glowing assessment of my lofty status. I granted Katy ample flirting space, avoiding eye contact, arm touching or seeping-through-cracks charm. John, on the other hand, easily conversed with a quietly centered confidence, without a hint of egoism or pretense, an unusual preternaturally nice persona. Not even on the same planet with any personality I had even been attracted to in the past.

As instructed, I gave Katy space to pounce when she dropped John off at his hotel, although he effused nothing but old-fashioned innocence during our meeting. Either he was already attached, was the best looking geek I'd ever met, or the most oblivious boy/man with his head in the clouds and his feet firmly on the ground, or all of the above.

A few weeks passed and I got a call from John, letting me know the *Johnny and Rose* project was available to pitch around town. Exciting news, since I had fallen in love with everything about it, the way his voice not only uncannily blended with hers, but expressed respect and admiration for her in every note. The freshness and integrity of the arrangements and instrumentation blazed light years ahead of most Nashville production. Ten years as a music executive and with the exception of Lewis, I'd never heard anything quite so uniquely compelling and artistic, yet commercially viable. I shuttled aside the nagging question of whether he was or wasn't THE John, not only because Katy still had her plans, but the music and getting it heard became paramount.

Business communication between John and me instinctively evolved to longer and longer conversations, and had begun to drift into more personal, tinged with spiritual overtones. One afternoon Katy noted the length of our business conversations and called me out.

"Why is it that John calls you to check on the progress of the project and not me?"

"Well … I don't know," I tap-danced, "maybe you need to ask him."

I adored Katy, but no bewitched spiel would help her understand or relate to the cosmic connection John and I had apparently committed, so, once again, I punted.

A friend from a women's support group, one of several I'd joined after the Big Split, had offered me her villa in Cancun as a retreat from my current Nashville reality. After a year of putting it off, I said yes. I invited a supportive couple, besties at the time who seemed firmly ensconced in their marriage to come along for ten days. I put off setting a date hoping I wouldn't have to be a third wheel on my own vacation. During the month of making up my mind, John and I were having deeper and more frequent conversations, sometimes lasting for hours. One, which ended with a spontaneous, "I love you" from him, caught me completely off-guard. I think I might have replied, "yeah, I love you, too," but more not to leave a hanging space than a meaningful response.

Finally my married friends and I narrowed down a few dates and the trip was officially on. In a rare afternoon conversation with John, as usual starting with business about his potential production deal and ending in an exponentially more personal tone, I heard myself blathering:

"I have a friend's villa in Cancun and have invited my favorite couple. Would you like to meet us there?" I channeled from somewhere in the Constellation of Pleiades.

"Sure, I'd like to do that; just let me know the dates," he rattled off in a roll of the dice. John later confided he'd caught buckets of shit from the band for missing a photo shoot to come to the Yucatan.

I knew why.

We had not seen each other's face since the discombobulated breakfast meeting two months previous. As if perfectly orchestrated by the Universe, my friends had a throw down the gauntlet fight, which sadly was the beginning of the end of their marriage. I was either going to paradise alone or with a man who said his name was John who had patiently waited in the ethers for me.

Shortly after moving to the first Big Marrowbone house, I was packing for the trip while pondering various renditions of bed attire, ranging from 'we got this' to 'meet my new friend.' I had no idea if John would actually show and if so, where our spiritual rendezvous would lead. I sought male advice from an artist friend, Michael Sokolis, who was adding seductive iridescent paint to my bedroom walls. I held up each nightie for a thumbs up, or thumbs down.

"Well, if he is actually a male, any of those will likely work!" Michael winked.

I built in a week to de-stress and work on my tan before my cosmic connection was due to arrive. Again, not knowing if I was picking up my new best friend or my forever love, I skirted the divide with low cut harem type pants, midriff top and a cap for the open top jeep, piled with snorkeling gear in the boot.

The Aero Mexico flight from LA was painstakingly slow to unload. Aiming for casual while defying my heart to flutter out of my chest, I noticed the disembarking was down to stragglers, then the crew.

In a single flash of fury, any testosterone-laden human being who had ever crossed my path condensed into a tsunami sized wave of rage. "FUCK MEN!" I bellowed sending a shock wave reverberating around the tiny airport, ducking as it echoed across the metal rafters and back with tears in the wake.

A female desk attendant who apparently witnessed the dismantling of my shaky trust glanced a half-knowing, half-pitying smile. I took it as an invitation.

"Was there a John Jorgenson on that flight?" I pleaded through still leaky eyes.

"Well, I'm not supposed to divulge the manifest, but apparently he did not make it on the flight," she who probably knew the scenario well, explained as she showed me the passenger list. "Maybe he is on the next flight, due in four hours?"

I knew that she knew the likelihood of whatever he was to become in my life arriving on the next flight was slim to none, but women, especially witchy women, know how to be present when circumstances beckon.

Four hours later, I repeated the same vigil with no pretense of nonchalance. John was the fourth person off the plane, looking all of eighteen years old, with a red sweat shirt, jogging pants and red high top sneakers … hot yes, but *young*. But what the hell, in that moment I was 27, at least warm on the Fahrenheit scale and ready for a romp in paradise. This man/boy traveled for a living, yet he missed a vacation flight for five days in the Yucatan with a possible paramour. Priorities? Fear? Shit happens? No, the musician who had traveled the world since he was eleven had forgotten his passport.

Cancun was blissful. There was visual beauty, spiritual togetherness and magical talismans all converging in the heart of the Yucutan Peninsula. The fully staffed, five bedroom seaside villa was a kindness from a generous friend, but the two mini, five-feet-tall pyramids on the roof were a gift from the Beneficent. Snorkeling in Xel-Ha Park was first on my preplanned agenda, where I noted that John not only had lovely gracefully digits but legs to compliment, and he silently noted that I was a hand full. Ending our first dinner at the villa, a typical taco affair, albeit handmade by our sweet but non-English-speaking staff, we both noted a small pile of mushrooms on either side of our plates. Affirmation number one that this could, indeed, be THE John.

That first full-moon-soaked evening was as magical as our pre-destined astral convergence might suggest. Brought together, most appropriately, by a song. My friend Rodney Crowell had written "Old Dancin' Couple" years before he knew he was my friend on my birthday.

John had been hired by the publisher of that and other Crowell compositions to re-demo the song, adding his guitar touch in hopes of the publisher snagging a cover by a major artist. John played the demo for me while we relaxed against twin personal pyramids under a luminous full moon. The antiquity of our connection was clearly narrated by Rodney in the words of the song.

The immensity and synchronicity was a Cosmic explosion, the kind that forms new planets and black holes.

I knew.

As the song ended, I wondered if John knew what I knew. I knew he did, he just didn't know that he knew what I knew, I mused, then reminded myself that it was John who came to me, not vice versa. I held my breath in hopes he'd suddenly remember and our love would blossom in a blazing burst of recall spurred by the song, the moon and the pyramids. Shaken, I struggled not to startle him with my awareness of just how infinitely, witchy and miraculous that moment was.

John stuck to obliviousness.

The moon had drifted to the other side of the ocean and John was tired from travel and snorkeling, so we attempted to say goodnight. As I reached up to hug goodnight, he is 6'2", John looked down. Two familiar lips met … yet again. No strangers here. No more questions, no more doubts. The 'which nightie dilemma' was rendered moot.

Our physical coupling was genuine, natural and tender, echoing the music I had just heard coming from him. Magic hands, he made love like he played, skillfully, confidently and sensitively. Afterward I felt as frightened as I was fulfilled. Frightened because I sensed I had just made love with an already married man.

"You're married," my mouth waged before my heart could catch up. "You're not available to me, you already have a love of your life."

"Uh, no, I haven't been in a relationship for months now." He pushed back.

"You're married to your muse, Guitar Man."

Outwardly he resisted, but I intuitively sensed it in his touch and knew it was deeply fortified in his identity. The omnipotent muse, his constant companion since he was four years old, was his paramour, sexual partner, and guiding light. She held his soul in her reserve. He had nothing he could offer except the gift of the moment. I was frightened. I knew I wanted more.

True, our four-day rendezvous in paradise was unmitigated magic, but more emphatically, it surpassed anything rekindling a new old love could possibly produce. We braved scaling the big pyramid at Chichen Itza, then spent hours rambling amongst the pre-Columbian Mayan ruins and the foreboding Sacred Cenote, where virgins sacrificed by the Mayans lay entombed. We stole kisses on the bluffs of Tulum overlooking the wildly beautiful Caribbean, and Christmas shopped at the Merida Market. To say our initial days together were coated in romantic platitudes and prolonged eye-gazing as one might surmise, not quite true. It became more and more clear that ours was a love forged in the ethers of time, a spiritual connection designed to be grounded to earth, not a physical connection destined to be actualized spiritually.

On our road trip from Cancun to Chichen Itza, I pulled out *The Book of Questions* by Gregory Stock and proceeded to pry John with crowbar probes, stumbling across an intriguingly appropriate question: If you had agreed to be assigned to spend six months in Antarctica with no other human around and could choose one person to go with you, who would that be? John barely blinked.

"Well, I guess it would have to be someone who played."

I closed the Book of Questions momentarily pinned to my seat. I had just found out all I needed to know about my cosmic love, validating my intuitive declaration after our first lovemaking. Our reconnected souls fit like long missing pieces of our life puzzle and our bodies followed that lead, but our hearts held on for dear life.

After leaving Cancun and feeding our escalating phone addiction for a month, I traveled to John's space in Southern California. M. L. Benoit, a witchy woman and deep friend was making a rough transition to the other realms and needed me by her side. I was curious to find if the alchemy of the Yucatan could sustain in the City of Lost Angels. Reality seemed to wear well. We laughed, we loved and we grieved. We shared M. L's recalcitrant exit from the earth. What was intended to be a weeklong visit turned into three. I was afraid of being the guest that wouldn't leave. Like our lovemaking, each moment was comfortable, communicative, fun and real.

I savored John's newly awakened intuition and untethered expression of his feminine, tucking it in my positive pocket. On the day before M. L. finally slipped out of her body, John suggested taking me to Disneyland, I had never been, so our inner children could escape the over arching aura of loss. Because my childhood past rode like a Disney roller coaster, John, whose child thrived front and center, guided us around the park. Having cut his musical performance teeth there, he knew the nooks and crannies of the joy grafted into the commercialism. At the end of a day of pure child's play, my jaw ached from grinning.

During those initial weeks I found myself acutely aware of swimming in the birth of a new life while drowning in the dying strains of my golden times with M. L. Sometimes the conflicting emotions were overwhelming and I was anesthetized to any feelings at all. My suddenly fragile heart aroused old fears, urging me to lunge for the exit door and the next plane home. I was adept at escaping into the night.

Vulnerability, feeling far too accessible to life's pokes and jabs, raised my neediness quotient and I struggled mightily not to abandon myself. I had not spent the past five years painstakingly finding myself only to abandon her for a relationship, not even one birthed in the Great Cosmos. My mind screamed not to fall in love with this man/child, while my body pulsed with the rhythm of just having been played like a fine instrument. Meanwhile, my trusted inner voice, in most harmonious tones, spoke unwaveringly with the admonition, "walk the shallow shores, don't venture into deeper waters; he can't swim."

Twice I took swimming lessons in the deep end. I could swim, though not strong enough to sustain either of my marriages.

Meanwhile, the Desert Rose Band cranked out number one records and John's visibility and credibility as a virtuosic musician won him numerous awards. I had not been seen in the biz world with a date since the Big Split five years before, so our debut as a couple at a number one extravaganza for DRB, played like an old Hedda Hopper column. Nashville and LA music folk were casting knowing smiles and raised eyebrows. I felt confident in our presentation as a couple, despite an age disparity. I recall loving the way John looked that auspicious night, sensual and innocent, with just enough edge to make you want to touch to see if it was velvet or steel.

He was both.

I returned to Nashville after M. L.'s memorial with plans to see John two weeks later when he came for studio work. Two days later he called.

"Do you want to meet me in New York for the Grammy's … tomorrow?"

We managed to walk literally into each other that evening in LaGuardia, arriving nearly at the same time, picking up where we left off two days previously on the other side of the country. The lights of the city were open and inviting, and the lobby of the Hilton was bustling with excited nominees and proud peep suits. Michael Jackson was the featured performer on the show, and although DRB did not win their nomination category, John and I sparkled in the inaugural New York launch of our couple-ship.

Although occasionally still dancing with some doubts about John's head-in-the-clouds innocence compared to my potholed path, the nagging voice of my original assessment that he was already in a committed relationship chattered relentlessly. This beautiful thirty-one-year-old was emotionally attached to his muse and had not yet found his heart.

Initially we flew around the long distance relationship, John in Southern California and me in Tennessee's serene Marrowbone Valley, with relative ease, spurred by his band thriving in the Nashville market. Success mounted in spite of the fact that the Music Row door was never completely ajar for West Coast country, as proven by talents like Buck Owens and potential superstars like The Maddox Brothers and Rose. Merle Haggard simply kicked the door in with his incredible voice. John took chart success in a calm stride, remaining focused on creating and performing, his essential self.

I, on the other hand, although deeply rooted on the beautiful Marrowbone was running out of money. Gamble Companies, my personally financed publishing venture created to sign Lewis had reaped nothing but several narrow misses for huge cuts by the reigning king, Garth Brooks. The goddess of music was not smiling and I knew it.

While my head tried to figure a way out of my financial crunch, my fear-induced emotions were vacillating beyond my control. My heart was in Southern California, my soul firmly anchored to my creek, animals and garden on the Marrowbone. A forty-year-old woman in an existential crisis, or one being firmly guided to her own highest good … a dueling dilemma.

I wasn't enamored with the follow-the-band, sit-with-the-band wives life style required to be in a relationship with a musician, mainly because I had been there and done that in my first marriage. Any residual music groupie luster had long since dulled. But when John invited me to join him in picturesque Lake Tahoe for a show—all of the wives were coming—I went because I missed him and we followed a twice a month protocol to see each other. Having nothing at all to do with the lovely women they are, I have never been more psychologically twitchy than sitting in a casino show room with the other wives. A dark feeling of déjà vu stalked the entire evening. By the time we were back in the hotel room, where ostensibly romance waited, I was admittedly distracted, but as with most new relationships, intimacy would have salved the fear. For whatever reason—John was tired from traveling, not happy with the show, distracted by something a particular band member said or did, or simply wasn't in the mood—whatever fueled choices made that evening kindled my doubts into a bonfire of vanity.

The next morning at breakfast, I ended our relationship.

Scheduled to fly back to Nashville early that afternoon, sobbing uncontrollably, I barely maneuvered through the airport. The woman at the airline desk offered to call for help. My heart suffered a deathlike loss. In spite of fighting for public decorum,

I wept with unconscious abandon all over the airport. Paranoid that I might have a forty-year-old heart attack, I called Sharon Dougan, a psychotherapist in Seattle, and inner circle friend, who also was in a relationship with a younger Cancer man, a whopping seventeen years her junior.

"I just broke up with John," I moaned through unmanageable mucous dribbling on the floor by the pay phone. "I don't know what to do, I can't stop crying."

"Well, you might as well fly up here, because I just broke up with Dan and we can cry together." Matter of fact, even in an emotional crisis, Sharon, a fellow Leo, and I traveled on mostly parallel paths without plans or intention. When my marriage to my boys' father ended in 1975, we shared a duplex in Nashville, Sharon and her two boys on top and me and my two on the bottom. Her boys were the same age as mine and we have remained close friends and traveling companions through the years. Over the next few days a couple of witches rescued each other from a cardiac event.

The dramatic, on my part, break up was interrupted when John had a show in Nashville a few weeks later. On a frigid night in January we shivered hand in hand strolling down Big Marrowbone Road with only a big hanging moon lighting our way, and with a single over the shoulder glance, my heart righted. Something about a female-receptive male wearing a vintage leather jacket, or maybe it was the chin dimple or the easy way he laughed, whatever it was, in that moment I lost my resolve to fight love.

My financial noose tightened to the point I was forced to close my Music Row office. I ghost-walked the humbling task of asking for a job, a highly public ego audit for a former corporate president. Thankfully, the previous five years of daily meditation and cosmic forays into other realms had created a manifestation maven. Not only had John and I finally found the right door, so did a job. An old friend in Durham, NC was starting a record label and needed an A&R person to feed the creative coffers. I commuted back and forth for nearly a year until the funding, as frequently happens, dried up for the fledgling label. A frightening path, one I had long denied loomed large, barely flush with immediate funds, I had no job.

By 1990, after nearly three years of long distance dallying both John and I knew it was in the cards to take another step forward, but I didn't want that step to be Southern California and he felt equally adamant about Nashville, a conundrum offering just one example of our plethora of contrasts and contradictions. We were two people who simply could not be more opposite: he, an extroverted performer destined for a world stage; me, an introverted closeted creative who needed a spatial environment. John had penetrated one constellation and his soul thrived in it: music. My soul, on the other hand, need a four dimensional space to inhale. Los Angeles had barely breathable air.

Air quality not withstanding, I leased out the Big Marrowbone house, packed my belongings, my yellow dog Ptah and off we drove in a U-Haul truck bound for a vintage Craftsman cottage in West Hollywood. One of the most beautiful of all spiritually sanctioned places to live, the magical Marrowbone Valley where I had spent the happiest few years of this life, receded in the rearview, for love forged from the ethers of time.

My heart was breaking.

Ours was not a soft landing. I was both impressed and depressed when John and I experienced our first homemaking disagreement. I had no previous conditioning with a man who actually cared not only about his furniture, but where it was placed in the house. We both assumed our collected treasures, mine through two marriages, his more recent, but none-the-less representative of his history, would fit into a 1700-square-foot house. A storage bin and fruitful compromise finally resolved our first major issue.

I could only wish it was that simple moving forward.

In 1991, after the Bush administration orchestrated the needless insanity of the Gulf War, black motorist Rodney King was captured on camera being brutally beaten by LA Police officers. The acquittal of those officers in 1992 triggered a five-day riot that left more than 50 dead, and 2,000 injured. Our sweet house sat a block off Sunset Boulevard, and just six blocks from the destructive flames of a burning city. My son Garin, who had just joined us in LA, had to perch on the roof of our home with a garden hose dousing flying embers, with a look of abject terror on his face.

In 1993, in the metaphorical smoldering embers of a torched city, fire struck again in Malibu, an end of times wantonly destructive menace called the Old Topanga Fire, which sent tiny bits of people's lives and animals snowing on our cars in West Hollywood. Sneaking in between the riots and our next biblical beast was the massive North Ridge earthquake. Measuring 6.7, the 4:30 a.m. toss-us-out-of-the-bed calamity was an angry giant, picking up a massive chunk of the city, shaking it up and down for nearly twenty seconds, then tossing it back to the ground, unamused.

I had no way to connect with our bed being lifted nearly a foot off the floor several times, and heard myself screaming from a deep sleep.

"What is it? What's happening to us?"

John, who is legally blind without corrective lens, was groping in pitch black to retrieve his glasses, which had been hurled across the room along with other nightstand paraphernalia.

"It's an earthquake," he established with far more calm than could be considered normal. "Get to the door frame," he instructed, attempting to hoist me from the arms of the giant.

By the time we hit the door jam, the beast grew bored and the violent earth convulsion abruptly stopped. We stood quietly holding each other in the doorway then confronted the damage to our sixty-year-old wooden cottage. Miraculously, as it likely had many times, our sturdy little architectural gem withstood the quake, with the notable exception of the chimney and the kitchen. Virtually everything in our cabinets was lobbed around the kitchen, painting a mire of broken condiment jars and tomato sauce, stirred with the contents of our red vintage lava lamp. Mayhem splayed the kitchen the color of bright new blood, looking like the set of a horror film.

Equally compelled and anguished to open our front door, I expected to not only witness a flatted neighborhood, but an entire city turned into a rubbish heap. As I stepped onto the front porch, tears sprang to my eyes and for a brief instant, I ascended into spiritual ecstasy. Every star in the heavens serenely winked back at me as if to say, 'don't despair; this is only a test.' I dropped to my knees in gratitude for our lives, the brightest starry sky to ever blanket LA, and the benevolent Universe who ignited them. We then pulled on our wading boots and went to work on the be-damned kitchen.

It's common knowledge in earthquake survival, that the initial shocking gut punch is not the end, but the beginning. Over the next two weeks, while John resumed his tour schedule, Ptah and I endured a nerve rattling daily onslaught of aftershocks. Coming on the heels of the previous two years of apocalyptic fires and the shocking recklessness of the Gulf War, my trial by terror indoctrination to Los Angeles proceeded to meet all of my previous expectations of doom. Both Ptah and I were suffering from a deep depressive state. He took to standing longingly by the front door for hours with big wet eyes pleading for me to take him back to the Marrowbone, while my soul sobbed, then furiously journaled in a desperate attempt to write my way out of the miasma that my catastrophe-magnet life had become. With every aftershock, I was convinced that I had brought my better self and my great dog to a verboten city to be summarily extinguished in the flames of hell. And I don't believe in hell.

Anguished and alone in an environment estranged from itself with no recovery in sight, I felt not only anxiety ridden to the point of panic, but overall concern for my sanity. When thoughts of being sedated in a 'quiet psych ward' become frequent visions, it's time for intervention. I was a practicing psychotherapist and meditation group leader engendered and informed to help lonely, frightened seekers find their way to the Light, but was bungling my own effort to get there.

In an impulsive moment, triggered by yet another 5 point aftershock, I grabbed a small bag, stuffed a few clothes, packed a cooler with food for me and Ptah, then jumped in John's hatchback Toyota for parts unknown. Anywhere but here was the intention. Eventually I noticed I was heading south toward Baja, thinking I might explore a fishing village or two along the Pacific coast, but then the car barreled on until I was deep into the peninsula, on the Sea of Cortez side. Washboard roads had long since deteriorated into unpaved pathways, so by ten o'clock that night, after traveling more than twelve hours with little sense of time or anything else, I pulled into a darkened area called Bahia de Los Angeles according to the atlas. Familiarity and exhaustion dictated the compartmentalized decision.

When I say darkened area, I mean it was impossible to see where I was or what the fishing village or whatever it might be looked like—not one light of any kind to give me a hint. I pulled over in what appeared to be a vacant unpaved lot, crawled into the back then zipped Ptah and my aching body into a sleeping bag. I remember it poured rain sometime in the night with big raindrops pounding the car, but the car didn't shake and the rain soothed. At first light, I raised up to realize I was parked in what must be a tiny school yard smack in the middle of a quaint cluster of buildings, that loosely could be called a village. But what a picturesque vision it was. A light sand beach encircled by placid turquoise sea called me near, then the seductive smell of beans lured me to the only café. I broke into tears of relief at how safe I felt in that moment, warranted or not.

Ptah and I moved into the only overnight accommodations, a six-room elongated shanty motel that was raw for a princess palate, but sparkling clean. Later in the day, after reading some of the hand-printed literature hanging on the walls about whale watching trips, I decided that was exactly what drew me so far south into Baja, I needed to commune with the whales. The Sea of Cortez is a spawning area for several whale species and apparently Bahia de Los Angeles was considered a good entry point for watching. The only options were a wooden boat called a panga or a rubber dingy, both with big noisy motors, which I considered detrimental to the well being of the mammals, and my battered psyche. As I sat pondering with Ptah snuggled beside me, by now used to my Lucy shenanigans, I spotted a single mast sail boat floating quietly toward the small dock.

"Now that's what we need to properly see some whales," I whispered to my psychic dog.

"Ohhhh, no, Mom, not a boat," Ptah shot back with a look of more than concerned consternation. Ptah, the Egyptian wonder dog had never fully bonded with water, Egypt being a desert and all.

As the single-mast boat sailed in, I sprang into manifest mode. We were going out to sea on that boat and we were going to frolic with whales, and so it is, and so it is! When the wild haired, hippy skipper disembarked, I reckoned he was harmless enough, after all how menacing could a sixties drop out to Mexico with more spaces than teeth be?

"I love your boat—the *only* boat of any description in the harbor—do you ever charter for whale excursions?" I inquired, noting the sharp distinction between my vocabulary and his appearance.

"No. I live on that boat; it's been my home for ten years and I don't hire it out." He was articulate but firm.

"I've just arrived from Los Angeles where my dog and I, (mentioning nothing about boyfriend) rode out a 6.7 earthquake. I seem to be in the throes of a nervous system upheaval that spotting a couple of whales might heal. Could you please help me out? I'd be happy to give you a more than fair charter price, plus any gas you might use."

"Let me think on it," the near-toothless salt-water-smelling dude called, as he ambled toward the café.

An hour later when he returned with a few provisions in a paper bag, he motioned for me to join him.

"Come on. I'll take you out, but stow the dog."

"Oh, no, I can't leave my dog behind; he is in worse shape than me from the constant aftershocks. Besides we're inseparable."

He looked me up and down as if deciding just how crazy I might be, then nodded in defeat.

Ptah, on the other hand, took one look at our rubber dinghy transport out to the anchored boat and started trembling violently. This was decidedly more than he bargained for, and quite possibly worse than the earth rattling. I heaved him into the dinghy shivering uncontrollably, whining softly as he eyed the disappearing shore.

Ptah was far more psychic than Hillary Ellers, did he know what I didn't?

The hippy home-craft did not hold up as well at close proximity, a tad rickety. She measured about thirty-two feet with a tiny galley area and slender sleep nook for the captain tucked under the bow. Congested with the owner's life, the living quarters, suitable for only one sailor, was relatively clean, comforting for a germ-phobic princess craving a whale communication. Gliding over the translucent azure waters, I felt the trauma melting off my body, draining over the side of the boat.

I smiled from a deeper well for the first time in four years.

Had I actually felt anything akin to joy since leaving the Marrowbone? Had Ptah? What the fuck had I done?

We were several hours into our sail when the somewhat contained Captain announced we would anchor near a small island for the night, and resume our sail to the breeding waters in the morning. Up until then, we had not discussed the length of the trip. As we neared an isolated island the size of a small football field to weigh anchor, the wind whipped up fairly large sized chops and the skipper abruptly made a call. Instead of taking my sleeping bag over to the island—it was too dangerous to try to get in the dinghy—Ptah and I should sleep on the boat with him.

Ok, admittedly, a glimmer of my human behavior training dampened my Pollyanna reverie, with the thought of bunking next to him on the dingy sheets, even with Ptah wedged between us. By now, the waves were lapping against the hull, rocking the boat in a lullaby motion that felt like anything but lulling. I capitulated.

"Hey, it looks like it's going to be a starry evening, I'll sleep out here on the side bench and Ptah can sleep on the deck floor," I volunteered, eluding the proximity of any intimate contact.

"Suit yourself," he grunted. "I'll crank up the generator and heat up the crock pot of beans, if you're hungry."

Suddenly realizing I was famished, soon I was, again, seduced by the smell of pinto beans, my hands-down favorite food. The Mexican bean confection he simmered was some of the most delicious food I had eaten since leaving my Marrowbone garden. I relaxed into a bean stupor hoping it didn't induce farting in the close quarters. We finally established eye contact over a cup of strong coffee, slipping into an easy after-dinner conversation under the silky Milky Way, the comforting Pleiades, and a canopy of constellations that the Skipper seemed to know intimately. For the first time in over two weeks, I didn't feel one twinge of anxiety. After wolfing down a can of doggydoms finest, Ptah snoozed on the deck as we finished our coffee and munched on a couple of stale cookies.

"So, tell me how you came to be a citizen of the beautiful Sea of Cortez," I pried with the skill any decent therapist needed to unlock a narrative.

"Oh, I came down here and bought this boat after I got out of jail," he dropped casually, directly eyeing me for a reaction.

While my heart turned a backflip, my eyes held his gaze without a flutter.

"Why were you in jail?" My carefully contained tone as casual as asking for a second helping of pintos … one of those times when therapeutic training comes in handy.

"Rape."

My heart leapt to my throat, my gut threatened to expel the beans, but I persevered to show nothing, in hopes of not triggering power issues. Ptah, picking up on the shift, stood up, shook, then sat down directly by my side.

"How long were you in jail?"

"Three years. It was statutory rape. I was twenty-seven and she was seventeen. Her parents didn't take kindly to the age difference and had me arrested," he held eye contact as if he was still working to get a reaction.

Inwardly, I yielded to his honesty, regretted his game-playing and not completely trusting his motivation, I smiled.

"Damn good beans. Any more in the crockpot?"

I slept on the deck, clinging precariously to a sixteen-inch bench, with my sleeping bag as a pillow. But as I lay there willing my eyes to stay open, I knew I was exactly where I was supposed to be, right there under a canopy of everything the Universe had to offer in the moment. While watching shooting stars dart across the heavens, I reminded The Other that this might be a fine time to reconnect.

Ptah snuggled with the Skipper.

At first light and a cup of steaming coffee, we weighed anchor and hoisted sail for a current of warmer waters where whales birthed their calves. Within forty minutes we were smack in the middle of several family pods joyously celebrating new births, while sucking in plankton to nurture their babies. I leaned over the side of the boat photographing the gigantic mammals as they swam back and forth beneath, in the thrall of their calming presence … in whale nirvana. I became not just a voyeur with a camera, but a family member celebrating the arrival of a new calf. At one point, maybe a half hour in to our discourse, a mammal swam under the boat so much longer and wider than the hull, that one hiccup and we would have been tossed overboard. Ptah whined as the enormous creature passed beneath us.

"What would happen if he decided to breach right now?" Holding my breath as I asked.

"Oh, they're sperm whales, vegetarians," the Captain grinned, "they'd have little interest in us, other than making sure we don't drown."

The whales laid healing on my shattered spirit during my three-day impulsive jaunt to Baja. I felt deep satisfaction in handing the captain enough money, minus any extraneous pot purchases, to supplement his simple way of life for a long while.

Returning to West Hollywood, fortified against a shuddering earth, I realized when I picked up John's string of 'where the fuck are you' messages, progressively escalating to what, for John, would be panic, Lucy had fucked up. No cell phones then, so I had disappeared and become so gone that I completely forgot he had no idea where I was. To this day, his incredulousness at my slip-away-into-the-night behavior far outweighs his understanding of what the whales did for my weary soul.

Penetrating the darkness of the first four years of my LA experiment was a ring. A beautiful vintage ring winged its way to John, who may or may not have been entertaining a proposal.

A friend who was all up in vintage jewelry called him about a particular ring she had found that looked like me, wanting to know if she should put it on hold for him see. He told her to buy it. Rather unceremoniously, in 1992, he slipped it on my finger after his thirty-fifth birthday party, while we lazed on a blanket in our back yard. There was no romantic knee drop, 'will you marry me?' simply a physical implication that we were engaged. It was and still is a perfect ring for my tastes and I treasured it as a symbol of hope for our relationship, but as the tumultuous darkness of the catalyzing events of those first four years receded into memories, the ring gradually transformed into not a symbol of hope, but doubt.

John is a hyper-focused musical prodigy who, in his thirties, still believed he was what he did, somewhat of a reoccurring male maelstrom. His work defined him, music his identity. There's nothing negative in that concept; it was exquisitely exampled for him by his conductor father, a music professor at the University of Redlands, forging musical careers for many of his students. Every concert was 'the most important' of Jim's career. Fair enough that John carried the mantle, although there was zero ego on his part. Perhaps his father's bountiful ego and arrogance, as conductors are prone to carry, was his fair warning.

As one who had wrestled with ego, I asked John how one of the world's preeminent guitar wizards managed to escape ego clutches.

"At four I sat on the living room floor, listening to the lesson my Mom was teaching my older sister, then wanting to keep up with her, would jump on the stool and try to play the lesson. At eleven, I played bass clarinet, then bassoon in my Dad's wind ensembles, sitting alongside college kids and adults, I had to keep up to not stand out. I guess I always felt I was simply trying to keep up with older musicians."

To this day I clearly see this pattern in my musical giant and how it drives him constantly to kick up his own bar. If he wants to learn to play a particular instrument, he masters it almost effortlessly, or what I might consider casually. He disappears into his studio for a few hours, caresses the instrument, then it gives him a new composition. I've witnessed this process for over thirty years, and am still awed by it.

My morning hours, set aside as my anchor to Center, began with an hour meditation, then yoga, followed by at least another hour of processing my doubts and concerns about John and me. Not that love was not present or that happiness was not part of our daily life—we loved each other without condition, and reveled in our time together. We didn't argue, respected each other's time and space, and John flourished in our West Hollywood lifestyle. But more and more, I found myself having to trust back to our first meeting in the ethers when he lowered down on me proclaiming he was John and had been waiting for me. That experience, I reasoned, could not, would not have occurred in a vacuum, but was created by my call for love, with John answering the call. I was convinced he was the more developed soul. Truth must prevail over emotional distraction, I cautioned myself over and over again.

The weaving in and out of the light and darkness, as life provokes us to do, became my observer's narrative poured daily into my journals. I couldn't seem to accept that a healthy relationship could be predicated on such a range of extreme opposites: John picked up *People*, while I trended to *Time*, he spoke in roadmap details, I forgo details for the big picture. John would eat most anything, having been raised on prepared casseroles—his Mom taught music lessons all day and had to improvise—I was fed from garden to spoon. My warm, Southern mama wore her heart on her apron, while John's mirrored the intricacies of musical perfection and baked sweets as a show of love. I favor a tidy space, free of clutter, while John is comfortable with all manner of Einstein piles breeding on any flat surface. We were raised on opposite ends of the country with opposing cultural norms, although that was more of a source of humor than hubris. John's lament came in the form of fear of 'not being able to catch up with me,' suggesting he felt a spiritual lagging behind, although it was him who found me. My deepest uncertainties were built on his consummated intimacy with his all-consuming, slay-the-competition, omnipresent mistress.

In 1994, amongst the rumbling vacillations, we were walking Ptah and our yellow cat, Lilly, around our picture perfect historic neighborhood, when I had a sudden flash of John playing under colorful banks of lights in a massive arena with some rock star.

"You are going to be on a big-ass tour next summer."

"I hope you're wrong; everything I'm putting out there is opposite of that. I'm happy with my career, doing so many varied jobs, getting to play diverse music," he quickly knocked back. "Besides, I turned down offers to audition for Dylan and Springsteen … can't imagine who it would be."

"Hey Babe, it's not something I wanted to see, I just flashed on it."

Three months later in Salisbury, while packing my mother's life for her move into assisted living, John called to check in then promptly put me on hold, knowing I have zero patience for listening to phone hiss for more than a two minutes. Twenty minutes later, he clicked back on.

"You'll never guess who that was?"

"I am way too pissed to play that game, who was it?" half-seething, half-smiling at his audacity.

"It was Elton John. He wants me to do a eighteen-month world tour for a new album called *Made in England*, which Gregg Penney produced, and you know Gregg produced the *Ingenue* album with KD Lang that I love." John always gives more detail that my brain wants to absorb. I was stuck on the eighteen month long tour.

"What did you tell him?" Determined to remain calm, not to inject an opinion in my question.

"I told him I'd have to think about it because I loved my life and career just as it is, so he suggested I come to the Four Seasons to hang out and listen to the record. Of course I'm curious because he was so excited about it. I have to ask for Binky Poodleclip, his alias, at the front desk. When I hesitantly replied Elton said, "it gets worse, Dah-ling."

The initial leg of the first tour was nine months, covering a good portion of the world. I tagged along for a couple of months that took us to exotic places I'd always wanted to visit: all of Europe, the Nordic Countries, and best of all, Moscow. During the day John and I fell into the spirit and cultures of magnificent cities that I'd always dreamed of visiting. Elton is a master performer who leaves his heart and soul on the stage, so each night this awestruck farm girl tripped the light fantastic down the Yellow Brick Road. The princess had no squabbles about being a 'band wife' on this tour.

I adored Elton from the minute we met. On first sight, we naturally embraced and as we held heart to heart I felt unconstrained love streaming wide open. Startlingly quick and brilliant with his irrepressible English humor poised at the edge, I found myself feeling and sounding dull when around him. As the weeks flew by, I got to know and love one of the sweetest, kindest most sensitive beings one could ever call friend. I also was privy to several of his infamous tantrums, when equally unbridled rage spews from his potty mouth.

A condiment on the dream travel was being a voyeur to my uncannily nice, gentle, balanced life partner, as we called ourselves, blazing into a sexy guitar god in tight leather pants with hordes of young ladies clamoring for him. Elton and the band quickly exited arenas as soon as the last note sounded to beat the crowd, and, for Elton, the clock on his private jet departure time, so it was unusual that the band was exposed to fans. One enchanting outdoor venue, carved from ancient coliseum ruins in the picturesque French village of Nimes, was within walking distance of our hotel, so John and I decided on a romantic stroll through the quaint streets after the show. Instantly, we were surrounded by a swarm of female fans rumbling for autographs. As John signed anything in front of him, the ladies in their excitement poured on the love, crushing us in the herd. I glanced over at John's face, sweaty, white, gripped in panic. Grabbing his arm, I was pinned between him and floating female flesh. A venue security person saw the fracas, ran to our rescue, shooing the suddenly large crowd back, freeing us.

John later said, "Just imagine what it would be like if I were really famous." We never tried that trick again.

The six years John toured with Elton and the band were some of the happiest of our lives, speaking for myself anyway. We not only explored a big chunk of an exquisite globe, listened to and played some of the best rock music ever written, but made lifelong friends. Elton's band and crew are a genuine, talented and kind-hearted family and we were privileged to have been welcomed as members. Certainly those joyful years stretched us both individually and as a couple, the shared journey offering a footstool to not only a broader world-view, but a path to deeper level of intimacy. I fell in love with him all over again.

While John continued to tour, I completed a BA in Psychology of Human Behavior and the better part of an MS in Spiritual Psychology all the while tending to the souls of some simpatico seekers in the LA area. But the ring, still a sparkling jewel on my left hand, reminded me that it had now been nine years of living, laughing, loving and learning without a commitment.

The ring began to sting.

My consistent meditation and journaling led me to a decision that I least expected, to a road not less traveled. One of my favorite quotes, which Einstein may or may not have said, and I quoted to clients working on codependency issues, 'The definition of insanity is doing the same thing over and over again, but expecting different results,' constantly stalked me. The lovely diamond was tarnishing my finger.

My heart nestled in the thrall of a man in progress who had committed his life trajectory to his career, not family life. I couldn't fix that, so I decided to move out. Not to move on, necessarily, because I was more in love than I had ever been with anyone. Although I tried, I couldn't argue the authenticity of our initial meeting and the fact that our connection was spiritually conceived and mandated, but treading water was wearing me thin. "If John is not the person I will be spending the rest of this life with, that person is out there waiting for me and I will open the door to truth," along with "this or something better for my highest good" became my daily mantras. I stumbled across a place near the ocean in Santa Monica that, though miniscule, was cute, had room for my practice and a bedroom that barely could hold a queen bed but, a nest of my own.

I don't recall if John was oblivious to my stirrings or if he was on an extended tour leg, likely the former, but for whatever reason, I don't think he knew I was looking for a place until I had found it. Perhaps the painful recollection of how soul-crushing our only breakup was, I couldn't trust myself to follow though if I shared my plan in advance … said the haunting child who slipped off porches into the night. At the time, with his hectic touring schedule and personal creative projects swirling around the house, I felt like it might be somewhat of a relief to him.

"I have found a small place near Santa Monica and am planning to put a deposit on it. If you are not the love of this life, then he or she is waiting out there and I need to unlock the door. I love you too much to quit us, but I can't continue to quit myself."

Whether it took minutes, hours or days for John to drop to one knee with a question on his lips, "Will you marry me?" I don't recall. I do remember tears glistening in his blue eyes, and a serene presence overtaking his face. Merging into the magic of the moment with him, "yes, I'll marry you" tumbled from my heart.

Later on our evening stroll, I asked why the sudden turn-around since we had no external forces like kids, or in his case, experience with wedded bliss that nudged couples toward matrimony, his answer was direct:

"Your pain pushed me to the next level."

During the wedding discussions, usually over morning coffee in our back garden, I began to sense my exuberance dragging John in the wake. I was driving the boat and he wasn't even up on his skis yet. I began second-guessing his motivation for proposing since it sure didn't seem like he wanted a wedding. Did he simply panic when I said I was moving out? After touring the inspirational Self Realization Center in Santa Monica and the enchanted Inn of the Seventh Ray in Malibu, John wasn't in the least inspired—until the idea sprang up "what about having it in England?"

"Let's ask Bob if we can have it at the Boathouse," I suggested.

BAM! That turned on a light that became the wedding that no one present will ever forget.

Bob Halley, our deep friend, who at the time was Elton's long-time friend and personal assistant, was, and is, the funniest person I know, besides Elton. The two of them were English peas in a pod, always goading each other into regaling, sometimes scathing, always snarky Brit humor, to the delight and horror of everyone in the room.

A quick call to the UK, and we were on for a ceremony in one of the most picturesque settings imaginable, the expansive gardens of a vintage Boathouse in Goring-on-Thames, England. The charming thatched roofed structure originally dating back to the 1600s nestled over the banks of the River Thames was a mystical fairy tale slice of British antiquity, complete with long-neck swans and British Border Terriers.

"Until we came up with the idea of a wedding in England, I was unexcited about having a wedding. I'd never been to one that I could see myself being a part of, they all felt like high school proms." With some prodding, John finally processed his obvious resistance that had nothing to do with his love for me. I marveled how fragile and projective female psyches can become around weddings, versus how practical the male psyche remains, and a what a damn good thing that is.

John and I were amicably able to agree to a guest list of fifty friends and family, anointed by us as the perfect open hearts to support our union. Everyone would sit in a circle with a special altar at the apex, creating a container for our vows, which we painstakingly wrote to each other. In lieu of a proper Vicar, since neither of us were religious, nor met resident requirements, we asked Sharon Dougan's partner Dan Hovee (remember they had a simultaneous breakup and rekindling), a kindred spirit couple in many ways, to officiate. Sharon and Dan are psychotherapists, as was I at the time. Over the next hectic months, we all thought of every imaginable obstacle, then smoothed every wrinkle.

The front of our wedding program we emboldened with *Out beyond ideas of wrongdoing and rightdoing, there is a field, I'll meet you there,* from the Rumi poem, "A Great Wagon," mitigating any provincial ideas or judgment from certain family members. By choosing England, we avoided having to invite the usual assortment of casual friends and family members as well as our business acquaintances. The control-oriented bride and the practical, laid-back groom-to-be dotted every proverbial i and crossed every t, because across the eons of time and space, this wedding was meant to be.

Except there were two non-controllable factors looming: the first was my precious mama had died the previous year, and although realistically there was no way she would have boarded a plane to England, since Tennessee was the extent of her flight frontier, I yearned for her presence; and number two, as Bob reminded us, "it always pisses rain in August, every day, Dah-ling."

The week before our departure, I was sitting at the kitchen table alone in the house, except for Benny, our Border Terrier (a fabulous gift from Elton) and Ptah. Suddenly I sensed a crowd in the room with me, so much familiar energy that I stood up, glanced around, expecting someone to yell out, 'surprise!'

Instead I heard a soft voice that sounded for the world like my mama say, "we've come with your wedding present."

"I accept," scanning the room, squinting to catch even a whisper of her. "What is it?"

"It will not rain on your wedding," was the reply, amid distance giggles and laughter. And with that everyone vanished, leaving me sitting there simultaneously laughing and crying, Benny and Ptah slurping at my legs in canine confusion.

Goring-on-Thames is a quaint British hamlet where the same charming thatched boathouses have graced the banks of the

Thames for hundreds of years. Bob Halley with his crackling charisma was a consummate host, sparing no generosity or expense for his guests. We were treated like royalty, up in my comfort zone all the way. Bob's crew decked out his handsome vintage yacht, the Amoreena, in white bridal ribbons and bouquets, along with his two Bentleys and lovely Cornish, which would transport our wedding party the few kilometers from the boathouse to our equally beguiling thatched restaurant down the river.

By August 30th, all our guests had arrived in Goring for an after rehearsal pub gathering for fish, chips and mushy peas. That evening, a clear star studded sky illumined our path from the boathouse to the pub, as we all strolled across the bonny bridge arching the regal Thames. After ample toasts and genuine appreciation to have our dearest closest, with the exception of my son Shannon and John's brother David, John and I returned to the boathouse brimming in ale, peas and glee. I decided to follow at least one wedding tradition by not sleeping with my groom on the night before our wedding, virgin that I am, so retired to my charming guesthouse, alight with naturally scented candles, sweet bouquets and thoughtful little wedding hearts from Bob.

This was my first third marriage. A no-longer-handicapped heart purred in my chest, and my romantic soul wore no blinders. For the first time, I was marrying with the certainty that I would spend the remainder of my life with this man. When Jesse Gamble and I married as teens, it was 'what the hell, we can always get a divorce,' and with Bowen, I had considered it a necessity for my young boys. With John, the fifty-year-old bride delivered a blameless heart and a refined romantic spirit to the altar of commitment.

I was free to be love.

Hoping to minimize eye bags and shadows, I fell asleep early,
only to be awakened at 1:30 by a blaring bedside phone. Barely
rousing, I figured it was Elton waking Bob up to chat about
nothing in particular if he couldn't sleep. At nine o'clock my
eyes opened to the happiest day of my life. I bubble-bathed
and groomed in the spa-like bathroom, then threw on shorts
and a top, practically cartwheeling like an eight-year-old, over to
the boathouse.

As soon as I slipped through the back door, I felt a pall over
the house, the kind that made my heart pound and my legs
limp. The service door led to the laundry room where I found
Jane, Bob's long time house manager, weeping softly into fluffy
white towels.

"Jane? What's going on?"

"Haven't you heard? The Princess of Wales died last night."

Embarrassingly, I have to confess, my initial thought, was 'oh,
no, not on my wedding day.' This was assuredly not on any list
of catastrophic events, falling way outside of my ability to
hyper-control.

I held Jane while she sobbed beyond what is natural for a Brit,
then joined Bob and John at breakfast. Bob was on the phone
with a completely distraught Elton. Once when John and I were
visiting Elton and David for a few days before a road trip to
Cornwall, Elton invited us us to stay over one more night for a
small dinner party, attended by close friends Diana and Gianni
Versace. Dinner conversation with Elton is intimidating enough,

lightening quick cleverness feeding itself, and he can out-snark any British rock star, even Mick, but three of the most renowned icons on the planet at the dinner table, while intriguing to John, kneecapped the redneck princess and we opted to hit the road to Cornwall.

Bob was doing all he could to console Elton, when I tiptoed in to hold John, who was also teary. I could see Bob's hand shaking as he quietly listened to his friend buried in sadness. I had once asked Elton who his best friends were, excluding Bob, since they behaved more like siblings than friends, without hesitation he answered Diana and Gianni. Tragically, he lost them both within six weeks of each other.

I cop to sounding like a peerless self-absorbed bride, but I have to confess: I was torn between sadness that Elton and David would not be coming to the ceremony, and relief that they would not be coming. On this one day, I wanted to be the star of the show. Without warning, my ego could still slip into the front seat and guilelessly grin like the Cheshire Cat.

Not quite able to wrap my emotions around what was happening on the third most important day of my life, I asked Bob if we needed to make other plans for the ceremony. He fired back in a British nanosecond.

"No, Dah-ling, the wedding will be in the garden as planned, if it doesn't piss rain."

"Well, Princesses and their boyfriends can fly away on my wedding day, but it is NOT going to rain!" I inwardly pouted. Though I was profoundly sad for Elton, Bob and all of England, I was determined to stay focused.

"Dah-ling," Bob, ever the master of smooth persuasion, was calculating the other bad news in the catastrophic shadow that had swallowed our day, "thunderstorms are due to roll down the river around four when we start the ceremony. I've already spoken to Jane about having movers come over to empty the great room and we'll usher everyone in here." Bob was more than efficiently adept at handling any crisis or tiara trauma Elton threw with genteel aplomb, a soggy wedding was a mere dawdle.

"Thanks, Bob, but it won't rain on the ceremony," I persevered as a few purple puffballs grouped over the River Thames.

Momentarily flashing on the myriad times my Mama told me something might happen, would happen, or that she would see if it would happen, that did NOT happen, I swatted at a nagging doubt.

My vintage pearl satin wedding dress, cut tuxedo style with tucking on the front and fitted sleeves, had a long coat overdress with a five foot long train, to be carried by eight-year-old twin sisters of John's Brit friend Andy McKenzie, hung regally on the door waiting for a thin, expectant occupant to shimmy in.

My early childhood friend Pat Pierce, who dutifully cried when told, was my attendant, along with Sharon Dougan. My soul mama Virginia Team reigned as person of honor. Virginia and Pat were helping me flower-power my hair after I had declined Bob's offer of a hairdresser. I tossed it up in a messy mock twist and my bridesmaids spotted in fragrant tuberoses. I was about to slip into my body hugging Rita Hayworth ensemble, when Sharon and Dan burst into the cottage shaking dripping umbrellas.

"We were wondering about plan B, it's raining, Seattle kinda raining." Dan's face wore the same mask of shock that all our guests would bear as they joined into our ceremonial circle. "No plan B; it'll stop. But we need to open the ceremony with a silent meditation then invoke the spirits of Diana and Do'di, freeing them to fly so we can ground in the joy of the day. Everybody will be in shock, especially our Brits, so we'll need to clear sad to make room for happy." I was speaking for myself and to myself.

A dark cloud of doom had just wept on the garden: now it was time to smile.

Fifteen minutes before downbeat, as our nattily attired guests paraded through the massive iron gates toward the ring of white chairs encircling a sparkling crystal and flower altar, the sun burst through the menace hovering over the river, illuminating a crisp blue and white cloud dance.

I prettied up like a Hollywood bride in the handsome gown ensemble, the same one that the vintage bridal saleswoman in Santa Monica had told me would be taken apart to be used as a pattern, because no on could fit in it. Pleading my case to let me try it on, I banked on a Cinderella outcome, and it was mine, made for a size 0 body, blending perfectly with my hair. She wouldn't agree to sell it, since it was invaluable as a pattern, so rent it, I did. I felt victorious, sucking in my poochie belly to caress the shiny smooth satin across my hips.

As the local parish tower chimed four o'clock, puffy cloudlets mirrored the swans floating below. Our musical director Andy, who hired a family string ensemble for our prelude music, cued a recording of John's I'd chosen as my wedding march.

Garin, with the help of elders, guardians, and a beneficent
Universe made it to Goring somewhat intact, with stitches in
his forehead—I didn't ask—and voices taunting his every step.
His valor in being there to 'give me away' with a fire raging
in his brain that no amount of alcohol or pot could douse,
comforted, while tearing at my heart. 1997 was the beginning of
the end of Garin's musical dreams, and our collective hope that
his prodigious talent would lead him to the big show. Glazed
haunted eyes, battling the most daunting of demons showed up
for my big day, but my huge spirited boy came through for me.
Less than ten years later I would laud that back to him.

Garin and I interlocked arms and stepped through a graceful
archway carved in the towering hedge between the guest cottage
and the main gardens, as Andy hit "play" on our wedding march.
I picked John's song, written about our relationship several years
back, to be the poetic strains that carried me to my man waiting
at the alter. The song is called "Black and Blue," but before you
break into snippy sniggers, check out his words:

> It's not that I don't want to go there with you.
> It's just that I never thought that I would go there at all.
> Live a life being just one part of two,
> take a walk to the edge and just fall.
>
> Into the love that's so true,
> into the arms that can hold
> a heart that's been fragile and cold
> surrounded by a wall, black and blue.
>
> I know that you've been ready for some time,
> tryin' to show me how to go there with you.
> Waiting for me to finally make up my mind,
> you'd think by now I'd have half a clue.

*To see a love that's so true,*
*to see the arms that can hold*
*a heart that's been fragile and cold*
*surrounded by hope that is new.*

*So don't despair I'm finally coming around.*
*No need to venture by yourself at all.*
*I'll be there with you right on solid ground,*
*so you can walk to the edge and just fall.*

*Into the love that's so true*
*into the arms that can hold a heart now stronger and bold,*
*no longer fragile and cold.*
*Surrounded by the love that is you.*

Holding strong to my unsteady son's arm, my soul expanded in to John's words as we strolled around the drive toward the circle, now bathed in the witching light of a waning sun. On first glimpse of John, my heart swooned at his radiance, backlit by a softening sun. A chiseled, elegant, powerful countenance projected across the sanctified gardens, all six foot two inches of his broad Norwegian shoulders filling out a custom white satin suit, like a Norse god. The man took my breath away.

John had waited then found me, then waited some more, then found himself, then waited again, then found us.

As the last verse of "Black and Blue" played through, we turned our souls inside out before our shrine, adorned in a flourish of massive towers of amethyst wrapped in softly hued flowers, artfully arranged around a front and center photo of my sweet Mama. We had waited ten years and many lifetimes to stand here with each other, with no blinders …

… off the edge we stepped.

The essence of our vows affirmed our souls' intention and hearts' commitment to honest communication as a path to compassion, compassion as a portal to understanding, and our willingness to be vulnerable, as a door to compromise. We stacked these alongside our promise to always bring our healthiest selves to our marriage.

We had asked Jim—John's Dad, Jim—to give a brief invocation without summoning Jesus and he managed beautifully with "Great God of us all," but was anything but brief. Dan's opening meditation for Diana touched what we each felt in our aching hearts, inspiring us to float above the painful fray. Rodney sang "Old Dancin' Couple," the soul-rattling song that brought John and me together in Cancun, penned on my birthday, August, 9, 1975, eight years before Rodney and I met.

*Dancin' girl your eyes are showing,*
*you're wondering if he's knowing,*
*you've never felt this much before.*
*You're thinking about the times you've hurt,*
*those soft and simple words,*
*make you feel like letting go this time.*
*Once a fool, you've always been one,*
*but then again you might just win one.*
*You never know if you don't take your chances.*

*He didn't have to have such an effect on you*
*as if your whole world is on fire.*
*I know you dreamed more than one time*
*that you were gliding across the floor.*
*You don't know that you look like some old dancin' couple.*

*Dancin' girl, the eyes upon you,*
*act as if they've never known you,*
*never seen the magic that you dream about.*
*The room is quiet, the floor is empty*
*perfect partners always will be*
*taking steps they never took before.*

Sentiments so profoundly prescient can only be carried from the Center of a knowing soul who has loved another through eons of time as Rodney and I have … from circus to circus, throughout many lifetimes.

Our union ceremony was intended not only to be fairy-tale romantic, but to be an exchange of love and creativity between our friends and family. John's Mom Lorraine, an extraordinarily gifted pianist and musical maven of the Jorgenson clan, performed Schumann's "Traumerei," a piece she played for her father as a young girl. Injecting a bit of loony theatre of the absurd into our carefully laid plans, John's strong-willed sister, Susie, hatched up a scheme to 'surprise' us by dancing in the middle of our circle as a wedding gift. For months, we adamantly eye-rolled and clearly informed her this was out of the question. Desperate not to lose her moment, at the rehearsal Susie took another stab at pleading her cause, sharing she had packed her tutu just in case. We managed to temporarily shelve it as a possible 'big maybe' for later, or as my mama used to say, "we'll see."

After Dan swept us all into tears with his inspired opening remarks, John realized my wedding band was still in the bedroom. Deftly, with minimal detaining, not something John is prone to, he sent Bob dashing in after it while Lorraine performed. I opted not to read anything into this other than pre-wedding jitters.

In lieu of any material gifts, we suggested our friends compose poems or affirmations supportive of our union to share in the circle, creating a container of positive energy we could tap as needed throughout the years. John and I took turns wiping tears from each other's faces. The power of words knows no bounds.

As John and I shared our first kiss as husband and wife, the setting sun caressed the Thames. Pat, Jim, Lorraine, Susie, Garin, John and I boarded the slipper launch, as the rest of the party found their spot on Bob's venerable yacht or, if boat-shy, settled into one of the chauffeur driven mighty-ass cars.

Slowly cruising down the placid river into my mama's sun, pockets of traditionally stoic locals glanced up from their grief, as our slipper launch and the Amoreena, escorted by families of long-necked swans, glided past. One by one, the bereaved villagers burst into applause as we motored past, partly in empathy that we carried on with our wedding on such a morose day, and partly in relief to have heavy hearts momentarily elated by the love flotilla. Each group of men, women and children clapped, waved and cheerioed us on, lifting our collective hearts to unite with them in the immensity of the day.

After docking in front of the Beetle and Wedge Boathouse, a few kilometers up river in Moulsford, Bob greeted us with the surprise that Elton had sent cases of Cristal, since he and David could not attend, this wildness after already having previously showered us with a thoughtfully generous gift.

The brilliant caterers, running a tad late, left us all with a few minutes to lounge outside on the mooring patio. Susie took this opportunity to pounce, determined to dance in front of her parents on our wedding day. To this day I'm still not sure what if anything it had to do with us, but there was no excuse stronger than her will, so after several glasses of champagne, we reluctantly capitulated to yet another plea to perform in her white tutu on the bank of the Thames. Susie, not known as a dancer but an accomplished flautist, still gracefully preened and careened as Saint Saen's cello opus "The Swan" blasted from the boom box that she just happened to have slipped into her purse. Probably a bit more awkward to her family members than our bemused guests ... twenty years on, while applauding Susie's courage, not one lovely middle-age pirouette has faded from the memory of anyone present.

Our crazy funny friend, comedian Dick Hardwick, cranked out a sidesplitting routine, and Pam Rose and Jill Colluchi gifted us with a tear-rendering version of the Kye Fleming/Mary Ann Kennedy song "Friends" as we dined on exquisitely-presented fare, laughing, crying, and toasting with Elton's Cristal into the wee hours.

Early the next morning, while most guests were sleeping off the champagne or making plans to stay in England for Diana's memorial, John and I presented Bob with an appreciation gift for one amazing fairy tale wedding that had far surpassed anything a redneck princess could ever dream up, then departed to Heathrow for our honeymoon in Paris. As soon as we dropped our suitcases at the Hotel de L'Abbaye, which we chose because it was a former monastery, we stepped into our walking shoes, and John, who speaks beautiful French, directed us to the Place de l' Alma, where Diana and Dodi Fayed had crashed while fleeing paparazzi. We lingered into the evening, blending our tears with all of Paris' as long lines of mourners, from tatted motorcycle gangs to sad-eyed cherubs, placed tokens of love and honor on a burgeoning altar for everybody's Princess. John and I left his wedding boutonniere attached to a note thanking her for lending her heart to the vulnerable.

Later at the hotel, John fended nerve-racking calls that were starting to look as if he might have to leave Paris the next day. I held my breath through various incarnations of how "Candle in the Wind" might be presented at Diana's memorial. We finally got a reprieve when Elton and Bernie decided to rewrite the lyrics as "Goodbye, England's Rose," and Elton opted to perform solo. Finally we could settle in for my first time in the sad but majestic City of Light for some "eat, walk, love."

Marriage is not a panacea for clashing opposites, but a quiet zone where contrasting personalities can embrace differences as space for expansion. Twenty plus years after our storybook wedding, John still converses in a dizzying array of details that wander down side streets, and at times I have surely rankled in these Witch Hairs, ducking vision-provoking descriptions for rousing big pictures. But that same detail-oriented brain can repair anything that needs a new working order, and I fair best with pigs and people.

For over thirty years, guitars and suitcases have plopped inside the front door, freeing strong arms to embrace waiting love, where they may or may not become vintage before being moved. The progeny of a chaotic past still shudders at piles and clutter, but as with all our opposing life messiness, our respect of each other's space and time offers middle ground.

Even the most intimate of conversations can swerve down a musical lane, the muse willfully commandeering the last word.

While still the most powerful force in his life, I have come to accept their relationship as contributing to the good of the whole, as those who follow John's music will attest. I lean ever more to the introvert, hungry for tiny spaces to fill with write. John, however, can create hanging upside down in Times Square, and compose complex orchestral pieces while changing strings on a guitar. He never quite understood the Bisbee cottage getaway, or the Crestone house, but he did and does realize and support an insatiable appetite to create.

In our opposing personalities, we reflect for each other the light of awareness, and the shadow of the unknown. Opposites attract for just this purpose, the sticky adhesive of contrast binding souls in evolution and expansion.

Although we are passionate, opinionated, fiercely independent people, our souls need each other. In that spirit, we seldom raise our voices or argue. Though we certainly don't always agree, we respect each other's right to disagree then tackle talking it through to resolution.

John and I chose compromise as the centerpiece of our commitment. Our reunion in this go 'round took place in the ethers, on the upper floors. Our task was to ground our spiritual connection down to an earth dance. Now the ol' dancin' couple minuet, best friends, fingers interlaced, weaving in and out of the dark into the light and the light into the dark, fortifying our humanity with each faltering step. Perfect partners who always will be taking steps we never took before.

Of course, I still give a good go at fixing him, I'm a fixer, but John, a patient being, knows the fixer will eventually mend herself. As we dance, we balance each other, smiling at our human frailties and foibles, while extending a hand out of potholes, and a leg up out of rabbit holes.

The music world esteems John Jorgenson as a maestro, for all his virtuosity on myriad instruments and pinnacles in performance, I treasure how my man loves my grown men that he has known since they were errant boys. Partnering with me down the darkest alleys of Garin's debilitating illness, John mirrors a beautiful example of manhood for Garin and Shannon. My husband adores our beautiful grands, Lili and Ella, and he loves me, the southern redneck princess, complex conundrum that she is.

John Jorgenson's character is equally comparable to his incomparable musical gifts. If you know him, you know that; if you don't, flip back through these pages to Garin's chapter, or meet him after one of his performances, you'll get it.

When John, as a celestially roving spark, initiated our reconnection in that morning meditation nearly thirty-five years ago, reminding me that he was John and he had been waiting, I replied, 'it doesn't matter who you are, this is everything.'

Love is everything. We are love.

And so it is.